THE IMPORTANCE OF PLAY IN EARLY CHILDHOOD EDUCATION

Psychoanalytic, Attachment, and Developmental Perspectives

Edited by Marilyn Charles and Jill Bellinson

Routledge
Taylor & Francis Group

LONDON AND NEW YORK

First published 2019
by Routledge
2 Park Square, Milton Park, Abingdon, Oxon OX14 4RN

and by Routledge
52 Vanderbilt Avenue, New York, NY 10017

Routledge is an imprint of the Taylor & Francis Group, an informa business

British Library Cataloguing-in-Publication Data
A catalogue record for this book is available from the British Library

Library of Congress Cataloging-in-Publication Data
A catalog record has been requested for this book

ISBN: 978-1-138-74992-4 (hbk)
ISBN: 978-1-138-74993-1 (pbk)
ISBN: 978-1-315-18009-0 (ebk)

Typeset in Bembo
by Taylor & Francis Books

THE IMPORTANCE OF PLAY IN EARLY CHILDHOOD EDUCATION

The Importance of Play in Early Childhood Education presents various theories of play and demonstrates how it serves communicative, developmental, and relational functions, highlighting the importance and development of the capacity to play in terms useful to early childhood educators. The book explicitly links trauma, development, and interventions in the early childhood classroom specifically for teachers of young children, offering accessible information that can help teachers better understand the meanings of children's expressive acts.

Contributors from education, psychoanalysis, and developmental psychology explore techniques of play, how cultural influences affect how children play, the effect of trauma on play, factors that interfere with the ability to play, and how to apply these ideas in the classroom. They also discuss the relevance of ideas about playfulness for teachers and other professionals.

The Importance of Play in Early Childhood Education will be of great interest to teachers, psychoanalysts, and psychotherapists as well as play therapists and developmental psychologists.

Marilyn Charles, Ph.D., ABPP, is a psychologist and psychoanalyst at the Austen Riggs Center, and Professor, University of Monterrey (UDEM), with a special interest in the intergenerational transmission of trauma. Recent books include *Psychoanalysis and Literature: The Stories We Live*, *Working with Trauma*, and *Introduction to Contemporary Psychoanalysis*.

Jill Bellinson, Ph.D., is a psychologist and psychoanalyst in New York City, USA. She has served as psychological consultant to preschools and child welfare agencies for more than 30 years and is the author of *Children's Use of Board Games in Psychotherapy* and numerous papers on psychodynamic treatment of children and adults.

'The role of play therapy and a psychoanalytic understanding of how early childhood trauma influences the way a child learns to learn is at the forefront of this major contribution to the field of early childhood education. *The Importance of Play in Early Childhood Education* is written for the frontline educator: the classroom teacher.'

–**Annie Lee Jones, Ph.D.,** Adjunct Professor and Co-Chair, Committee on Ethnicity, Race, Class, Culture and Language (CERCCL), New York University Postdoctoral Program in Psychotherapy and Psychoanalysis

'Trauma in early childhood, including complex trauma and its transgenerational transmission, disrupts and precludes secure-base attachments and healthy development. To the extent that young children are "resilient," it is due to supportive and understanding relationships with parents, teachers, and early care-givers. This compilation of insightful chapters contributed by psychoanalysts and early childhood experts is a "must-read" for all who work with young children, promoting attunement, an understanding of the meaning of behavior and play, and preventing "burn out."'

–**Thomas F. Barrett, Ph.D.,** Psychologist, Child Psychoanalyst, Consultant and Professor of IECMH

'Early stress, adversity, and trauma impacts an unthinkable number of young children in the United States. We know that children exposed to uncontrollable stress may suffer effects that may last well into adulthood and impact not only learning, but lifelong health. Educating all adults who touch children's lives in how to buffer the effects of stress and trauma equips those adults with the tools they need to make a significant impact in a child's life. This volume provides those invaluable tools and insights.'

– **Linda C. Mayes, M.D.,** Arnold Gesell Professor and Director, Yale Child Study Center

CONTENTS

ILLUSTRATIONS

Figures

Tables

CONTRIBUTORS

Sophie Alcock is a Senior Lecturer in Education at Victoria University of Wellington, New Zealand-Aotearoa. Her professional background includes being an early childhood teacher, researcher and academic; thereby combining pragmatic, philosophical, and theoretical approaches to understanding and interacting with young children. She is interested in children's emotional well-being from relational and sociocultural perspectives that prioritize the systemic attachment contexts within which children live, play, and learn. The ways in which music and musicality can mediate children and all people moving, feeling, and connecting with themselves and with others are an extension of this interest in emotional well-being and the feeling of feelings. Sophie particularly enjoys the complexities that emerge when reflexively observing children moving and playing alone and with others as well as in early childhood care and education settings.

Ana Archangelo is an Associate Professor at the Faculty of Education at the University of Campinas (UNICAMP) in Brazil, where she teaches undergraduate and graduate courses and supervises Master and PhD students. Her research interests focus on Social Exclusion, Psychoanalysis, and Education. She has investigated children who have shown what she has coined as "the capacity not to learn" for the past 15 years. Author of several academic papers and book chapters on education, she has also co-authored a book series on *The Meaningful School*. She has undertaken psychoanalytic training with the Brazilian Psychoanalytic Society of São Paulo, an affiliate of the International Psychoanalytical Association. She has been a member of the editorial board of the journal *Psychoanalysis, Culture & Society*, as well as a member of the *Association for the Psychoanalysis of Culture & Society*.

Jill Bellinson is a clinical psychologist in private practice in New York City, working with children, adolescents, and adults. She trained at the William Alanson

White Institute, where she was one of the founders of the Child and Adolescent Psychoanalytic Training Program and continues to serve as faculty and supervisor. She supports new therapists by supervising in clinical psychology doctoral programs and postgraduate training programs in the New York City area. She has served as psychological consultant to many agencies over the past 30 years, including pre-schools and clinical treatment programs serving children from birth to five years old. She is Associate Editor of the *Journal of Infant, Child, and Adolescent Psychother-apy* and author of *Children's Use of Board Games in Psychotherapy* as well as numerous papers about understanding and treating children and adults.

Peter Blake is a clinical psychologist and Tavistock-trained child and adolescent psychotherapist. For 25 years Peter worked in child and family teams in Commu-nity Health Centres in England and Australia. For the last 15 years he has worked in private practice in Sydney. He was the Foundation President of the Child Psy-choanalytic Foundation, a charity based in Sydney. He is currently Director of the Institute of Child and Adolescent Psychoanalytic Psychotherapy (ICAPP). This is a training body offering child and adolescent psychotherapy, based in Sydney but offered via Zoom. He has lectured in a number of Australian universities and has given workshops to professionals across Australia. He has published a book, *Child and Adolescent Psychotherapy* (2011), with IP Communications (Australia) and Karnac books (London), and has contributed to numerous publications and journals.

Marilyn Charles is a psychologist and psychoanalyst at the Austen Riggs Center in Stockbridge, Massachusetts, affiliated with Harvard University, University of Monterrey (UDEM), Boston Graduate School of Psychoanalysis, and Chicago Center for Psychoanalysis. As Cochair of the Association for the Psychoanalysis of Culture and Society (APCS) and Past-President of Division 39 (Psychoanalysis) of the APA, she actively mentors and promotes community involvement and psy-choanalytic training, outreach, and research. Interests include creativity, psychosis, resilience, reflective function, and the intergenerational transmission of trauma. Books include: *Patterns: Building Blocks of Experience, Constructing Realities: Transfor-mations through Myth and Metaphor, Learning from Experience: A Guidebook for Clin-icians, Working with Trauma: Lessons from Bion and Lacan*, and *Psychoanalysis and Literature: The Stories We Live*. Edited volumes include: *Introduction to Contemporary Psychoanalysis, Fragments of Trauma and the Social Production of Suffering* (w/ Michael O'Loughlin), and *Women & Psychosis: Multidisciplinary Perspectives* and *Women and the Psychosocial Construction of Madness* (w/ Marie Brown).

Stephanie Creekpaum, PsyD, is a child and adolescent clinical psychologist. She received her doctoral degree from the University of Indianapolis in 2009 after completing an internship with The Institute of Living in Hartford, Connecticut and a postdoctoral fellowship with the Riley Hospital for Children in Indianapolis, Indiana. She currently lives in Moab, Utah and is developing a psychological test-ing service for the rural area of southeastern Utah Kids on the Move, a company that provides early interventions and services for children diagnosed with autism spectrum disorders. In addition to general child and adolescent work, she specializes in psychological testing, intellectual and developmental disabilities, including autism spectrum disorder, early severe mental illness and prodrome phases, LGBTQ issues, and comorbid medical conditions.

Athena A. Drewes is a licensed psychologist, certified school psychologist, and registered play therapist and supervisor. She recently retired as Director of Clinical Training and APA-Accredited Doctoral Internship at Astor Services for Children and Families. She has over 40 years of clinical and supervision experience with sexually abused and traumatized children and adolescents in school, outpatient, and inpatient settings. She is a former member of the Board of Directors of the Association for Play Therapy and Founder and President Emeritus of the NY Association for Play Therapy. She has written extensively and is an invited guest lecturer on play therapy in the United States and around the world. She has eleven books on play therapy with the most recent being *Play Therapy in Middle Childhood*, co-edited with Dr. Charles Schaefer, published by the American Psychological Association, and a companion DVD showing Dr. Drewes' integrative prescriptive play therapy work.

Alexis W. Lee, MA, is a fourth-year graduate student in the Clinical Psychology PhD program at Case Western Reserve University in Cleveland, Ohio working under Dr. Sandra Russ, PhD. Her research focuses on pretend play, predictors of creativity and creative self-perceptions, and creativity and ADHD. Dr. Russ and Alexis Lee have collaborated on research projects in the past few years with a number of schools in Northeast Ohio. They investigated the predictive validity of Russ's Affect in Play Scale in a longitudinal study by asking, 'Does early pretend play predict creativity across seven years?' They have also carried out a pretend play intervention with a sample of preschoolers from a Head Start center to increase play skills and creativity. These projects have resulted in presentations in three national conferences and one publication: Lee, A. W., & Russ, S. W. (2018). Pretend play, divergent thinking, and self-perceptions of creativity: A longitudinal study. *The International Journal of Creativity & Problem Solving, 28*(1), 73–88.

Brenda Lovegrove Lepisto, PsyD, is a clinical psychologist and adult/child psychoanalyst and devoted a 35-year career to working with children and their families. Her Child Clinical Psychology Fellowship led to supervising Michigan State University (MSU) clinical psychology doctoral students along with maintaining a private psychotherapy practice. Dr. Lepisto is Past-President of The Michigan Psychoanalytic Council. After serving as faculty in internal medicine for over 20 years, she recently joined the core faculty in the Obstetrics and Gynecology Department at Hurley Medical Center. As a member of the faculty of the Academy for Communication in Healthcare, she teaches workshops on patient- and relationship-centered communication. She is a coauthor of the 4th edition of *Smith's Patient-Centered Interviewing:*

An Evidence-based Method. Other publications include topics on child psychodynamic treatment, empathy, and medical curriculum development. Dr. Lepisto is the President of The Sophie L. Lovinger Memorial Fund, a nonprofit dedicated to the education of professionals treating children and adults.

Norka T. Malberg, PsyD, is a certified child and adolescent psychoanalyst, who is an Assistant Clinical Professor at the Yale Child Study Center, Department of Psychiatry. She is in private practice in New Haven, CT. Her affiliations include Clinical Tutor at the Anna Freud Center and Clinical Consultant at Carrot Patch Preschool in Hamden, CT. She is a member of the Contemporary Freudian Society and the Western New England Psychoanalytic Society. Her editorial positions include being the coeditor of the Child Section of the *PDM2*, and of the Lines of Development Book Series for Karnac. She also serves on the editorial boards of the *Journal of Infant, Child, and Adolescent Psychotherapy* and *Psychoanalytic Study of the Child*.

Ann-Marie Mott is the retired Coordinator of the program for young children at the Bank Street School for Children. She still teaches the Art Workshop for Teachers in the Bank Street College Graduate School. She also teaches art to three- and four-year-old children at the Town School in New York City. She is an artist and a photographer.

Deborah Mugno, EdD, has spent over 30 years working with children with special needs, from birth through high school. She has been a classroom teacher, in-home early intervention service provider, adjunct college faculty member, and an administrator over the course of her career. Dr. Mugno received her undergraduate degree from the University of Maryland and her masters and doctorate degrees from Johns Hopkins University in Baltimore, MD. For the last 20 years her area of concentration has been working with children with social and emotional difficulties. She is currently the Director of Education and Operations at the Lucy Daniels Center in Cary, NC, a mental health agency that serves children from birth through age 11, with a therapeutic school program, an outpatient clinic, and in-home mental health services.

Tia Neha is a descendant of the Ngā Puhi, Ngāti Porou, Ngāti Kahungunu and Te Whānau Ā Apanui Māori tribes that are located in New Zealand. She is the Māori and Indigenous Lecturer and a Fellow of the Centre for Applied Cross-cultural Research team in the School of Psychology, which is based at Victoria University of Wellington, New Zealand. Her main research interests include Māori-centred developmental, community, theoretical, and longitudinal psychological work. The emphasis of her work is that it is of benefit to the Māori, research, and international indigenous communities.

Michael O'Loughlin is Professor in the School of Education and a Professor and clinical and research supervisor in the Ph.D. program in Clinical Psychology at

Adelphi University, New York. He has authored, co-authored, or edited eight books, four of which concern the emotional lives of children, and he has published extensively on matters to do with childhood. Past Cochair of the Association for the Psychoanalysis of Culture and Society, he is currently co-editor of the journal *Psychoanalysis, Culture, and Society*. He is also editor of a new book series, *Psychoanalytic Interventions: Clinical, Social, and Cultural Contexts*, from Rowman & Littlefield.

Elaine Reese has taught and researched child development for over 25 years in the United States and in New Zealand. She is the former editor of the *Journal of Cognition and Development* (Taylor & Francis) and the author of a book for parents, *Tell Me a Story: Sharing Stories to Enrich your Child's World* (Oxford University Press, 2013).

Jennifer Reid began teaching as an early childhood Montessori teacher in New York City in 2001. She received her master's degree in Early Childhood and Elementary Education from New York University in 2003. Since 2005, she has worked at the Lucy Daniels School in Cary, North Carolina, as a therapeutic teacher in preschool, kindergarten, and elementary school classrooms. She currently serves as the Director of the Early School and provides guidance and mentoring to therapeutic teachers through their fifth grade, coordinates the students' clinical treatment with therapeutic intervention in the classrooms, and facilitates collaboration between teachers and clinicians. As a certified psychoanalytic teacher, she is particularly interested in using a psychodynamic understanding of development to help children reach their highest potential as learners and members of a group.

Sandra W. Russ, PhD, a clinical child psychologist, is a Distinguished University Professor of Psychology at Case Western Reserve University and holds the Louis D. Beaumont University Professor chair. She has served as President of the Society for Personality Assessment of the Clinical Child Section of Div. 12 in APA and of the Division of Aesthetics, Creativity, and the Arts (Div. 10) in APA. Her research program has focused on relationships among pretend play, creativity, and adaptive functioning in children. She developed the Affect in Play Scale, which assesses pretend play in children and, with her students, developed a play facilitation intervention. She is author of *Affect and Creativity: The Role of Affect and Play in the Creative Process* (1993), *Play in Child Development and Psychotherapy: Toward Empirically Supported Practice* (2004), Russ & Niec (Ed.) *Play in Clinical Practice: Evidence Based Approaches* (2011), and *Pretend Play in Childhood: Foundation of Adult Creativity* (2014). A recent honor was being appointed as a Distinguished University Professor at Case.

Ionas Sapountzis is an Associate Professor at the Derner School of Psychology of Adelphi University and the director of its School Psychology program. He is a faculty member and supervisor in the Psychoanalytic Psychotherapy and in the Child, Adolescent, and Family Psychotherapy programs of the Derner School of

Psychology. His articles have been published in the journals *Psychoanalytic Psychotherapy*, *Psychoanalytic Review*, and in the *Journal of Infant, Child, and Adolescent Psychotherapy* (JICAP). He has worked with emotionally disabled children and students in the spectrum in school and community settings and maintains a private practice in Garden City, New York.

Steve Tuber is Professor of Psychology, director of Clinical Training, and program head of the doctoral program in clinical psychology at City College, CUNY, where he has taught for over 30 years. He is a diplomate of the American Board of Professional Psychology in clinical psychology, the editor of the book series, *Psychodynamic Assessment and Psychotherapy for the 21st Century* (Lexington Books), and on the editorial board of five different journals, including *Psychoanalytic Psychology and Contemporary Psychoanalysis*. He has authored and/or edited seven critically acclaimed books and written over 150 papers in the intertwining fields of assessment and treatment of children and adolescents.

Kirkland C. Vaughans, PhD, is a licensed clinical psychologist and a psychoanalyst with a private practice in New York City. He is the founding editor of the *Journal of Infant, Child, and Adolescent Psychotherapy* and co-editor of the two-volume book, *The Psychology of Black Boys and Adolescents*. He is a senior adjunct professor of psychology at the Derner Institute of Advanced Psychological Studies at Adelphi University and Director of the Postgraduate Program in Child and Adolescent Psychotherapy, where he also serves as the Director of the Derner/Hempstead Child Clinic. He is also a visiting faculty member and Honorary Member at the Institute for Psychoanalytic Training and Research (IPTAR). He is a retired school psychologist and the former Regional Director of the New Hope Guild Centers for Child Mental Health of Brooklyn. He is an active member of the Research Council of the New York City Young Men's Initiative and the Chairman of the Board for The Harlem Family Institute: a multicultural psychoanalytic training institute.

Renee Vaughans received a BS in Applied Mathematics from Long Island University, C.W. Post Center, and a master's degree in Clinical Psychology from the Institute of Advanced Psychological Studies at Adelphi University. In addition, she also holds a certificate as a school psychologist and a second master's degree and certificate in School Leadership and Administration at both the building and district level. She was a school psychologist and currently is a chairperson for the Committee on Preschool Special Education (CPSE) and the Committee on Special Education (CSE) for school-aged students for a cumulative of 21 years. She has presented on numerous panels on topics related to early childhood education and advocacy for educational rights for children of color.

Fabio Camargo Bandeira Villela is an Associate Professor in the Department of Education at UNESP (Brazil). He has a bachelor's degree in Psychology. His master's degree and PhD are in Education from the Catholic University of São Paulo (PUC-SP) and the University of Campinas (UNICAMP), both in the state of São Paulo in Brazil. He has done research in Psychoanalysis and Education and coordinated projects related to playful activities for children with difficulties in emotional development. He has written a book series with Ana Archangelo about *The Meaningful School*, a pedagogical concept constructed with contributions from psychoanalysis.

ACKNOWLEDGEMENTS

We would like to acknowledge the extraordinary work being done by early childhood educators across the globe, particularly that of the teachers of Gunawirra in New South Wales, whose valiant efforts and desire for further learning gave rise to this volume, and of John Jay College in New York City, who demonstrate what it takes to be an early childhood educator.

We would also like to acknowledge the contributors, for their very rich offerings to early childhood teachers everywhere, as they work to bring playful engagement into the learning of their students in spite of ongoing adversities.

And we want to recognize the children we have met and worked with, for opening their minds and hearts to us and trusting us to offer them our best efforts on their behalf. We are grateful to our teachers and supervisors and above all to our patients, who taught us much about their lives and everything about how to help them.

This book is dedicated to young children everywhere, who deserve the energies of our entire village of caregivers to raise their bodies, inform their minds, and comfort their pains.

INTRODUCTION

Marilyn Charles

Teachers of young children are at the frontline, charged with perhaps the most important challenge one might take on: to nurture, educate, and protect. For teachers who work with children living in stressful environments, these challenges are compounded. Teachers are expected to help their young charges learn, but often those children are not in a position to learn. Stress, deprivation, and traumatic experiences all interfere with the child's capacity to learn. In this volume, we contend that because the young child's play is learning, the early childhood teacher is in an important position through which both to make sense of the child's play and to further the child's capacity to play so essential to learning.

In my engagements with early childhood educators in Australia who were working with Aboriginal children living under stressful conditions, I could see how difficult it was for them to try to meet the challenges of teaching under such circumstances. Through our conversations, I could see that many of the ways that I made sense of the children's – and the teachers' – dilemmas were culled from literatures not easily accessible to anyone who did not know the jargon. In addition, some of the literature was geared towards a therapeutic environment, which is not the province of the classroom. How then, I wondered, might we offer up potentially useful ideas to early childhood educators in language accessible to the teacher and technique appropriate for the classroom?

My ideas are framed by psychoanalysis, which helped me to recognize ways in which trauma I encountered in my adult life exacerbated fault lines I had carried from childhood, a childhood infused by transgenerational issues that had not yet been worked through and parents who were too stressed to accommodate to my needs in a given moment. In helping me to accept myself and to better meet life's challenges as I encounter them, psychoanalysis has also taught me to be utterly respectful of the person I am working with, to try to see the world through that person's eyes, and to listen for echoes of past history that may be haunting them.

This effort helps put the focus where it must be, on *their* lived experience. In learning to recognize my feelings as potentially useful signals, if I can attend to them and think about them, I am also giving space for the other person to reflect as well.

Such a stance is critically important for teachers of young children whose development is waylaid by trauma. I use the term *trauma* broadly because disruption is a function not so much of any particular event but rather depends on our resilience and ability to withstand and master difficult experiences. Experience becomes traumatic *because* it derails, when it takes us off center and we are unable to regroup. Studies show that when children are not the focus of parental attention, they attend to the needs and feelings of others over and above their own. More particularly, trauma results in difficulties distinguishing between positive and threat-related cues (Cichetti & Curtis, 2005; Chu, Bryant, Gatt & Harris, 2016). From that off-center position, the child learns to be vigilant about external forces rather than making sense of her own needs, feelings, and desires in ways that are fundamental to identity development and to the development of empathic concern.

A child in such a position cannot truly play. Play depends on sufficient safety in one's environment to be able to try different feelings and characters on for size. Watching a young child at play, we can see how he or she narrates a story alongside the play. The child is both making sense of how the world works and also building a sense of his or her own identity through these narratives (see Chapter 10: Reese and Neeha and Chapter 11: Charles).

In our first section, **Theories of play**, we look at the functions of pretend play and its importance in child development. In particular, we invite the teacher to recognize the important functions of play in early development and how the early childhood teacher can support those crucial developmental functions. In Chapter 1, **Child development through play**, Stephanie Creekpaum provides an overview and describes forms of pretend play in relation to stages of child development. In Chapter 2, **Pretend play in the classroom: Helping children grow**, Sandra W. Russ and Alexis W. Lee look at relationships between pretend play, creativity, and well-being, with a particular focus on ways in which the teacher can incorporate pretend play into the classroom setting.

Play is the child's means for engagement with the world and also provides a window onto the child's experience. In Part II, **Understanding play**, we offer two vantage points on what the child might be communicating through his or her play. In Chapter 3, **Play as communication**, Brenda Lovegrove Lepisto takes up the issue of play as communication most broadly, describing a method of child-centered communication that assists children in elucidating and expanding their communication through play. Tools are offered to help teachers and parents to more accurately recognize and respond to children's wishes, dreams, fear, and aspirations, as they are enacted through play. In Chapter 4, **From reaction to reflection: Mentalizing in early childhood education**, Norka T. Malberg introduces the teacher to the concept of mentalization, the ability to understand behavior as a function of the state of mind of self and others.

Self-development depends on the development of mentalization or reflective capacities, the ability to recognize and differentiate one's own feelings and then to be able to do the same with others who may be both similar and different than oneself (Fonagy, Gergely, Jurist, & Target, 2002). That differentiation process is set in motion from the earliest moments of life, as caregivers monitor and moderate the child's emotions sufficiently to keep them from being overly stressed but also allow sufficient frustration that the child can be an active agent as well. Overwhelming emotion is itself traumatic, particularly for the young child who has no way of reassuring herself that the distress will, indeed, end. In meeting and then soothing the child's distress, the attuned adult shows the child her importance and also helps her to learn to soothe herself, thereby facilitating the development of autonomy and individuation.

In Part III, we look at **Play in the classroom**, exploring ways in which play manifests in the classroom environment and suggesting ways in which the teacher might creatively engage with such play. In Chapter 5, **Play in the emotional and cognitive life of a preschooler**, Steve Tuber highlights ways in which the possibility of play is enhanced in an environment that actively supports the provision of a safe and nurturing play space. To this end, he directly addresses classroom factors that enable the child's capacity to play to be most usefully developed, including suggestions regarding how to enhance children's play in the classroom. In Chapter 6, **Being a Playful Teacher**, Peter Blake focuses on the teacher as a valuable model for students, suggesting that the teacher who appreciates the value of play and playfulness not only enhances a child's cognitive and social skills, but also enables the child to learn about their inner world and the inner world of others, in this way enhancing the development of mentalization. Imaginative play, from this perspective, is vital for problem solving and also for identity development. Tensions between self and other are taken up by Jill Bellinson in Chapter 7, **Mine! No, mine! Interaction in children's play**, in which she addresses the important developmental achievements entailed in negotiating conflict. Turning a fine-grained lens on ways in which conflicts between children can be adaptively recognized and worked through, this chapter illustrates conflict as an essential part of living and learning, inviting the teacher to make use of conflict as it arises in children's play. In this way, the teacher models the types of behaviors that lend themselves not only to effective dispute resolution but also to more respectful and pleasurable interactive play.

In Part IV, we look at **Techniques of play**, ways in which an understanding of child development can help teachers to provide learning-enhancing play experiences. Chapters 8 and 9 focus on ways in which the teacher's sensitivity to rhythms of emotional meanings can support the child's efforts to use art in its various modalities in support of their own development. Emotions have their own particular patterns that are recognized and communicated through multiple sensory modalities (Charles, 2002). Soothing functions become a type of melody that can be invoked through sound, touch, or facial expression. We see that internalized soothing function in the child who croons to her doll, "It's all right, Mama will be right back." The attentive teacher can also notice the child who freezes, and becomes withdrawn and silent or oppositional and aggressive when challenged. When we watch a child at play, we can see by their movements and expressions something about how they are managing, and we can try to be with them in ways that might help them to feel safe and perhaps develop greater trust. There is no substitute for paying attention to the impact our behaviors and actions have on those we work with, and to learning from those experiences, thereby modeling the importance of being present and attentive to the lived moment as it occurs. Through a process called *embodied simulation*, we take in information directly from our experiences with others about how the world works (Gallese, 2009; Gallese, Eagle, & Migone, 2007). These nonverbal channels are primary for children.

For children who have not sufficiently internalized self-soothing functions, art, music, and other expressive or repetitive activities can provide avenues towards the self-soothing so essential to learning. In Chapter 8, **Art-making experiences for young children affected by trauma**, Ann-Marie Mott focuses on art-making as a means for symbolizing and working through traumatic experiences. The teacher is offered suggestions for encouraging a playful interactive engagement with the child around the experience of making art, and also developmental guidelines through which to contextualize the child's productions. In Chapter 9, **Young children's musicality: Relating with rhythm**, Sophie Alcock attempts to expand and enhance the teacher's understanding and awareness of children's musicality that may be present in their daily play. Also included are suggestions for more actively providing events that enhance children's musicality. In Chapter 10, **Promoting identity development through memory narrative**, Elaine Reese and Tia Neha focus on the importance of storytelling as a tool for transformation in childhood. The authors note ways in which adults contribute to identity development by encouraging the evolution of a life narrative in which the child plays the leading role. They also offer suggestions of ways in which teachers can actively facilitate the development of children's life narratives in ways that enhance self-development.

In Part V, **Specialized needs for play**, we turn explicitly to the difficulty of working with children whose development has been disrupted by trauma. When children are living in chaotic environments, their needs and feelings may not easily be recognized. The child whose parents are not able to meet, tolerate, and soften excessive emotion is in a precarious position. Trauma and unresolved mourning can leave even good parents preoccupied and inaccessible, which is confusing and disorienting to the child. The literature on disorganized attachment shows that it is precisely *these* parents who can be *most* frightening because the child does not know whether she will encounter the responsive face or the empty one (Main & Hesse, 1990). Without the parent as a secure base to reliably return to, the child may become hypervigilant to the emotions of others. That external focus makes it hard to make effective use of internal emotional signals. Self-regulation depends on our ability to track our feelings sufficiently that we can negotiate challenges as they arise. The teacher might be alerted to signs of disorganized attachment in the child who is overly compliant; or who freezes; or whose speech, movements, or play become disfluent or chaotic at times. Such a child has not been able to rely on adults for assistance. The attentive teacher provides a needed mirror by recognizing the child's distress and then providing soothing attention that helps the child to settle a bit so that he or she can begin to engage once again in classroom activities.

Hypervigilance to others affects the child's cognitive development as well. Verbal communication depends on the categories that build up over time as we notice patterns in our experience. Chaotic households impede this process by making it difficult to integrate external signals with internal ones. Studies show that when individuals are offered discrepant data, they can become confused even regarding the contours and limits of their own bodies (Petkova & Ehrsson, 2008). In families preoccupied with trauma, there can be mixed messages that make it difficult for the child to learn to generalize their intentions in accordance with categories of experience (Knox, 2009), thereby interfering with the developing capacities for abstraction and generalization that facilitate learning. At the extreme, rather than being symbols that can be played with and matched against experience, words become empty placeholders, inviting mindless compliance rather than engagement with the regularities of experience through which children begin to elaborate and integrate increasingly complex meanings about self and world.

Psychoanalysis is fundamentally a theory of development, a way of trying to understand what goes wrong (and right!) for the person. Freud developed a method for listening very carefully, to try to make sense of what was said and what was left unsaid, or perhaps spoken in ways beyond words. Much as a dream or a story can allow us to tell difficult truths indirectly, children can often show us, either through their symptoms or their play, something about the truths that cannot yet be named. As we saw in previous sections, allowing children to show and then tell us their story at their own pace, in their own way, helps *them* to discover that story and, in the process, to learn to make use of, and to believe in, their own capacities. Child researchers show us that, with children, it is the 'beyond words' that is often most important in making sense of what children may be trying to tell us. All those who work with children know something about that nonverbal language, the child who tells us about his troubles through silence, or the one who speaks through what we might term 'bad' behavior.

For children living in oppressive or marginalized conditions, in particular, it is important for the teacher to be able to recognize and reflect on conditions that may be undermining the child's capacity to learn (Charles, 2014a; Charles, 2014b). In Chapter 11, **Trauma and identity**, I look more specifically at ways in which trauma can impede identity development. In Chapter 12, **Working with difficult children in schools**, Ionas Sapountzis looks at ways in which seemingly difficult or troubling behavior may help the teacher to recognize trouble that the child cannot communicate through other means. He stresses ways in which empathic responsiveness can help to deescalate troublesome behaviors or invite withdrawn children into greater engagement.

In Part VI, **Culture and play**, we invite teachers to look through the lens of culture to better understand aspects of the environment that may help or hinder the child's development. In Chapter 13, **Creating reflective space in the classroom**, Ana Archangelo and Fabio Camargo Bandeira Villela suggest that conversations about how teachers might best work with and address diversity issues are complicated by a lack of recognition of the internal forces at play. If, they suggest, these tensions are not so much about what is unknown in others but rather with what is unknown in ourselves, then we are pointed towards self-discovery as crucial in promoting respect for others. In Chapter 14, **Cultural issues in relation to play for teachers**, Athena A. Drewes highlights ways in which play has a significant impact on the continuation and development of culture. While play is universal, the way play looks and works and the degree to which it is encouraged or attended, as well as the forms and modes of expression, vary according to each society and cultural group. This chapter helps to highlight for the classroom teacher issues of culture as they emerge in children's play. By setting up a culturally rich and inviting classroom, children can explore their own culture and those of their peers, thereby lessening the likelihood of bullying or isolation and increasing tolerance and acceptance. In Chapter 15, **Culture and play as key elements of identity formation and academic performance for children of color in primary education**, Kirkland C. Vaughans and Renee Vaughans look at ways in which children who are 'othered' in exclusionary ways within the culture face particular challenges, not only in relation to identity development but also in terms of academic performance. The authors stress the importance of educators' recognition of play as embedded in and mediated by cultural meanings, so as to convey a respect and sense of care that enables their own cultural identity to serve protective, valuable functions.

In Part VII, we turn more directly to **Teachers and play**. In Chapter 16, **Engaging children in healing work**, Michael O'Loughlin looks at ways in which teachers might make use of their own emotional experience to inform their work with children in ways that are empathic, meaningful, and potentially healing. The author suggests how teachers of traumatized young children can make use of the child's narrative capacities to assist them in developing new self-actualizing life narratives. In Chapter 17, **Teacher stress: Impact, challenges, and solutions**, Deborah Mugno and Jennifer Reid look at sources of teacher stress, offering suggestions for ways in which teachers, in attending to and diminishing their own stress, can create less stressful environments in which the children are more free to play and to learn. In each chapter, we try to speak directly to the early childhood teacher in ways that invite greater appreciation for some of the problems faced in the early childhood classroom and also propose interventions that might help to more playfully resolve or alleviate some of those difficulties.

References

Charles, M. (2002). *Patterns: Building blocks of experience*. Hillsdale, NJ: The Analytic Press.

Charles, M. (2014a). Trauma, childhood, and emotional resilience. In N. Tracey (Ed.), *Trans-generational trauma and the aboriginal preschool child: Healing through intervention* (pp. 109–131). Lanham, MD: Rowman & Littlefield.

Charles, M. (2014b). The intergenerational transmission of trauma: Effects on identity development. In N. Tracey (Ed.), *Transgenerational trauma and the aboriginal preschool child: Healing through intervention* (pp. 133–152). Lanham, MD: Rowman & Littlefield.

Chu, D. A., Bryant, R. A., Gatt, J. M., & Harris, A. W. F. (2016). Failure to differentiate between threat-related and positive emotion cues in healthy adults with childhood interpersonal or adult trauma. *Psychiatric Research*, 78: 31–41.

Cichetti, D., & Curtis, W. J. (2005). An event-related potential study of the processing of affective facial expression in young children who experienced maltreatment during the first year of life. *Developmental Psychopathology*, 17:641–677.

Fonagy, P., Gergely, G., Jurist, E. L., & Target, M. (2002). *Affect regulation, mentalization, and the development of the self.* New York: Other Press.

Gallese, V. (2009). Mirror neurons, embodied simulation, and the neural basis of social identification. *Psychoanalytic Dialogues*, 19:519–536.

Gallese, V., Eagle, M. N., & Migone, P. (2007). Intentional attunement: Mirror neurons and the neural underpinnings of interpersonal relations. *Journal of the American Psychoanalytic Association*, 55(1):131–175.

Knox, J. (2009). Mirror neurons and embodied stimulation in the development of archetypes and self-agency. *Journal of Analytical Psychology*, 54(3):307–323.

Main, M., & Hesse, E. (1990). Parent's unresolved traumatic experiences are related to infant disorganized/disoriented attachment status: Is frightened and/or frightening parental behavior the linking mechanism? In M. Greenberg, D. Cicchetti, & E. M. Cummings (Eds.), *Attachment in the preschool years: Theory, research, and intervention* (pp. 161–182). Chicago: University of Chicago Press.

Petkova, V. I., & Ehrsson, H. H. (2008). If I were you: Perceptual illusion of body swapping. *PLoS ONE*, 3(12):e38–e32. doi:10.1371/journal.pone.0003832

PART I
Theories of play

1

CHILD DEVELOPMENT THROUGH PLAY

Stephanie Creekpaum

Play is important in children's development, as they learn about the world through play (Sherkow, 2004). In the earliest play relationships between a caretaker and a child, caretakers help children cope with their emotions (Gilmore, 2011). As adults, we have the experience and the language to understand emotions that children are not yet able to process. We are able to understand that when children cry when their mothers drop them off for day care they are sad or anxious to see her go. Through play with another trusted adult we are able to help these children calm and through these interactions, children learn more about themselves, their feelings, and being in relationships with others (Bergman, 1993).

The earliest forms of pretend play begin when children are about a year old. Around this age, children are exploring their worlds through sensory and motor movements (Fischer, 1980). They look closely at items, hold them in their hands, feel their shape, bang them on things, feel them in their mouths, etc. Around a year old, they also start to use objects to imitate things that are familiar to them (Fein, 1975), such as pretending to drink from a cup. For children around a year old, it is important that the objects they use in play are similar to the objects they use in the real world. They can pretend to use a play phone to talk, but they cannot yet use a banana in a similar manner. However, starting around 18 months, they begin to move from playing with items in a functional way (e.g., pushing a car or rolling a ball) to a more creative and representative way (e.g., putting a bowl on their heads as a hat) (Ungerer et al., 1981; Pederson, Rook-Green, & Elder, 1981). Around this age, children are not only starting to move toward having objects represent other things, but they are also beginning to incorporate others more into their play (Fein, 1975). A child may now use that banana to have a conversation with mama and then pretend to feed a doll their favorite food.

When children are around 2 years old, through their experience playing, they have a greater understanding that they are separate and independent from other things and people around them (Watson & Fischer, 1977). Very young children do not have a sense that others and their surroundings are separate from themselves. When they cry because they cannot reach the toy that fell on the ground and their mother hands it back to them, they experience it as magically appearing again as though they made it happen. They do not understand that someone outside of themselves, i.e., mother, was the one who saved the day. Everything that happens is experienced as though the child caused it to happen. However, through play, toddlers start to experience others and the world as separate from themselves. When they cry because they cannot reach their toys that they threw behind the couch and their mother retrieves it, they are delighted not only to have their toys back but also because they can now experience the connection that it was in fact mother who saved the day.

Also, around 2 years old, children begin to recreate the actions of others, primarily family members (Bretherton, 1989). They now start to pretend to shave like dad or cook a pie like grandma. Children are able to start imitating these adult actions because they have developed a mental image or representation of others through memories they have with them (Mayes & Cohen, 1992). They use memories of their interactions with others in their lives (e.g., parents, grandparents, siblings, day care providers) to form an image in their mind of that person. Once they have this mental image of a familiar person, they are then able to represent this person and their actions in order to pretend to act like them and play in a similar manner. For example, after children see their mothers driving them to day care every day, they may start to pretend they are driving their stuffed animals to day care. They have memories of all of the times their mothers drive them to day care, and from these memories, they have developed a mental image of what mother is like when driving to day care. With these memories and representation, children can now bring up the mental image of their mother even when not actively driving to day care to be able to re-enact her actions and this routine in play.

In addition, once children have the capacity to develop these mental images, they are able to bring up the memories they have with their caretakers to help them cope when separated from them (Mayes & Cohen, 1992). Children who have reached this developmental stage are able to bring up the mental image of their mother signing their favorite lullaby or their father giving them the biggest bear hug when they drop them off at day care to help them cope with being separated from them. They also start to use play to master their feelings around separations, and they may play through the same script or scene repeatedly as they work through their feelings (Lillard, 1993). Let's go back to the example of children re-enacting mother driving to day care with their stuffed animals. After children drop off the stuffed animals at day care, the animals may start to cry that they do not want mommy to go. Children who have a mental image of their mothers comforting them may then start to comfort their animals saying, "Mommy will be back. I love you." Children may also express their anger that mommy is leaving them and have the animals scream and hit or they may express their fear and have the animals cower and hide. They may go back and forth between re-enacting a comforting mother and their anger or fear, playing through their feelings while also using the mental image to help cope.

Children may also attempt to cope with their feelings about separations and reunions through games such as peek-a-boo and hide and seek (Bergman, 1993; Mayes & Cohen, 1992; Neubauer, 1987). These games are a safer place to re-enact these separations as the child has more control over the separation. In these games, children tend to take the lead in determining when it is ok to hide and be separated. They then also use the mental image of their caretaker to tolerate the separation. In these playful games of separation and reunion, children are able to learn to rely on others returning and also on themselves being able to tolerate the separation, and this is all made possible by their ability to develop mental images or representations of their loved ones through the memories they have of them being comforting and consistent in meeting their needs. Through play, children are not only able to remember positive interactions with their loved ones to help them cope, but they also use playful games to master feelings around separations. These games are safe ways to work through these feelings because when the child pulls down the sheet, they see the smiling face they love. In this way, they learn that even when separated, this separation does not last forever.

In addition, around 2 years old, with this greater sense of themselves as separate from others, children start looking toward their caretakers for clues on what to think about a situation. When they trip over their truck, fall and bump their knee, they often look to their caretakers first to see their reactions before starting to cry or getting back up to run around again. This is not because their knee does not actually hurt. It likely does hurt, but children are learning how to cope with situations by looking at the reactions of those around them. If their caregiver looks very anxious about the fall, screams and runs after the child, the child sees this is a scary situation and begins to cry loudly. If on the other hand, the caregiver calmly acknowledges that the child bumped a knee and provides comfort and assurance that the child is okay, the child will get a kiss from mommy and continue to play. The child in this situation is learning how to cope in these situations. They are also building an ability to imagine others' thoughts and feelings. In this way, they are starting to understand not only that others are separate from them, but also that they have separate thoughts and feelings from them (Mayes & Cohen, 1992).

It is also around this time that children may develop an imaginary friend. Through imaginary friends, children are playing with the idea of being separate from others and having different thoughts and feelings, while still being in control of this creation (Mayes & Cohen, 1992), and as they grow in their independence from their parents, they may increasingly have times where they want others to watch them play rather than interacting or seemingly interrupting (Sherkow, 2004). Thus, having imaginary friends is seen in typical child development. One in which the child is playing alone without being alone. Children can progress in developing more socially based play through imaginary friends. In a stage where they may not yet be ready to negotiate the compromises that happen in social play, children can practice playing with others in a situation they still have control over.

When children are 2 years old, they begin to pretend that dolls can perform an action, and by 3 years old, children start to have dolls perform several actions related to a role they are playing (Watson & Fischer, 1980). Thus, children move from pretending a doll is talking to pretending a doll is a teacher in a classroom who is teaching others. When children are around 3 ½ years old, they understand the meaning of objects and are able to pretend without needing to have an actual object in reality (Elder & Peterson, 1978). They can now pretend to be talking on a phone without needing a toy phone or pretend to drink from a cup without needing an empty cup. Thus, as children's understanding of the meaning of objects grows, they are better able to symbolize an object without needing it to exist in reality (Ungerer et al., 1981). Around 4 years old, children start to act out social roles (Watson & Fischer, 1980), such as playing doctor, and around 5 years old, children engage in more coordinated and complex play with others (Lillard, 1993). Thus a 5-year-old can coordinate a play scene with her friends by pretending she is the doctor and the other children are the patients who need to come to the clinic to get a shot. By the time children are 6 years old, they are often able to have one figure pretend to perform several roles at the same time (Watson & Fischer, 1980). In this play development, a child may pretend to be the parent bringing the child to the clinic one moment and the nurse assisting the doctor the next. Their desire to switch and try on different roles is an important stage of development and should be encouraged. It also allows for children to continue working on playing with others, as the success of social play depends on the playmates' ability to cooperate in developing the shared meaning (Gilmore, 2011).

Throughout play development, children are moving from solitary play to play-ing with others. Up until children are about 2 years old, they tend to play alone. They initially examine the sensory and motor aspects of toys and then begin to engage in early play, such as pushing cars and drinking from cups, but this play tends to be solitary. Children then move to engaging in parallel play around the ages of 2 to 3. During this phase of development, children play beside others, usually with the same toys, but not interacting. For example, they see another child playing with cars, they sit down to also play with the cars but do not talk to or play with the other child. This then progresses into cooperative play with others around the age of 4. Children can engage in pretend play alone, beside others and with others. When playing with others, children can impersonate other people, such as imitating actions of adults in their lives or actions of favorite characters on shows, and they can play other roles, such as pretending to be a teacher and teaching other students. This latter form of pretending can be done alone, as the child plays the teacher and teaches to his stuffed animals, or with others, as the child plays the teacher and teaches her friends who are playing the role of the students (Lillard et al., 2013).

Now that we've explored some of the stages of development through play, let's look at some of the different forms of play. Play can take the form of unstructured free play, which is created by the child, and semi-structured play, which is guided by parent and child (Milteer & Ginsburgh, 2012). In free play, children follow their own line of creativity. In semi-structured play, another individual comes in to suggest different play themes or roles, working with the child to incorporate them into the child's play (Lillard et al., 2013). For example, in free play, a child may pretend to be a lion that is being chased by a spaghetti monster who the lion then eats. In this play, the caregiver would not suggest that she is also a lion and not a spaghetti monster but would go along with the roles the child creates. In semi-structured play, the caregiver may suggest that she is another lion and they are running in a field chasing each other. For this situation to work, though, it is important to remember that it is guided by both the adult and the child. The child and the playmate (i.e., the caregiver) need to both agree on these roles or the play is likely to stop prematurely and in an unsatisfying way.

There are multiple roles that objects may take when a child is pretending. Children can use an object based on what it is. For example, they may take an empty cup from a cabinet and pretend to be pouring and then drinking apple juice, so they are using the cup for what it is actually intended. Children may pretend one object represents something else. With this, they may find the empty box from the new vacuum, get inside it, and pretend they are driving a car to go to the store. The box now represents their car. Children can pretend an inanimate object has living characteristics. They may find the broom in the closet and start riding it around the room, pretending it is a horse as it bucks and neighs, so the broom has the characteristics of a horse. Children can pretend they are doing something that does not exist in reality. For example, they may pretend they have magical powers and are able to make things they love appear and things they do not like disappear. They may also reference a situation that is not actually happening currently (Matthews, 1977). Children who wish they were fishing can sit on a chair in their living room and pretend they are on a boat in the ocean, catching the biggest fish.

While toddlers learn about rules and boundaries through play, older children use play to break free from the rules and reality (Sherkow, 2004). Children can use play to safely separate themselves from reality, explore their thoughts and feelings, satisfy needs that they may not be able to do in reality because of rules, and work through different situations. A child who is not allowed to have a cookie before dinner can go to his pretend kitchen and make himself 20 cookies and pretend to eat them all. A child who is fearful of an upcoming doctor's appointment because of a shot can put on her doctor's stethoscope and give her teddy shot after shot, reminding teddy each time to think about a favorite memory and that teddy is brave.

Children have control over their play world in a way they do not in reality, and they base their play more on reality or fantasy as they play through different situations, thoughts, and feelings (Neubauer, 1987). If a situation is challenging or emotionally intense, they may rely more on fantasy as a way to have greater control and distance while they work through their thoughts and feelings. As the situation becomes more manageable and understandable, their play may shift to being more reality based. Through play, children can explore different meanings of a situation and change the outcome or the way things are represented (Lillard,

1993). This allows them a space to safely explore, work through, and cope with these thoughts and feelings. Children at times need to change the facts of a situation and use fantasy to make it more manageable for them emotionally as they find ways to work through their feelings and come to a better understanding of what a situation means. As children do not have the same level of cognitive processing adults do, there are times where they need to rely on fantasy to figure out a situation. It is not because they are lying. It is because they do not yet understand something, usually a highly emotional situation to them, and they need the space of fantasy to protect themselves from feelings they do not understand as they work on understanding. A child who is worried about what it means to have to move can practice his feelings about it through play. He can explore the different ways a house looks and the different ways a family occupies it. Depending on how anxiety-provoking this situation is, he may begin by pretending it is a different family—maybe it is his stuffed animals who are moving or he may pretend that they are not moving at all, and then he may move toward playing as though it is him and his family who are moving. He may arrange and rearrange his new "room" while having his parents reassure him that they will be there and all of his belongings will be coming too.

Pretend play also has impacts on other areas of child development. It seems linked to early language skills in that children who have more advanced pretend play when they are a year old tend to have more advanced language skills when they are 2 years old. In addition, exposure to play materials such as plastic letters, seems to increase literacy. Pretend role play increases children's memory for stories, and when retelling stories, children tell more elaborate stories when they have toys to accompany their stories. Construction play with building materials is associated with increases in problem-solving for other building-related tasks. Finally, it is possible that pretend play impacts emotion regulation as well as increases creativity (Lillard et al., 2013). Children's ability to represent another person's thoughts and feelings may be related to perspective-taking, cooperation, and competence in social skills (Lillard, 1993). In a similar light, when adults join children in play directed by the child, these adults have an opportunity to better understand the child's world. Children who have verbal delays may be able to better express themselves through play, allowing others to better understand them (Milteer & Ginsburgh, 2012). To foster this exploration, it is important that adults do not become too concerned with reality (Moran, 1987), allowing themselves to enter into the child's play world without imposing their own rules and boundaries.

When children are able to engage in activities they experience as play, they have an increase in emotional well-being (Howard & McInnes, 2012). They are also able to try on many different feelings, learn to tolerate those feelings, and then express them to others without the confines of reality. Children use play to seek pleasure, reduce tension, and cope with conflict. Through play, they try out different approaches to situations (Solnit, 1987), they are able to satisfy needs that may not be allowed in reality (Moran, 1987), and, as they try on those different approaches, children come to a new level of competence (Neubauer, 1987).

To foster the development of these competencies, it is important to provide children an environment to fully make use of play. Within a preschool classroom, this would mean providing a playful environment where children have many opportunities to explore through play. This can be done by providing different toys as well as different play situations. Children need a variety of toys to explore. Some examples of toys that may be available are cars, trucks, blocks, kitchen foods and utensils, doctor's kits, clothes for dress up, dolls, doll houses and furniture, animals, and drawing materials. Children should be encouraged to explore toys freely and use them in any way they see fit. Teachers within a classroom should have times where they encourage unstructured free play, where children are allowed to explore and express as they wish. Teachers may become involved in play, but it is important to remember to be open to the roles children choose and the ways they play. Inserting oneself prematurely into the play or changing the play without the child's consent will likely lead the play to end and to possible behavioral acting out, as children try to preserve their sacred space of play. It is truly an honor to be allowed into the play of a child where we can have a better glimpse of their inner world, learn from their sense of playfulness, and foster their social, emotional, and behavioral development.

References

Bergman, A. (1993). To be or not to be separate: The meaning of hide-and-seek in forming internal representations. *Psychoanalytic Review*, 80(3):361–375.

Bretherton, I. (1989). Pretense: The form and function of make-believe play. *Developmental Review*, 9(4):383–401.

Elder, J.P., & Pederson, D.R. (1978). Preschool children's use of objects in symbolic play. *Child Development*, 49(2):500–504.

Fein, G.G. (1975). A transformational analysis of pretending. *Developmental Psychology*, 11(3):291–296.

Fein, G.G. (1981). Pretend play in childhood: An integrative review. *Child Development*, 52(4):1095–1118.

Fischer, K.W. (1980). A theory of cognitive development: The control and construction of hierarchies of skills. *Psychological Review*, 87(6):477–531.

Gilmore, K. (2011). Pretend play and development in early childhood (with implications for the oedipal phase). *Journal of the American Psychoanalytic Association*, 59(6):1157–1182.

Howard, J., & McInnes, K. (2012). The impact of children's perception of an activity as play rather than not play on emotional well-being. *Child: Care, Health and Development*, 39(5):734–742. doi:10.111/j.1365–2214.2012.01405.x

Lillard, A.S. (1993). Pretend play skills and the child's theory of mind. *Child Development*, 64(2):348–371.

Lillard, A.S., Lerner, M.D., Hopkins, E.J., Dore, R.A., Smith, E.D., & Palmquist, C.M. (2013). The impact of pretend play on children's development: A review of the evidence. *Psychological Bulletin*, 139(1):1–34.

Matthews, W.S. (1977). Modes of transformation in the initiation of fantasy play. *Developmental Psychology*, 13(3):212–216.

Mayes, L.C., & Cohen, D.J. (1992). The development of a capacity for imagination in early childhood. *The Psychoanalytic Study of the Child*, 47:23–47.

Milteer, R.M., & Ginsburg, K.R. (2012). The importance of play in promoting healthy child development and maintaining strong parent-child bond: Focus on children in poverty. *Pediatrics*, 129(1):e204–e213. www.pediatrics.org/cgi/doi/10.1542/peds.2011-2953

Moran, G.S. (1987). Some functions of play and playfulness: A developmental perspective. *The Psychoanalytic Study of the Child*, 42:11–29.

Neubauer, P.B. (1987). The many meanings of play: Introduction. *The Psychoanalytic Study of the Child*, 42:3–9.

Pederson, D.R., Rook-Green, A., & Elder, J.L. (1981). The role of action in the development of pretend play in young children. *Developmental Psychology*, 17(6):756–759.

Solnit, A.J. (1987). A psychoanalytic view of play. *The Psychoanalytic Study of the Child*, 4(2):205–219.

Sherkow, S.P. (2004). Further reflections on the "watched" play state and the role of "watched play" in analytic work. *The Psychoanalytic Study of the Child*, 59:55–73.

Ungerer, J.A., Zelazo, P.R., Kearsley, R.B., & O'Leary, K. (1981). Developmental changes in the representation of objects in symbolic play from 18 to 34 months of age. *Child Development*, 52(1):186–195.

Watson, M.W., & Fischer, K.W. (1977). A developmental sequence of agent use in late infancy. *Child Development*, 48(3):828–836.

Watson, M.W., & Fischer, K.W. (1980). Development of social roles in elicited and spontaneous behavior during the preschool years. *Developmental Psychology*, 16(5):483–494.

2

PRETEND PLAY IN THE CLASSROOM

Helping children grow

Sandra W. Russ and Alexis W. Lee

Pretend play is a terrific resource for children. For children who can already engage in pretend play, giving them opportunities to pretend in the classroom will help them develop in a variety of ways. For children who cannot pretend very well, teaching these pretend skills to them can provide a tool for the future. The classroom is an ideal place for children to play – especially in preschool and kindergarten. However, even in the early elementary school years, building in pretend play periods can be useful. This chapter will review the role of pretend play in child development and will suggest how pretend play can be incorporated into the classroom setting.

Pretend play, creativity, and well-being

What do we mean by pretend play? Pretend play is an activity during which children make up stories, use objects to represent other things (a block is a telescope), and express pretend emotions in the story narrative. Krasnor and Pepler (1980) thought pretend play involved nonlinearity, positive affect, intrinsic motivation, and flexibility. All of these components are important in creativity. Fein (1987) stressed the "as if" quality of children's play – an object is treated "as if" it was something else. She thought that imagination in play is intertwined with emotions and that both processes are essential to creativity.

What is creativity? Creativity involves the production of a product that is determined to be creative because it is novel, of good quality, and appropriate to the task (Sternberg, Kaufman, & Pretz, 2002). People often ask the question, 'Can children be creative?' It is unlikely that a child can make a contribution that is truly original or that has an impact on a field because they have not been able to gain the knowledge necessary or the developmental maturity. However, children can produce ideas or products that are novel and creative for their age group. They can develop the seeds of creativity important for their future.

Pretend play in childhood has been recognized as being important in child development by many theoreticians and clinicians. Erik Erikson (1963) thought that one function of play was creative expression and a second function was resolution of problems. A. Freud (1927) thought that pretend play was similar to free association in adults. In pretend play, children could take a leave of absence from reality and let their imagination roam. Primitive images and ideas with negative emotions, such as scary monsters or sad events, could be thought about and expressed in a way that was manageable (Waelder, 1933). Rather than "repress" or not think about uncomfortable thoughts and memories, children could express and integrate these issues. During play, children could learn to process emotions.

When children engage in pretend play, they are expressing a variety of cognitive and emotional processes. Russ (2004; 2014) has identified a number of processes that occur in play that overlap with processes that occur in creativity. Some children are more imaginative than others, tell better stories than others, can generate more ideas than others, and express more emotion in their stories. Many of these individual differences can be observed and measured in pretend play. Russ, Fehr, and Hoffmann (2013, p. 50) described these processes, which are presented as follows:

Cognitive processes in play that are important in creativity are:

- Fantasy/make-believe – the ability to engage in "as if" pretense. Children are making things up from scratch, pretending to be in a different time and place.
- Symbolism and transformation – the ability to transform objects into representations of other objects.
- Organization – the ability to develop a narrative with plot sequences and cause and effect.
- Divergent thinking – the ability to generate a variety of ideas, story themes, and symbols. Divergent thinking is especially important in creative problem solving.

Affective processes in play that are important in creativity are:

- Expression of emotion – the ability to express affect in a pretend play situation. For example, one puppet happily says to the other, "Whee. This is fun!" Both positive and negative affect can be expressed.
- Expression of affect themes – the ability to express affect-laden images and content themes. For example, one puppet says, "Let's have a snowball fight." This is aggressive ideation, even though no fighting has occurred.
- Enjoyment of the play activity – the capacity of experiencing joy and deep involvement in a task. This deep enjoyment and immersion in a task is often referred to as a "flow" state that is commonly reported by creative adults (Csikszentmihalyi, 1990).
- Cognitive and affective integration – regulated emotion and the ability to switch between emotion and well-organized thinking in a narrative.

Why is the link between play and creativity important? We know that children who have a good imagination can use it to problem solve. They can generate more coping strategies in stressful situations. They are better able to understand the viewpoints of other people. They can also use their imagination during play to express negative feelings in a safe place and to reduce anxiety. In different ways for different children, the ability to engage in pretend play is a resource that can enhance adaptive functioning.

Research findings

A large number of studies have found support for the association between pretend play and creativity in children (See Russ, 2014 for a review). For example, in an early study, Lieberman (1977) found a relation between playfulness in play and divergent thinking in kindergarten children. In a series of studies by Russ and colleagues, imagination in play was associated with divergent thinking, creative storytelling, and teacher ratings of imaginative ability.

In most of the play and creativity studies, play is associated with creativity independent of intelligence. This finding is important because it implies that the abilities we can measure in play are different than what our intelligence tests measure. Intelligence tests measure what we have learned and the ability to think of the correct answer – convergent thinking. Problems are defined and have one answer. Divergent thinking, which is the ability to think of many ideas, is a different cognitive process and is especially important in creative problem solving. A typical item on a divergent thinking test is "How many uses can you think of for a newspaper?" There are many acceptable answers and the more broadly one can associate, the more answers and more novel answers one can think of. Pretend play is an ideal vehicle for expressing and practicing divergent thinking. Blocks and Legos can become many different objects and stories can change in many ways. Children who are imaginative in their play are flexible in their thinking.

There is also evidence that early pretend play is predictive of later divergent thinking. Russ, Robins, and Christiano (1999) found that imagination in pretend play in first and second grade children was associated with divergent thinking four years later. With a different sample of children, Wallace and Russ (2015) found that imagination and positive affect in early play predicted divergent thinking after four years. In both studies, the association between play and divergent thinking was independent of verbal intelligence. Mullineaux and DiLalla (2009) reported that realistic role-play at age 5 predicted divergent thinking in early adolescence.

Studies have also found support for the association between pretend play and aspects of well-being and adaptive functioning in children. For example, Russ, Robins, and Christiano (1999) found that imagination predicted coping ability over time. Fehr and Russ (2016) found that pretend play was related to teacher ratings of prosocial behavior in the classroom. Hoffmann and Russ (2012) found an association between pretend play and emotion regulation.

Pretend play is associated with many abilities important in adaptive functioning. An important question is whether engaging in pretend play actually facilitates these abilities? Can we demonstrate cause and effect in our research programs? Russ (2004; 2014) theorized that, over time, engaging in pretend play helps children become more creative in the following ways:

- Practice with divergent thinking.
- Practice with making broad associations.
- Practice with manipulating ideas and images and story-themes. This contributes to cognitive flexibility.
- Practice with transforming objects into pretend objects.
- Express and experience positive emotions. Positive affect is important in creativity. Joy in a task is important in creative activity and in well-being. Children also report using play to improve their mood when they are stressed (Kenealy, 1989).
- Express and experience negative emotions. As Singer and Singer (1990) have emphasized, children can pace themselves in expressing anger or sadness so that they can modulate the affect and manage it.
- Express and think about affect themes and images.
- Practice making up ideas and stories from scratch. This kind of self-generated thought is important in creative production.

What does the research say about whether play can facilitate creativity? Research findings are mixed. There is some evidence that play facilitates divergent thinking. For example, in several well-done experimental studies, pretend play did facilitate divergent thinking in preschool children (Dansky, 1980; Dansky & Silverman, 1973). In the Dansky and Silverman study, it was found that children who played with objects during a play period gave significantly more uses for those objects than did a control group.

Lillard et al. (2013) criticized the rigor and conclusions of many of the play facilitation studies. There are different opinions about how the results of individual studies should be interpreted, but there is a consensus that methodologically rigorous studies with large samples, blinded experimenters, adequate control groups, and valid measures of play and creativity are needed (Lillard, Russ, Hirsh-Pasek, & Golinkoff, 2013). One important factor is the "dose" of the intervention. How many play intervention sessions are needed to demonstrate an effect? Christie (1994) has cautioned against brief one-trial studies in the play intervention area. It may take time for the development of processes in pretend play that would, in turn, facilitate creativity tasks. There is evidence that when pretend play occurs in multiple sessions over time, increases in components of creativity occur. For example, Kasari, Freeman, and Paparella (2006), in a randomized controlled study with children with autism, found that a play intervention resulted in increased symbolic play. These were young children from 3 to 4 years of age. This was a rigorous study that began the intervention at the child's current developmental level. The training involved modeling and prompting. Children received 30 hours of intervention weekly for six weeks on a daily basis. This was a rather intensive intervention but is necessary for children with autism. Children in the playgroup, compared with children in joint attention and control groups, had increased symbolic play that generalized to play with mothers.

In the Russ research program at Case Western Reserve University, we have been developing a protocol that uses story stems and a variety of unstructured toys. The play facilitator plays with the child and uses different standardized prompts. In a pilot study by Russ, Moore, and Farber (2004), first and second grade children in an inner-city school with a high degree of poverty received five individual 30-minute play sessions following a standard play intervention protocol. Different examiners blind to the group assignment assessed baseline play and outcome play on the APS. There were two playgroups (imagination and affect) and one control group (puzzles and coloring). The playgroups had a variety of toys available and played with the adult facilitator. They were asked to play out specific story themes that focused on imagination (have a boy go to the moon) or affect (have a girl be happy at a birthday party). The adult played with the child and followed the child's lead in the story but also praised, modeled, and asked questions. We controlled for adult interaction in the control group as well (coloring sheets and puzzles). The major result of this study was that the play interventions were effective in improving play skills on the APS. The affect play condition was most effective in that, after baseline play was controlled for, the affect playgroup had significantly higher play scores on all play processes. These children had more affect in their play (both positive affect and negative affect), a greater variety of affect content, and better imagination and organization of the story than did the control group. The imagination playgroup also had significantly more positive affect and variety of affect than the control group. Another major finding was that, on the outcome measure of divergent thinking, there were significant effects for group. Children in the playgroups had higher divergent thinking scores. Although the individual contrast comparisons did not reach significance, inspection of the profile plots indicated that the playgroups (usually the affect play group) had higher scores on the divergent thinking test. However, one limitation of this study was that no baseline measure of divergent thinking was obtained. In a follow-up study of these children four to eight months later by Moore and Russ (2008), the imagination group had improved play skills over time. The affect group did not maintain the play changes over this period. It may be that an increase in affect expression from a play intervention is temporary, whereas an increase in imagination and pretend in play could be longer lasting. In the follow-up study, there no longer was a significant group effect for divergent thinking. In fact, the control group now had higher scores. Perhaps booster sessions would have been useful in maintaining the initial group effects.

In a group adaptation of the play intervention, Hoffmann and Russ (2016) found that small group play sessions, when compared with a control group, did result in increased imagination and affective expression in play after six sessions. In addition, there was a transfer effect in that below average players increased in play creativity and also increased on a divergent thinking task. In the Russ research program, we have been able to increase imagination and affective expression in pretend play with standardized play intervention sessions with elementary school children. There have been transfer effects to a divergent thinking measure in two studies.

Implications for classroom settings

Assessing creative potential

Pretend play can be a window into a child's creative potential. As the research has shown, a child's ability to organize a story, use fantasy, think divergently, and express emotion and emotional themes in pretend play is related to measures of creativity. By observing children at play, a teacher can assess their capacity to pretend, to use a block to represent a stove, to express emotion in the fantasy, to make things up, and to enjoy an activity. Because these abilities in play are different from intelligence, children who are average or even below average in IQ can be creative in pretend play. Children high in intelligence, on the other hand, can be average or below average in imagination and emotion expression. The creative potential of many children is being overlooked because of problems with intellectual abilities or learning disorders. By identifying creative potential early, we can help these children develop processes important in creative production. One of the ways we can nurture creativity is through pretend play.

Facilitating pretend play in the classroom

Teachers and teacher aids can help children improve their play skills with a variety of play activities in the classroom. Depending on the needs of the child, play could be with one child, a small group of children, or with a teacher. There is evidence that children are more imaginative in play by simply playing with an interested adult play partner (Zyga, Russ, Ievers-Landis, & Dimitropoulos, 2014). What follows are some suggestions based on our play facilitation studies for encouraging play in the classroom.

Classroom setup and toys

Unstructured toys that allow for imagination and fantasy are best for encouraging pretend play. For example, blocks, Legos, human figures, plastic animals, and dolls allow the child to transform objects and develop their own associations. Toy cars and trucks, action figures, a play house, or play kitchen can allow for many different stories. It is important to note that these toys can be very inexpensive. In addition, arts and crafts such as play dough and drawing materials can also easily be incorporated into play stories, depending on the needs of the child.

It is best to designate a space in the classroom, like a rug or table, set aside specifically for pretend play. Having toys and play props in a special place, especially for preschool children, can help differentiate between playtime and other more structured and rule-based activities.

Guiding the play

In play with one child, the child is free to play out any theme that he/she chooses. Teachers can provide prompts and suggestions if needed. Some children need help getting started so the teacher could suggest a story and start playing along too. In group play, the teacher can help children take turns deciding what the story will be about and initiating the play. Teachers can encourage children to be open to other children's ideas and creativity. Additionally, children are encouraged to work together to play out the stories in such a way that each child's ideas are heard and implemented at some point in the storyline. Pretend play allows a space where children can practice taking alternative perspectives from their own. Group play can facilitate turn-taking, cooperation, sharing, and recombining many different ideas.

Each story has an organizational framework/sequence

Teachers can prompt for ideas about what happens first, middle, and last in the story (how the story resolves). As such, teachers help guide young children to think about cause and effect as well as consequences of behavior. Additionally, teachers can encourage their students to practice divergent thinking by generating and playing out alternative endings to stories. For example, each child's idea for a story ending could be played out.

- Include themes/stories with a variety of affect categories (happy, scared, angry, surprised)
- Include themes/stories with varying levels of structure:

   a   Outer space mission
   b   Day at school

Encourage playing out feelings with the character

- Negative feelings can be played out with the characters but not directed at other children.
- Both positive and negative emotions are encouraged by teachers.
- Children can take turns adopting different roles, i.e. mom, dad, brother, friend, to think about how one character's feelings might be different than another's.
- Incorporate specific praise for child's ideas and emotion expression.

- Foster a safe, accepting space where each child is free to express and enact a variety of different behaviors.
- Model pretending and expression of feelings. Modeling pretend or expression of emotions by the adult in play can be especially helpful.

Prompts to encourage emotion regulation and affect expression

- How is he feeling?
- It sounds like he feels . . . xx
- How does xx make her feel?
- What else could she say/do?
- How could he feel better? What could she do to feel better?
- How could she help him feel better?
- How does she want to feel?

Increase creativity and use of pretend

- What, how, what if, and so what questions
- What is your idea?
- What do you think?
- Let's play it out
- (As an aside) What should she do/say?
- Follow child's lead; minimal restraints, rules, and limitations
- What could we use this for?
- What could we use to be . . . xx?
- Children can learn that one object can represent another from an adult play partner or from other children in play.

Examples of play facilitation of child with adult play partner

In our work with children, we have a number of facilitation studies with different populations of children. The following are examples from transcripts of how specific interactions and prompts can facilitate play in the child.

F Facilitator (adult)

P Participant (child)

All names have been changed to protect identities.

Demonstrating questions, reflection, and specific praise

7-year-old boy

F: So, a story about having superpowers!

Huh, who are you gonna be in this story?

P: Uhhh . . . uhhh . . . this guy!

F: That guy? Nice! Who should I be?

P: Uhhh . . . this one!

F: This one?

P: He doesn't have superpowers.

F: He doesn't have superpowers? Aw man. Does your guy have superpowers?

P: Yes.

F: And what are your superpowers gonna be?

P: Strength.

F: Strength? That's a cool one. Nice.

   Hmm . . . I wonder how this story's gonna start . . .

P: That's a little thingy here.

F: Are these guys friends . . . or . . . brothers . . . or . . . ?

P: Friends!

F: Friends? OK. [Lots of setting up] You're getting something set up here? What is this?

P: This is . . . his house!

F: Their house? Or your house?

P: Uh . . . his.

F: Oh! Oh, it's his house. I see.

P: That will go here. They will fit . . . like that.

F: Very nice. You are getting it all nice and set up.

   I like how you made the blanket on the bed nice and smooth.

Demonstrating modeling and summarizing

F: So, he woke up because he's scared and he heard a noise, but he didn't find anybody and somebody took his box. What happens next?

P: And this guy comes out and says, "I found this box on the street, is it yours?"

F: Yeah, hey that's my box! Where'd you get that?

P: It was on the street.

F: Ohhhh! Thanks for bringing it back for me!

P: You're welcome.

F: That's so nice of you! Ah, I feel so much better now, thank you!

P: Why do you have a bear trap?

F: Well, that's just in case somebody decides to come and break into my house, so I can trap them in it.

P: You tried to trap me?

F: Not you! You were nice and brought me my box back, thank you.

P: No, I had the box and I threw it on the street!

6-year-old boy

F: So, Jack, look at me, Jack, remember this story is about having . . . what? Do you remember?. . . Do you remember what the story's about, Jack?

P: A boy having magical powers.

F: It's about having magical powers, yeah! So, what are your powers going to be?

P: Anything, when you have magical powers you can do anything, except if you want to choose a power.

F: Do you want to choose a power?

P: No, so I have every power!

F: You have every power? Woah!

Demonstrating modeling pretend, following child's lead, labeling, and summarizing story

7-year-old boy

F: Matt, I think, I think I see an elephant in the house!

P: Where?

F: Right over there, what is it doing?

P: I don't know!

F: What should we do about it?

P: Hmm, keep it?

F: Keep it? Ohh, we can keep it as a pet?

P: Yeah!

F: Oh, ok! I like that idea. I've always wanted an elephant as a pet.
   [To elephant] Hey, Mr. Elephant, wanna be our pet?
   [Aside to boy] Can the elephant talk?

P: Mm no.

F: No? OK.

F: Maybe this could be a bed for the elephant.

P: This could be an art project!

F: Or it could be an art project! That's true.
   Alright, so let's play out what's gonna happen in our story . . .
   First, we got our room and our house all set up and you had a really good
   idea with making those so they are even, and then . . .

P: See?

F: Oh cool! You have our art project all set up.

F: And we have a pet elephant in our room!

F: What's gonna happen next in our story?

P: Oops!

F: Uh oh, good thing it didn't break!

P: I'm gonna put this here.

F: OK, will it stay up? Nice.
   Oh, you're using that as a little prop for it to help it stay up? You got it! Cool.
   Alright, I think we're all set up, what should we do now?

P: Umm, put the books on the shelf?

F: Alright!

P: This is . . . um OK

P: Here we go, there.

F: Oh no! I dropped the books!

P: I just put this right there.

F: That's great. I think that looks really nice right there. Good spot for it.

P: Alright, this guy's gonna flip the pages.

F: Ohh, yeah . . . what is that story about?

P: This could be a chapter book!

F: It could be a chapter book!

What do you think that book's about?

P: Dragons!

F: Ohhhh, cool!

P: So that's more books over there. You get those.

F: Alright, got them.

P: I'll get these too.

F: OK, I got the books! Should I put them on the shelf?

P: Yeah, let's put them up here.

F: Oh, up there? Up top. OK, I can jump really high and put them up there.

P: Hmm . . .

F: OK, we got our books all set, cool. This is looking really nice in here.

P: Yeah.

F: What's that?

P: Uhh, just a brick.

F: Just a brick?

P: Yeah.

F: Do we need to do some repair in our house?

P: Nah

F: OK

P: I wonder where the surfboard could be . . .

F: Ohh, I don't know!

P: Found a place!

F: Hm?

P: Found a place! Or it could just be right here.

F: It could just be right there? Yeah, that looks good.

P: I wonder what the bathtub could be?

F: What the bathtub could be?

P: This could be the bathtub! Like in there. [Points to inside the jet ski]

F: Oh, yeah! Great idea. I like that!

P: The bathtub could be right here.

F: Uh huh.

P: Or right here, like you could play right here, if the bath is right here.

F: Uh huh and the bath is right here and these things maybe, could those be like the jets and we could make like a Jacuzzi sort of?

P: Yeah, like a little pipe that goes onto there?

F: Ohhh . . . that makes it like bubbly!

F: Ohhh makes it all bubbly in the bath? Like a bubble bath? Cool! I like that bubble bath.

F: Alright, are you gonna take a bath, Matt?

P: Sure!

F: Alright, I'll be over here, playing with our pet elephant over here.. . . OK, so we got our house all set up, we hmm, we got the piece of artwork and the books all on our book shelf and you had that really cool idea to use that thing as our bathtub, and now you're taking a bath. How's our story gonna end?

P: How 'bout us driving to the beach!

F: Ohh OK!

P: I'm gonna change into this guy since like he's more beachy.

F: He's more beachy? He's got his beach clothes on? That's true.. . .P: This could be like a cool submarine thing.

F: Oh, yeah, that's a good idea!

P: Still also like a bathtub too.

F: Oh it could like be both? It could transform from a bathtub to a submarine?

P: Yeah!

F: Alright!. . . How are you feeling right now?

P: Good.

F: You look like you are having so much fun!

What cannot be relayed in these examples, but is so important, is that the adult play partner *enjoys* the play with the child. The adult must be engaged in the play and attentive to the child. The adult should always follow the child's lead rather than introduce plot points. The adult play facilitator can model uses of pretend and emotion expression but should avoid generating ideas for how the story unfolds.

It is important to tailor the play interaction to the individual child. Some children, especially in the 6- to 9-year-old age range, just need the time and space to play. Other younger children do best with a play partner who engages with them using different encouraging prompts. Some children may benefit best by playing in a small group with other children. Paying attention to pretend play in the classroom, finding ways to help children develop play skills, and providing tools for future development of children's creative potential are crucial skills on the part of teachers and play facilitators.

References

Christie, J. (1994). Academic play. In J. Hellendoorn, R. Van der Kooij, & B. Sutton-Smith (Eds.), *Play and intervention* (pp. 203–213). Albany: State University of New York.

Csikszentmihalyi, M. (1990). *Flow: The psychology of optimal experience.* New York: Harper & Row.

Dansky, J. (1980). Make-believe: A mediator of the relationship between play and associative fluency. *Child Development,* 51:576–579.

Dansky, J., & Silverman, F. (1973). Effects of play on associative fluency in preschool-aged children. *Developmental Psychology*, 9:38–43.

Erikson, E. (1963). *Childhood and society*. New York: Norton.

Fehr, K. K., & Russ, S. W. (2016). Pretend play and creativity in preschool-age children: Associations and brief intervention. *Psychology of Aesthetics, Creativity, and the Arts*, 10(3):296–308.

Fein, G. G. (1987). Pretend play: Creativity and consciousness. In D. Görlitz & J. F. Wohlwill (Eds.) *Child Psychology. Curiosity, imagination, and play: On the development of spontaneous cognitive motivational processes* (pp. 281–304). Hillsdale, NJ: Lawrence Erlbaum Associates, Inc.

Freud, A. (1927). Four lectures on child analysis. In *The Writings of Anna Freud* (Vol. 1, Introduction to psychoanalysis: Lectures for child analysts and teachers, 1922–1935, pp. 3–69). New York: International Universities Press.

Hoffmann, J., & Russ, S. W. (2012). Pretend play, creativity, and emotion regulation in children. *Psychology of Aesthetics, Creativity, and the Arts*, 6(2):175–184.

Hoffmann, J., & Russ, S. W. (2016). Fostering pretend play skills and creativity in elementary school girls: A group play intervention. *Psychology of Aesthetics, Creativity, and the Arts*, 10(1):114–125.

Kasari, C., Freeman, S., & Paparella, T. (2006). Joint attention and symbolic play in young children with autism: A randomized controlled intervention study. *Journal of Child Psychology and Psychiatry*, 47:611–620.

Kenealy, P. (1989) Children's strategies for coping with depression. *Behavior Research Therapy*, 27:27–34.

Krasnor, L., & Pepler, D. (1980). The study of children's play: Some suggested future directions. *New Directions for Child Development*, 9:85–94.

Lieberman, J. N. (1977). *Playfulness: Its relationship to imagination and creativity*. New York: Academic Press.

Lillard, A. S., Lerner, M. D., Hopkins, E. J., Dore, R. A., Smith, E. D., & Palmquist, C. M. (2013). The impact of pretend play on children's development: A review of the evidence. *Psychological Bulletin*, 139:1–34.

Lillard, A., Russ, S. W., Hirsh-Pasek, K., & Golinkoff, R. (2013). Probing play: The research we need (Guest editors' afterword). *American Journal of Play*, 6(1):161–165.

Moore, M. & Russ, S. W. (2008). Follow-up of a pretend play intervention: Effects on play, creativity and emotional processes in children. *Creativity Research Journal*, 20:427–436.

Mullineaux, P. Y., & DiLalla, L. F. (2009). Preschool pretend play behaviors and early adolescent creativity. *Journal of Creative Behavior*, 43:41–57.

Russ, S. W. (2004) *Play in child development and psychotherapy: Toward empirically supported practice*. Mahwah, N.J.: Lawrence Erlbaum Ass.

Russ, S. W. (2014). *Pretend play in childhood: Foundation of adult creativity*. Washington, DC: American Psychological Association.

Russ, S. W., Fehr, K., & Hoffmann, J. (2013). Helping children develop pretend play skills: Implications for gifted and talented programs. In K. Kim, J. Kaufman, J. Baer, & B. Sriraman (Eds.), *Creatively gifted students are not like other gifted students: Research, theory and practice* (pp. 49–67). Rotterdam: Sense Publishers.

Russ, S. W., Moore, M., & Farber, B. (2004, July). Effects of play training on play, creativity and emotional well-being. Poster presented at the Annual Meeting of the American Psychological Association, Honolulu, Hawaii.

Russ, S. W., Robins, A. L., & Christiano, B. A. (1999). Pretend play: Longitudinal prediction of creativity and affect in fantasy in children. *Creativity Research Journal*, 12(2):129–139.

Singer, D. G., & Singer, J. L. (1990). *The house of make-believe: Children's play and the developing imagination*. Cambridge, MA: Harvard University Press.

Sternberg, R., Kaufman, J., & Pretz, J. (2002). *The creativity conundrum*. New York: Psychology Press.

Waelder, R. (1933). Psychoanalytic theory of play. *Psychoanalytic Quarterly*, 2:208–224.

Wallace, C. E., & Russ, S. W. (2015). Pretend play, divergent thinking, and math achievement in girls: A longitudinal study. *Psychology of Aesthetics, Creativity, and the Arts*, 9(3):296–305.

Zyga, O., Russ, S., Ievers-Landis, C., & Dimitropoulos, A. (2014, September 21). Assessment of pretend play in Prader-Willi syndrome: A direct comparison to autism spectrum disorder. *Journal of Autism and Developmental Disorders*, 45(4):1–13.

PART II

Understanding play

3

PLAY AS COMMUNICATION

Brenda Lovegrove Lepisto

After table work, Ms. Taylor, Rachel, and Jason's kindergarten teacher straightened her classroom supply closet. She smiled to herself hearing Jason's loud, belly laugh with intermittent giggles. Vaguely, she heard toys banging and crashing as the children played. As Ms. Taylor turned around she saw Rachel dumping the last of six bins of toys on the ground. Frustrated, she first thought of scolding the children: one for dumping and the other for laughing, yet she calmly stated, "Well, we are going to need to pick up these toys." Rachel answered adamantly, "Not now, I am too tired." Jason disappeared among the other children, some who were witnessing the incident and others who continued playing. Aware of her feelings of irritation, Ms. Taylor walked away repeating that the toys would need to be put away. What was being communicated here? Ms. Taylor decided to try another tactic. She approached Rachel and repeated that these toys belong in the bins, not on the floor. Rachel said, "I am too angry to pick them up now." Ms. Taylor said, "I understand. I feel a little irritated, too," and again walked away. Ms. Taylor appreciated that some of the other children were watching. She noticed Rachel picking up one of the toys. Ms. Taylor knew that Rachel became a big sister to a baby brother about three months ago, she said, "Oh Rachel, I saw you picking up a toy. Thank you so much!" Rachel said, "No, I didn't." Walking away Ms. Taylor remarked, "Thank you for picking up that toy! That is great." Rachel said, "Don't look!" as she picked up more toys and began putting them back in the six bins. Then she asked Ms. Taylor to admire her work. Ms. Taylor fussed over her cooperation and work and then the other children started showing Ms. Taylor that they, too, were helpers.

Ms. Taylor responded acknowledging and respecting Rachel's need for agency as she enhanced the solid sense of classroom community. The children cautiously watched and listened to Ms. Taylor, taking in both the tone and tenor of her message to Rachel and Jason. Through recent parent conferences, Ms. Taylor learned of Rachel's life circumstance, sharing parents and living space with a new brother. Appreciating how wonderful making someone giggle feels, she resonated with Rachel's desire to keep the laugh going. She also enjoyed Jason's delight in the toy dumping. Listening sensitively, though, she heard Rachel's important unstated communication, "I love feeling powerful by causing delight in Jason. I can make him laugh so hard. I need to feel agency in my life." Ms. Taylor could have scolded Rachel, demanded that she and Jason pick up the toys, or worried that if she was not strict and tough the other children would not respect classroom rules. Limits and boundaries are crucial to classroom functioning. Instead, she listened to Rachel's communication, putting her observation into the context of Rachel's life as she monitored her own feelings. Through play, Rachel communicated her plea for agency and the desire to bring joy to others. Fortuitously, Ms. Taylor saw more than a disobedient child dumping toys on the floor.

This chapter offers teachers a perspective of play as communication. Viewing children's play with an appreciation for the communicative value play possesses and appreciating the life context in which play occurs, enriches teacher-child relationships. Paying attention to what is said, not said, done, not done, as well as knowing the child's life situation provides necessary information to communicate effectively with children. Once we hear what they say, see what they play, we can know how to best respond to facilitate children's development, our relationship with them, and their understanding of themselves. This chapter describes a method of child-centered communication that assists children in elucidating and expanding their communication through play and the tools that adults, teachers, and parents can use to more accurately understand and respond to children's wishes, dreams, fear, and aspirations.

Introduction

If we truly understand children's play, we can gain a real understanding of what they are thinking, feeling, and generally what is going on inside of them. In other words, play is like theater where a complex story is told. Child psychologists who are play therapists agree that play is the natural medium of children's communication and self-expression (e.g. Lovinger, 1998). Further, viewing play from a communication perspective contributes richness to observations of children's play behavior. Adults can facilitate children's communication by adjusting their own play communication, enhancing the opportunity for the child's psychological growth, and the strengthening of the adult and child relationship. Due to children's immaturity, the capacity for verbal expression is limited—children are better at showing than telling. "When viewed from this perspective, toys are used like words by children and play is their language" (Landreth, 1991, p. 14). Hence, play offers a glimpse into a child's mind.

With astute communication skills, children's play can be expanded to illuminate unique mental workings and emotions. Likewise, children react with actions and feelings to our play with them. They develop ideas, experience emotions, and draw inferences from our verbal and nonverbal behavior, so we can communicate with them using the medium of play. When we play with them, or respond to their underlying thoughts and feelings, they begin to develop thinking about their own thinking and others' thinking.

Throughout this chapter, we will focus on children's and adults' play communication to achieve sensitive listening that allows us access to children's inner most feelings and thoughts. We will accomplish this task systematically using practical tools and guidelines that enhance play and communication by: 1) gathering data through listening and observing play, 2) allowing and facilitating the expansion of play, 3) paying attention to our own feelings, and 4) choosing a level to react to the play using our own play communication. These techniques are illustrated with vignettes. In summary, we **gather data, listen to children, remain self-aware**, and then **make decisions how to react**.

Gathering data and expanding the communication

To understand children's play we first need to gather background information. Teachers observe actions and language, learning crucial information about children, individually and collectively in the classroom. Parents and caregivers contribute significant information about family life, unique personality, and background. During early childhood before children begin using internalized, private speech, they spontaneously tell us through play exactly what is on their minds. With close observation and facilitation, we can learn what children think and feel. Additionally, we can better understand and help them if we hear their voices when informed by context and circumstance such as concerns about siblings, conflict in their homes, health worries, etc. That background information provides context to understand their play behavior. The best source for a child's perspective, attitude, and feeling is the child her/himself, which means that adults need to learn to listen more accurately and respectfully, then use context and history to develop understanding.

In an article advocating listening to children during child development research, Brooker (2011) discussed talking and listening seriously to children as imperative to protect the rights of children. Thus, she suggested we conduct research "with" rather than "on" children. Mistakenly, some adults think listening to children is a simple, unimportant event because they think that they know better than children or what in is their best interests. Furthermore, disingenuous listening harms children and further reinforces the power and status differential. Children quickly learn that their concerns are not taken seriously so they stop telling us what is important to them. Sometimes, adults view seriously listening to a child as an act of beneficence rather than a child's right to be heard. For example, allowing children to *only* make inconsequential, trivial decisions about clothing or color rather than hearing them out on important matters suggests that their ideas are unimportant. Once children deem their ideas as unworthy of consideration, they will not risk telling adults their genuine thoughts. Genuinely and respectfully listening to children does not equate with taking their advice on all matters, especially matters that are beyond their capacity to determine. Rather, we can listen, appreciate, and respect their ideas—not to be taken as orders to carry out but rather a discussion of important matters.

In this chapter the premise lies in showing respect by attentive listening that seriously considers what the child is saying, exploring, and communicating. Sometimes I hear comments like "Oh, don't get him started on that because he will never stop asking for the new truck." How does exploring his interest in trucks determine whether a truck is going to be purchased or not? Could the problem lie with the listener who does not want to experience feelings of guilt for not buying the beloved truck or just doesn't want to buy another truck or is bored with the conversation? Who does not want to talk about a passion? What I am suggesting here is that we can always listen—we do not have to agree, act, condone, disagree—just listen with intent, authenticity, and seriousness. Naturally and fortunately, we like to teach children, yet when we change the topic of conversation or play because we are bored, uncomfortable, or feel the need to instruct, we interfere with the communication between us. The child will follow our lead rather than reveal thoughts and feelings. Our agenda may include curricular learning intentions, a wish for a specific outcome in conversation, quell discomfort and a need to "not hear" what a child is trying to tell us. When we interfere with children's play agendas, we lose the message they are telling us about what is important to them. Do we only listen to children's agenda? Teaching, of course, involves imparting knowledge, yet there is room in our relationship with children for them to tell us openly what concerns them. Life's lessons taught through respectful, engaged listening represent the lessons that guide lives. Learning to listen, observe without steering the conversation, and play becomes vital to hearing what children communicate.

In an article, aptly titled, "Getting Under Their Skins? Accessing Young Children's Perspectives through Ethnographic Fieldwork," Warming (2011) suggested two listening techniques when dealing with children. First, as adopting the "least adult role" where the adult tries to play with the child in a childlike manner. Basically, this is refusing to take an adult role of informing, regulating, ordering, and educating. Using this approach, the adult observes, participates, yet does not intervene in an adult way, allowing the child full rein of the play. The second approach described is that of "the detached observer" or "other adult." Here, the adult watches the children but holds back from actively participating as a group member or playmate. Interpretation from observable data then provides information regarding the child's mental working. Yet, another role for learning about children's lives, experiences, feelings, and thoughts through play is to adopt the "interested adult friend" role. The adult separates herself from the usual adult role, engages the child, yet does not instruct, educate, discipline the child but rather is a "friend" (Thomas & O'Kane, 2000). These various roles speak to the power imbalance between children and adults that exist in any conversation, often inhibiting the child from freely expressing her thoughts, ideas, or feelings. The balancing act involves having the best of both worlds: remain in charge yet allow children open self-directed communication. An adult can accomplish this task only if self-aware and self-reflective. As with all communication skills, self-awareness makes for better communication with others.

Listening to ourselves/listening to children

Better communicators are self-aware, they track their own feelings during conversations. Often our feelings push us to respond with an answer, tone, or words. Being aware of our feelings and thoughts, allows us to consciously steer the conversation down a growth-producing path. As adults do, children arouse feelings in us and themselves as they talk about subjects important to them—sometimes uncomfortable, upsetting, or irritating feelings, along with joyful, delightful feelings. Paying attention to our own feelings as we talk with children aids in sensing emotional landmines along the way. We learn about ourselves. Do you feel your heart pound as the child begins to hit the baby doll with the adult doll? Do you want to know what she has on her mind? What is being played out? Do you want to know more? Will more feelings be allowed to emerge or encouraged? Or will we stop listening by telling the child to stop hitting the baby—it is not nice. Importantly, if we feel and acknowledge our feelings and we are truly interested in communicating with the child, we can thoughtfully engage in the play, allowing the child to share her/himself without censorship. However, when adults shut down the play or conversation due to negative emotions, we never learn what children think, feel, or need help with. Being aware of our own feelings guides us to respond more thoughtfully and strategically to children's communication.

In the next two sections—tools for observation and common themes of childhood—we will gather techniques to better understand communication with children. Then when reading the next two vignettes, identify which tools and themes were present. You may think of more tools and themes.

Tools to facilitate communication in children's play and conversation

This section offers some tools that adults can use to enhance communication with children.

Checklist for observation

Physical

Child's tone of voice: Sharp, excited, intense, bored, happy, dull, angry, etc.
Child's chosen words: Children use words they have heard. For example, "Get your butt over here," and, "Come over here. Hurry." convey related, although different meanings.
Facial expressions: Type of eye contact, lacking, intense or fleeting eye contact, clenched jaw, relaxed face, drools without knowing, etc.

Emotional expressions: For example, a child may talk about being "mad" vs. "annoyed," which suggests finer more distinctive understanding of feelings.

Gross and fine motor movements: Smooth, clumsy, changes in patterns, regulation of motor movements, etc.

Toys: First chosen, pondering over toys, use of toys (conventional, novel, incidental), clothing of characters, children's handling of dolls' bodies, etc.

Contextual variables

Circumstances: Where the play occurs, with whom, why (at recess, at the desk, etc.)

History: Background information to aid in understanding play in context.

Changes in patterns of play: Often abrupt changes in play signal conflict or distress. Repetitive play suggests the child repeated attempts to master a situation or feeling.

Dynamics and relationships among characters with adult or self: Dynamics are behaviors, thoughts, and feelings that are linked together through association, often by time.

Motivation: Motivation includes the child's possible reasons for whatever happens in the play. For example, in the previous example Rachel's motivation was to entertain Jason rather than to make the teacher angry.

Mood and affect: Affect includes emotions and feelings of all play characters.

Teacher reactions—Self-awareness

Feelings generated in teacher

Toward child: Do you like this child? Does this child's behavior frustrate the classroom procedure? What feelings are you coming into the situation with?

Seemingly from self: What feelings do you have about yourself today? (Just a quick check—are you tired? Feeling enthused? Eager?)

Toward others in play: How are you feeling about the others in the play, either children, toy figurines, or pretend characters? For instance, is this imaginary friend demanding? Are the other children cooperating with the play theme, appropriately enhancing the story or obstructing movement of the story?

Acknowledgement of attitudes

In oneself, possibly newly discovered: Feelings of revenge and retribution surprise you. Understanding why children get in trouble after being in trouble—you recall a time when you were angry and subsequently caused some trouble yourself. Kindness and love well up when witnessing a child lovingly care for another child or figurine. You become sensitized to feelings, thoughts, and attitudes that reside inside of you.

Toward abstractions, society: Sometimes children play themes of injustice based on belonging to a group (all sheep cannot be a part of the farm because they are stupid or for every wrongdoing a stronger wrongdoing is deserved, etc.).

Toward authority figures: In play with a child, you notice how angry you feel when playing the student who is always in trouble. Then you reflect on this attitude in yourself and the child especially in the child's life circumstances.

Toward children: Maybe you discover feelings and attitudes that you did not know you had about children (i.e., impatience with their dawdling, tendency to pick at fabrics, etc.).

Physical sensations

Stomach ache, headache develops, pains in various parts of the body: A common physical sensation is needing to "run to the bathroom" just when the play gets intense. These physical sensations inform us of underlying feelings, often. Sometimes, children come to the session when they are "sick" and are not "sick" when they leave. Clearly, there were other factors playing a part in the child not feeling well. Sometimes, we have the physical sensations—develop a headache after playing a theme, etc.

Free association

Following the thread of our own thinking called free association helps us think of what comes to mind when the child does this, I feel like this or have this thought when a child does this or says this. These somewhat random thoughts provide clues to what the child is trying to tell us. By paying attention to your own thoughts and feelings, you can develop this skill. Just listen for what thought follows which thought regardless of logic. Our free associations are linked but not always transparently or logically linked.

Now let's list some common themes of childhood. You may come up with your own list by adding themes you observe in the children you teach.

Common themes of childhood

Developmental stages in children suggest themes that often appear in their play and conversation.

Various body themes: Anatomical differences, bodily damage, bodily functions, illness: Children seem to never be too old for bathroom talk or curiosities. Bodies are of great interest to children.

Power: As discussed previously, playing school where the teacher has the power or house where the mother or father have the power. How is this power handled? Where does the power lie? Who has strength, lack of it?

Abandonment, loss of a loved one, and death: For example, one child adopted after her mother and father lost custody, drew "lost" signs "Help wanted: Please help me find my mom." Another child played burying all the sand toys, only to resurrect them, over and over.

Imitation of adult functions and roles: Playing going to the office. Recently, when given a new book a 3-year-old told me she would take it to her office (like her mother and father have often said to her). She packed up her backpack and "left for the office."

People's or self's comings and goings: Themes of packing for a trip, going to the work, and coming to visit are common themes.

Exclusion, rejection: Children sometimes practice not letting others play, even stuffed animals, or they negotiate who can watch and who can play (adapted from Marans et al., 1991).

Lastly, we will consider questions to ask ourselves and children to facilitate the communication. Then we will practice these skills by identifying them in the previous and following vignettes.

Questions and comments to facilitate communication

  i Tell me more.
 ii What story are we playing today?
iii What should s/he do next?
 iv I wonder how s/he is feeling.
  v Um, what is s/he thinking?
 vi Maybe s/he is feeling a feeling.
vii What happens next?
viii I hear s/he is crying. I wonder what s/he is crying about.

Vignettes

Vignette 1

Max, age 2 years old, witnessed his nanny fall against a sharp statue at the museum. To protect Max, she remained calm, mostly shielded the wound from Max's view, phoned for help, and luckily Max's father worked in the building and arrived to take him home. Max's attentive parents were concerned over Max witnessing such an upsetting event as his nanny was hurt and bleeding. After reassuring him that nanny will heal, they sought to further shield him from the memory of the event, yet to no avail. Over time and with a concerted effort by his parents and his nanny, the incident remained in the background of parental/nanny conversation. Max's mother cautioned others to not speak of the unfortunate event in fear of drawing attention to the incident further upsetting Max, who seemed unscathed by the entire situation—no sleep or unusual eating disturbances. A few days later, observant Max noticed his Mickey Mouse figurine's broken arm. With furrowed eyebrows, concerned expression appearing that he was about to cry, he brought Mickey to his father, Justin. With limited verbal skills, he pointed to the broken arm. The unsuccessful taping of the arm to Mickey resulted in a one-armed

Mickey. Justin wondered how Mickey feels. Max responded, "Crying" as he thoroughly examined Mickey, pointing out his wounded arm. "What happened to my arm?" says Mickey through Daddy's voice. "Boo-boo," replies Max. Justin spontaneously played out Max's feelings of sadness over losing the arm. "Waa, Waa, Waa," cried Mickey through Daddy's voice. Max watched intently as Daddy cried for Mickey, then dressed Mickey's wound assuring him that his boo-boo would heal. Max examined the arm. "Again, again," squealed Max. He and Daddy played the scene repeatedly until Max "lost interest." Next, after Max showed Nana how to play, she noticed the cue by crying, "Waa, Waa, Waa," and fixing up Mickey until Max lost interest.

In their discomfort and concern over Max's potential trauma of witnessing nanny hurt, bleeding, and paramedics arriving, they attempted to shield Max from emotionally processing the experience, yet he persevered. Fortunately for Max, his loving, attentive father's empathy responded to his worry and through play he attended to Max's questions and concerns. These concerns extend beyond the nanny getting hurt to his own vulnerability and the safety of the environment. In this vignette exists the opportunity to explore, illuminate and elaborate a play theme of critical importance to the child at this moment.

Now let's think about Max's father's (Justin) experience of the play. First, when Max handed broken Mickey to his father, Justin inquired for more information. He read and responded to his son's portrayal of Mickey's injury. Because Justin's empathic attunement, he responded on a level that tapped into Max's worry about body integrity, his own and his nanny's welfare. Justin noticed Max's furrowed eyebrows, intent stare and he remembered what the experience Max had with the nanny's injury, Max's experience with boo-boos, and then decided to follow suit with "crying."

Once the play communication has been explored, elaborated, and illuminated, how do we respond? Max's father chose to demonstrate the crying and then when Max suggested he provided the assurance that Mickey will recover. This repetitive healing narrative brings forth the possibility of comprehending the event and feelings. Expanding the child's communication by inviting the child to determine and elaborate what is on his mind by asking, "Now what happens?" "What do you want Mickey to do?" "What do I do now?" The control gives the child permission to alter, augment, or change the theme. Max learns important life lessons of people getting hurt, people getting better, how to get help, and helpers helping, through play, not verbal explanations. Most of life's lessons are first learned through play. We learn what he has on his mind, his history, how he interprets the world, what his experience is, his feelings, and his idea of how situations can change.

Next, Max began to focus on his acquired boo-boos, crying over minor scratches, needing a band-aid, observing, pointing out and commenting on others' boo-boos. With a worried expression on his face, he points to a boo-boo on Nana's thumb and asks, "boo-boo?" Max received a doctor's kit that he enthusiastically used to examine all family members. After Max discovers that the conversation about Mickey's body is acceptable and taken as legitimate, he feels secure enough to question others' boo-boos in vivo. From displacement to real-life demonstrates the confidence he feels to question directly.

Analysis

What observations do you have of the previous vignette? Look over the observation tools and common themes listed previously before reading the following section. You may discover more observations and themes than are listed.

Checklist for observations

- Context/history of nanny getting hurt at the museum
- Parents concerned
- Chose broken toy and then pointed to missing arm
- With furrowed eyebrows, intently watched father playing
- Father played out the getting hurt
- Max squealed "again, again," letting us know he needed to work out feelings.
- Repetitious play

Questions and comments to facilitate communication

- Father took Max's concerns seriously.
- Father read behavioral cues indicating Max's concern about bodily integrity
- Father asked for elaboration.
- Nana followed communication, so she could respond to Max's concerns.
- Doctor kit was purchased so Max could take the role of the helper.
- Emotions were expressed by father, Max, and Nana.
- Roleplaying of event occurred until Max felt ready to move to the next developmental level.

Common themes of childhood

- Bodily integrity and missing anatomical part in displacement (in the toy)
- Healing in displacement (toy)
- Focus of play shifted to his own body integrity (boo-boos) and keen awareness of others' boo-boos
- Healing of own and others' bodies
- Taking on role of caring for others by asking about boo-boos
- Using doctor kit to examine family members

Vignette 2

Maria, age 3 years old, moved to a new home across the country, left a beloved caregiver, and began attending a new preschool. Her parents and teachers describe her as confident, happy, sturdy, and independent. Since the move and beginning a new preschool, Maria cries fearfully when she notices a fly, bee, or bird. Flapping her hands, she runs away. Simultaneously, she begins to withhold bowel movements, becoming anxious when she feels she need to have a bowel movement. Isolating herself, straining to hold in, and themes of preoccupation with others' bathroom habits emerge. The wind frightens her. Looking at the moving clouds, she remarked, "The sky is moving." Play themes are disrupted as a bug or bird fly by. Parents' and teachers' reassuring comments go unnoticed. Her parents and teachers work together to understand Maria's feelings, thoughts, and behavior. Understanding her communication as a feeling of loss of control, they follow her lead through play. When he sees a housefly, her teacher, Mr. Solomon, in a playful tone tells the bugs, "Go away, bug. I am not a flower" or, "Shoo fly." She and her classmates laugh and begin imitating him. At school Maria became a bug hunter and catching bugs in a special jar, allowing her to observe the bug under her control. Bug hunting became a sought-after activity. Then having the role of naming and observing the bug, she began to feel some control over the uncontrollable life. She and Mr. Solomon discussed the bug's possible feelings about the new home and old home, helping process her experience. Similarly, waving at the birds flying by converts the scary unknown into a friend. Searching for bird nests in the wooded area next to the playground becomes a favorite activity for her and other children. Conversations about where the birds live, with whom, what they eat, and their life habitat transform birds into interesting rather than scary creatures. Drawing bird and nest pictures, not only provides mastery over the experience of birds, it also provides a window into her experience. What colors are chosen, where on the page, and what is included in the picture are all further communication of how Maria experiences the uncontrollable.

Next, the need for control was experienced through her bodily functions. Suppressing bowel movements became another expression of the need for control. Looking at poop, talking about poop, watching videos about poop, having dolls and animals sitting on the potty, watching her aunt's cats go potty, and flushing her own poop down the toilet waving goodbye achieved a feeling of control. All of this was communication through play from her and to her. Now that we have the hypothesis that the family relocation jarred Maria's feeling of security, we can understand why she felt afraid of the dark. She needed her grandmother to check on and she wanted to see the dark, "Just a little bit of dark" she says as she holds her fingers to show how much. Moving from the East to the Midwest, the daylight hours are extended resulting in her uncertainty when it is bedtime. She plays putting the baby to sleep, going through the tradition of bedtime, being quiet so the baby can sleep, and sleeping with the baby and other friends. Maria's grandmother visited her at her previous home, so when she sees her, Maria asks, "Abuela, let's play baby like when you visited me, okay?" She orchestrates the sequence just like at her previous home. She pretended to be a baby and to be put to sleep as a baby. In other words, her play regresses to a safer time, so she can catch up psychologically to where she is now. Her parents expressed concern over the regressive play, thinking that if they participated she would not want to grow up. This confident young child needed to express her feelings, feelings that were upsetting for her parents to witness due to their own guilt over causing her distress by the family move. Again, as stated previously, nothing serves us better than knowing ourselves and being able to be thoughtful about our communication to children.

Later, parents reported, "Maria is back to normal, happy, no problems with anxiety." During Facetime her grandmother said, "Maria when you come to visit Abuela at the lake house, this will be where you sleep," showing the bunk beds. Maria says, "Abuela, check me?" Abuela says, "You know Abuela will always check you, Sweetie." When Abuela showed her the bed where her parents will sleep she reacts with anxiety and breaks off the conversation. Then as her father and grandmother finish their conversation in the background, Maria begins singing "Good night mousie, good night mousie" until several toys are put to bed. Then she wanted her father to witness the mouse asleep. This play communicated the anxiety just under the surface. She is not "over it and back to normal"—she is coping and actively mastering her anxiety at having been uprooted with no real understanding or choice.

Analysis

What observations do you have of the previous vignette? Look at the observation tools and common themes listed previously before reading the following section. Again, you may discover more themes than listed here.

Checklist for observations

- Context/history of moving to a new home
- New fears and interests
- New fears
- Interest in bodily functions
- Fear of darkness
- Regressive play
- Repetitious play
- Change in pattern of conversation regarding sleeping

Questions and comments to facilitate communication

- Adults took Maria's concerns seriously.
- Teacher expanded play with bugs.
- Parents allowed and expanded regression to assist Maria in marshalling her resources to confront loss of control.
- Adults recognized the developmental growth as Maria mastered levels of control.

- Parents monitored their own feelings about Maria's anxiety and loss.

Common themes of childhood

- Themes of loss of home and control over environment.
- Feelings of lack of power.
- Maria identifying with the parents putting her to bed by putting Mousie to bed. She takes good care of Mousie.
- Loss of control: fearful of flying insects, bodily functions, the dark.

Discussion

Common themes of childhood include body integrity, control, and security, hence the extensive conversations about boo-boos, bodily functions, and flying creatures—their origin, severity, location, and experiences. Establishing the theme and then the child's unique perspective and experience of the theme act as a guide to learning more about the child's understanding. In discovering the theme, we need to guard against demanding too much cognition rather than the experience. In other words, the danger with sophisticated verbalizations and interpretations of play is that "children get caught between the words and their experience" (Saxe, personal communication, November 11, 1996). She explained, "Words don't articulate the experience at the moment. If you are talking to their cognition, which undermines their experience, it doesn't help them move their experience to one that is better articulated." In other words, providing more verbal detail, instruction, and education often build cognition at the expense of the child's better-understood personal narrative, which remains the foundation of acquired knowledge. Asking the who, what, where, when, and how can appeal to cognition, not elucidation. Rather, we may be imposing our own wish for details, expansion, or content on the child, instead of allowing and facilitating the child telling her own story. Exploration, when successful, opens the conversation and is best accomplished using open ended questions about what the child has already said.

Often, I hear adults assume the child's feeling and the intentions by commenting on a crying doll, "Why is the little girl sad?" The little girl may not be feeling sad but rather angry. A better indirect question would be, "I see the little girl is crying." And if that does not facilitate more comments, open the conversation more by wondering, "I wonder what the little girl is crying about?" This allows for frustration, anger, sadness, and joy to be a reason the little girl is crying. Staying with observable behavior and what the child has brought to the conversation allows the child to lead the story. Imagine a table where you can only talk about what the child has placed on the table or you have seen placed on the table. This means only what the child has said or you have seen, excluding your interpretations of what you saw. The child then has room to feel, say, and expand the play theme in any direction without concern of contamination of what the adult has said. Of course, we will have thoughts about the child's experience, yet we do not have to verbally share our thoughts with them. We can first follow the child's direction.

What if during the busy classroom, we do not have time to give the one-to-one attention to a play theme that emerges? Classrooms of children present a wonderful opportunity to discuss many child-led topics. For instance, one day in a classroom when children drew and colored pictures to accompany the story the teacher read, a bird flew into the window. The teacher stopped the lesson, focused on the bird, and discussed feelings they had about what had just happened. The children spoke about how the bird's mom would be sad and maybe would cry, how the bird lay there scared and hurt, how the bird would go to heaven, how dumb it was for the bird to fly into the window, how they might stop birds from flying into the window, why birds fly into the window, what happened to the birds' body, etc. The teacher gave the children a wonderfully rich opportunity to describe their thoughts and feelings about the incident. She showed them a book from the library describing bird habitats and development. Then the children resumed their art lesson. Over the next week during recess the teacher noticed the children running and falling and children aiding children who were pretending to be hurt, building nests, and pretending to fly. She witnessed the power of communication, the discussion she and the children had about the bird. The play represents the children's internalization of the lessons of vulnerability, fear, hurt, help, kindness, empathy, compassion, and care. These lessons are learned through the teacher's willingness to follow the children's communication lead.

Summary

Communicating to children and listening to children takes courage. As adults, we sometime unintentionally quell raw emotions and the direct, uninhibited expression of primitive feelings, urges and thoughts. Mistakenly, we think if we steer the child's conversation away from uncomfortable subjects and feelings, that the issue is resolved. Yet, if we listen and listen closely we are privileged to learn the child's private thoughts and feelings. Sensitive listening, observing, and nonintrusive conversation and play, facilitates children's development and understanding of self, others, and the world in which they live. Once we learn their feelings, we will know how to respond to help them learn about themselves, and we, if we are lucky, learn about ourselves in the process.

References

Brooker, L. (2011). Taking children seriously: An alternative agenda for research? *Journal of Early Childhood Research*, June:137–149.

Landreth, G. L. (1991). *Play therapy: The art of the relationship*. Muncie, IN: Accelerated Development Inc.

Lovinger, S. L. (1998). *Child psychotherapy: From initial therapeutic contact to termination*. Northvale, NJ: Jason Aronson, Inc.

Marans, S., Mayes, L., Cichetti, D., Dahl, K., Marans, W., & Cohen, D. J. (1991). The child-psychoanalytic play interview: A technique for studying thematic content. *Journal of the American Psychoanalytic Association*, 39(4):1015–1036.

Thomas, N., & O'Kane, C. (2000). Discovering what children think: Connections between research and practice. *The British Journal of Social Work*, 30(6):819–835.

Warming, H. (2011). Getting under their skins: Accessing young children's perspectives through ethnographic fieldwork. *Childhood*, 18(1):39–53. doi:10.1177/0907568210364666

4

FROM REACTION TO REFLECTION

Mentalizing in early childhood education

Norka T. Malberg

It is 8 am on a Monday morning; teachers have been getting ready for the day since 7:30 am. Mrs. Tina says she hopes today will be a better "Jenny day" . . . Miss Gena sighs and comments: "we should be so lucky!" A feeling of dread invades the room for a second followed by the usual active and fast-moving morning pace of the Little Apple Daycare. A minute later Jenny, a shy looking 3-year-old, walks in while holding her mother's dress, her face hiding under a cascade of blonde hair. Mom looks at Miss Gena and says Jenny had a tough night; she did not sleep very well, so she has been fuzzy. In response, both teachers exchange glances as Miss Gena acknowledges Mom's comment and says, "That means nap time might be a welcomed time" (in a relaxed and inviting tone). Mom looks at Miss Gena in despair and sighs, sharing her helplessness. Miss Gena asks Jenny if she is ready to put her things in her cubby. Jenny hides further behind her hair and her mother' dress. Miss Gena stoops down and tries to make Jenny smile while pretending to try to find her. Jenny looks out from under her hair but quickly hides again. Mom stays quiet, just lending her body to Jenny. Mrs. Tina comes over after a few minutes and tells Miss Gena more children are coming and classroom activities need to get underway; maybe Mom and Jenny can figure out how to say goodbye on their own. Miss Gena tells Jenny to hurry up so she can help her greet the other children. Mom begins to push Jenny with her body in quite an abrupt manner and tells Jenny she needs to go to work, she will be late. Jenny struggles and begins to hit her mom ever so gently at first, then with more force. Mrs. Tina, a grandmotherly figure, tells Jenny, "Hands are not for hitting in the classroom, and that includes Mommy." Jenny stops. Mrs. Tina asks Jenny if she remembers the first thing they are doing today because she has forgotten; she needs Jenny's help. Jenny appears from under the cascade of hair with a big smile and replies, "We are going to sing in circle time." "Ok then!" Mrs. Tina remarks, "Then you don't want to be late, do you?" Jenny pulls Mom, asking for help to transition to the cubby and then circle time. Children are coming in and settling down. Jenny's mom feels the looks from the other mothers . . . it is another "Jenny morning" . . . Mom lets go of Jenny and leaves the preschool, leaving Jenny crying in front of her cubby. Both Mrs. Tina and Miss Gena feel the dread of "another Jenny day" as the other children begin to comment and react to Jenny's behavior.

This example illustrates the challenges of **thinking while feeling** in the context of multiple agendas. What do we mean by that? The thoughts, feelings, intentions, beliefs, wishes and needs of the child, teacher and parents, as well as the influence of the larger community in which they exist, all clash. Trying to **listen, reflect and be curious** about all the individual agendas involved is central to managing a situation like the one described previously. Furthermore, it requires checking one's own thoughts, feelings, beliefs, intentions and attributions while thinking of those of the others simultaneously. In simple terms, it requires "**looking at ourselves from the outside and others from the inside**." This is what *mentalizing* means: our capacity to think of and imagine what is causing Jenny's behavior and emotional state while keeping in mind our own and that of other adults involved.

What is mentalization and how does it develop?

Mentalization is a developmental capacity inherent in all human beings very much dependent on the quality of a child's relationships (Fonagy, 2001). By the time children are 6 years old, if they have been exposed enough to the experience of adults trying to understand who they are (what they need, want, fear, etc.) they develop what developmental psychologists call **theory of mind** (Bartsch & Wellman, 1995). The best way to explain how theory of mind manifests itself is by briefly sharing the "**false belief experiment**." In it, a researcher shows a 3-year-old a box of crayons and asks, "What is in here?" The child says, "A box of crayons," and then opens the box to see candles inside. The researcher closes the box and asks, "If your friend came in and I asked him what is inside this box, what would he say?" Most 3-year-olds will say candles! Three-year-old children believe that what they think and know is what others think and know. If we ask the same of 6-year-olds they will answer, "Crayons of course!" indicating their capacity for perspective-taking. It is during this time that children begin to understand that their being angry does not mean that others are angry too. Just because they know something, others don't necessarily know it too. This capacity lays the foundation for a child's mentalizing abilities.

Mentalizing begets mentalizing

When educators mentalize a child, they are offering a valuable emotional learning experience. Miss Gena's attempts to find Jenny's face is a way of saying, "I care, I want to understand you." However, her capacity to go a step further has been inhibited by the repeated experience of failing to help Jenny. Mrs. Gena fails to mentalize Jenny's experience more explicitly, perhaps by saying something like: *"Oh boy, I don't understand why Jenny is so worried today? Hmm . . . I am going to guess (with a funny tone and face). Could it be she is worried about being away from Mama from such a long day? Could it be she is worried she won't find someone to play with?"* In this way, Miss Gena would offer herself as a **mentalizing partner** who is both curious and resourceful in offering a safe place to think and feel away from Mama's dress. Instead, Miss Gena might be thinking: *"Here we go again, another Jenny morning. My boss must think I can't manage kids. What are all the incoming parents thinking?"* and this is inhibiting her natural capacity to be playful and flexible in her response. Her **reflective functioning** capacities are lowered by the stress of the situation . . . We have all been there!

The concept of mentalization is also known as **Reflective Functioning** (RF). Good reflective functioning is characterized by the following characteristics (Malberg, 2015):

1 **The capacity to understand that we don't ever really know what others are thinking and feeling.** For example, Jenny's hiding might mean she is afraid, embarrassed or perhaps feeling shy. The point is, we don't really truly know what is behind someone else's behavior unless we ask them and explore it. We can, however, imagine it and offer "guesses" to the child, to help her in the process of putting feelings into words: *"Jenny, could it be that you worry about Mama not coming back?. . . Did that get it right?"*

2 **The understanding that child's thoughts, feelings and intentions are very different from those of adults.** This helps us to *not* make assumptions such as, *"That child is just manipulating,"* without putting it in the context of the child's current developmental level and family culture.

3 **The capacity for appropriate use of humor and playfulness.** This is important since it helps to communicate to the child that things are okay; it is safe. Moreover, it allows the adult to feel relaxed and continue to think while feeling the strong feelings children's challenging behaviors evoke. For example: *"Oh my Jenny! I lost my way to the cubby! Do you know how to get there? Can you help me find it?"* It is very important, though, to be mindful of children who may have a propensity towards feeling shamed or made-fun-of.

4 **The ability to have a curious and inquisitive attitude about the child's behavior and the thoughts and feelings that lie behind it.** We observe some of that in our opening example but not enough, as all three adults seem concerned about "moving on," and getting things to work instead of trying to understand why it is happening. There is in fact a place for both a task-oriented and a curious stance to coexist: *"I think Jenny is having a hard time saying goodbye to Mom after such a nice weekend, but it is now time to say hi to all her friends who missed her so much. And then, after playing and helping me all day, she will be able to say hello to Mom again."*

A **reflective classroom** is one in which, *observing, reflecting, checking* and *clarifying*, creates a safer environment for all. In the following pages, we intend to share with the reader the basic principles of attachment theory and how they can be useful to those working with young children and their families in early educational settings.

One of the difficulties in translating attachment theory to work in educational settings has to do with the language of attachment. Like many psychological modalities and theories, its language can often feel foreign and distant from the reality of the classroom. In the following pages we will define briefly the main theoretical concepts of attachment theory alongside examples from situations often witnessed and experienced by teachers. Following that, the chapter concludes with the description of the main mentalizing techniques/ principles and their potential application to working with young children and their caregivers.

The history of attachment theory

John Bowlby (1969), the father of attachment theory, studied children who exhibited antisocial behavior and became curious about the connection between the absence of consistent and predictable parenting figures and children's behavior. Furthermore, he began to observe the impact of loss and separation in children's development of self-esteem and overall functioning in relationships. His work impacted the way we think about schools and hospitals and understand separations between parents and children from the child's perspective. Later on, Mary Ainsworth (1978) developed more scientific ways of exploring these issues across cultures. Her studies were very important as they showed that attachment is universal, that we find it in all humans across cultures. These two pioneers developed the basic language of attachment theory. The field of attachment has been influenced by other disciplines—like developmental and cognitive psychology, neuroscience and anthropology. Contemporary theorists and researchers have expanded the language of attachment as a result of this cross-fertilization. Of importance to early childhood educators are the following:

- the importance of the quality of the relationship,
- the impact that alternative attachment figures (teachers) can have during the first five years of life and
- the ways in which developmental research can help the technique of teaching young children.

What do we mean by secure base?

"In homes where the baby finds no mutuality, where the parent's face does not reflect the baby's experience and where the child's spontaneous gesture is not recognized or appreciated, neither trust in others nor confidence in the self develop" (Hopkins, 1990).

Mary Ainsworth (1978) first used the phrase **"secure base"** to describe the environment created by the attachment figure for the attached person. The essence of the secure base is that it provides a springboard for both *curiosity* and *exploration* (Goldberg, 2000). When we perceive danger, we seek and cling to our attachment figures (mom, dad, grandma or sibling). Once danger passes, their presence enables us to work, relax and play, but only if we are sure that the attachment figures will be there if we need them again. Ainsworth emphasized the importance of a caregiver's response to the infant's signals (cry, cooing and facial expressions) as the main influence that determines the attachment pattern that children develop.

Let's return to Jenny for a minute in order to apply an attachment lens. Jenny clings to her mom the same way she clings to her teachers during the day. This behavior can be motivated by several things. Jenny might be concerned about her capacity to behave well and follow the rules of the classroom and might be dreading coming to preschool as much as her teachers dread her presence. How would we know the answer? We might be able to observe and inquire about how long she has been attending her preschool. Have there been any recent difficulties with being in the class or interacting with other children? Feeling frustrated and angry might be making Jenny feel afraid, and so she clings to her mom. However, Jenny's behavior does not occur in isolation; her mom seems to be unable to **reflect and adapt** to what she imagines her daughter might be needing. Instead she goes to things that can be seen and fixed and speaks of lack of sleep as the main reason for the behavior. Mom's sudden departure might be an important cue to Jenny's experience of her mom as an unpredictable attachment figure. Faced with this reality, Jenny becomes desperate and angry but mostly afraid. Jenny does not know what she needs, she just feels it.

Attachment behavior

Attachment behavior is often triggered by separation or threatened separation from the attachment figure (Holmes, 1993). As in Jenny's case, hitting and crying sends a signal, which hopes to be met with a soothing tone, a hug or a gentle touch. Miss Gena seems to respond to Jenny's distress by lowering her body and trying to be playful; however, Jenny is more tuned to her mother's frozen body and helpless response to her despair and is not able to accept the invitation to play extended by her teacher's curious attitude.

Development of attachment system

A teacher's perception of the young student shapes and mediates the contact between them and profoundly affects the teacher's efforts to engage and motivate the child. In many ways, we can think of the relationship between child and teacher as paralleling that of the parent and child. The way in which a teacher interprets and responds to a child's nonverbal communications, for instance, is very important in creating a secure base in the early childhood setting. As small children are still very dependent and yet still learning how to decipher adults' nonverbal cues, it is important to have a developmental understanding (Malberg et al., 2012)

Psychiatrist Daniel Stern (1985) spoke of the importance of the *"mutual looking"* between mother and baby as a key element in the development of the internal world (how we see ourselves in the world of relationships) in which attachment can be represented and regulated. Simply put, the quality of the relationship infants—and later on small children—have with grown-ups who take care of them lays the foundations for learning how to think about feelings and how to manage feelings especially anxiety. Sometimes early childhood teachers are in a special position to offer children the possibility of learning new ways of relating. This is particularly true for children whose families might be affected by mental illness, poverty, marital conflict and other difficulties affecting parents' capacity to be a consistently secure base. As children become older, their emotional reactions become more their own and increasingly complex. By the time children reach preschool, they begin to understand implicit rules (there is no need to use words) about displaying emotions and seem to have deliberate control of facial expressions. The way in which teachers and parents respond and react to this new capacity is very important in terms of letting the child know that expression of feelings, positive and negative, is allowed and most importantly that adults make an effort to understand what is behind them. *What is the motivation? Is the child showing us he is feeling afraid, alone, confused?*

Jenny's teachers begin Monday morning dreading Jenny's tantrums and clinginess. Unfortunately, this makes them already predisposed to a certain way of understanding her behavior. In attachment terms, their capacity to mentalize Jenny, to think of what she is feeling, thinking and needing, and what is motivating her behavior, is being influenced by their feelings of dread and helplessness both towards Jenny and towards her mom who often stands, waiting for them to sort it out. It is difficult to pay attention to both their own feelings and those of Jenny. In response, both teachers make attempts to **reach out and recruit the child**. In this example we observe both teachers' intuitive attempts to calm the child's attachment behavioral system by using their tone of voice, their face and their body.

The quality of the relationship: What is good enough?

Attachment theory tells the story of how a caregiver and an infant learn to communicate with each other. In the context of that "**relational dance**," children begin to discover themselves away from those who take care of them and build their **emotional muscle** (Novick & Novick, 2010); that is, their capacity for frustration tolerance and managing difficult feelings, among other socio-emotional capacities. The following are important aspects/qualities of that dance which can be applied to the way teachers reflect and respond to children in the classroom. A child needs to have more experiences of working things together than experiences of things falling apart and never being repaired in order to have enough data to help her emotional muscle grow and develop. In other words: *"I make mistakes, Mama makes mistakes and my teachers too, but we work on making it better and in the process, I learn to feel independent, yet trust that adults will help me and do the best they can."*

Connecting via empathy

When infants cry, caregivers copy their facial expression, change their tone of voice, move differently, and try to both soothe and understand what is behind the infant's cry. In the same way, we observed Miss Gena trying to find Jenny's face from under her hair when she gets on the floor at her level. However, Jenny seems to need more, in this case from her main caregiver. She needs someone to actively try to understand and verbalize what might be happening inside of her. For example, Mom could have said: *"Oh Jenny, I am also sad that our great weekend is over, but maybe we can think of something fun we are going to do together after I pick you up."* Sometimes, when children and parents are stuck, we can help them by speaking to the parents so they can feel they are *"the mentalizing team."* For instance, Mrs. Tina, who is an authority figure in the preschool, could say something to Mom like: *"You have a little girl stuck to you, I think she might be worried about when you will return, but you always do, Mom. You remember last Friday, you were so happy when you saw each other."* In this way, Mom would feel helped by Mrs. Tina, and Jenny would hear both Mom and Mrs. Tina acknowledging together that Jenny shows her thoughts and feelings through her behavior.

Furthermore, according to researchers in the field of neuroscience and attachment (Gergely et al. 2002), in order for an infant to truly feel understood and thought-about as separate with his own intentions, wishes and desires, the caregiver needs to be attuned but also try to imagine what the infant is experiencing and "return it" to the child with her facial expression and with words: *"Oh! I think you are feeling alone."* To exemplify this in Jenny's case, Mom could try to imagine what is going on for Jenny and put it into words: *"It is always scary to say goodbye on Monday morning, but I will be back this afternoon and you can tell me all about it. No worries, Mama will be back,"* followed by helping Jenny to transition to the cubby. In this way, Mom would be speaking to what she thinks is behind her daughter's behavior—anxiety over separating after a weekend together.

Rupture and repair

All human interactions have their highs and lows, what attachment and neuroscience refer to as **rupture and repair**. The baby cries and Mom tries to figure out what he needs, but her stress and feelings of guilt get in the way and she becomes flustered and unable to soothe the baby. She walks away and returns moments later after taking a minute away and returns *"online"* ready to think of her babies' needs as separate from her frustration. The baby feels calmer when a mom feels calmer. The student feels calmer when she sees in her teacher's face someone who is trying to understand her and "be with her" while trying to sort it out. The same way parents need support from friends and family, so do teachers. They need to help each other reflect when children's behaviors make them feel *"offline"* and not able to mentalize. In the opening example, we see how the teachers are able to support each other and communicate verbally and nonverbally.

However, there is one element missing: Mom's participation in the efforts. Is it that Mom feels embarrassed? Does she feel teachers don't welcome her input? Or does she want the teachers to witness the behavior and perhaps find solutions she has not? We don't know.

Rupture and repair in the relationship between educators and caregivers is important, as children's challenging behaviors have potential for dividing and creating a *"non-mentalizing"* environment of finger pointing and competition. In Jenny's case, Miss Gena could spend a few minutes with Jenny and acknowledge that the beginning has been tough, but recruit the child to engage in an activity that will help her feel strong, competent and in control of something in the class, such as walking her friends to their cubbies. Helping children to "save face" and recover from the shame and fear of retaliation they might fear are mentalizing activities.

Attachment behavioral styles

Attachment styles are clusters of behaviors that develop based on the quality of the relationship between babies and those who take care of them. The quality of the relationship can be observed by paying close attention to some of the things we have just explored: *empathy and capacity for rupture and repair*. These are all linked to the parent's own history of relationships and capacity for reflective functioning, meaning to the capacity to think about the child as separate with his/her own emotional experience from the very beginning.

Attachment classifications are not meant to be used diagnostically: instead, they are designed to help us when we are trying to understand a child's behavior in relationships, especially when the behavior does not seem to make sense or seems to be a repeated pattern, such as the child who seems to shift his behavior suddenly and with no obvious trigger, leaving his teacher wondering what is going on every time. We will briefly describe the different behavioral patterns of attachment and offer short examples of how these children might manifest in the classroom. Further, we will think about ways in which assuming a "mentalizing" attitude in the classroom helps children who struggle to find a "secure base." A mentalizing teacher creates an opportunity for a new way of relating that can make all the difference in children's future relationships and self-esteem as learners.

The securely attached child

Children who have felt mentalized by their caregivers achieve higher self-esteem, capacity to adapt, less clingy behavior towards teachers and overall positive attitude towards learning. As they develop, these children tend to be more curious and sympathetic to others, more effective in play and more cooperative. Securely attached children are able to retrieve the experience of someone being curious and caring about them and be creative and flexible to manage the feeling of threat or the experience of a potentially traumatic experience.

Classroom example: *JJ begins to make a project with paper and tape in the creative corner. He seems very involved in developing a strong and big invisible man. When his teacher tells him it is time to move to circle time, he throws himself on the floor and cries in protest: "I must finish my monster! I need to!" In response, his teacher tells him she could see this was important and allows him to finish the project and put it in his cubby with the help of one of the assistants. JJ seems relieved and is able to join in the class activities for the rest of the day.*

Implications for teachers: Securely attached children are able to recover when they feel understood by an adult. A teacher should always try to understand the behavior in the context of what she knows of him. This facilitates the process of waiting and observing, which leads to a mentalized response to the child's demands and needs.

The insecurely attached child

Children who fall into this category seem to react with less confidence when they feel threatened by new interpersonal experiences and contexts (e.g. a new school). Researchers (Sroufe, 1983) have found these children to be more dependent, display more negative emotions and show less positive behaviors towards others. Children displaying insecure attachment fall into three categories:

a   Avoidant
b   Resistant/Ambivalent
c   Disorganized

The avoidant child

The main characteristic of these children is that they seem to have difficulties managing and expressing their feelings of anger. They don't feel it is safe to be angry, as they often experience a caregiver who has not responded with predictability to their attempts to express negative feelings. The avoidant child stays away in order to "keep things safe" while still desiring very much the closeness.

Classroom example: *Joey, a 3-year-old boy, settles easily in the morning when dad drops him off. He cries at naptime, saying he misses his mom, but when she picks him up, Joey ignores her and "makes her work" for his attention. With teachers, he seems very self-sufficient, running away from adults. However, when coaxed by a smile or a welcoming classroom song, he seems to enjoy himself. His teacher is confused by his behavior—he seems to be wanting comfort but then pushes her away with rejecting behavior such as mean faces and small pushing.*

Implications for teachers: The aim is to respond as consistently as possible to the child's attempts to express himself, to reinforce verbalizing feelings both positive and negative, and to model it for the child. Most important is the way in which the teacher reacts to these children's pushing-away behavior. Usually the presence of another trusted child helps the adult to approach these children in a more efficient way. The main goal is to "prove them wrong" and offer different responses to their behavior by verbalizing, modeling, checking and clarifying.

The resistant/ambivalent child

Children exhibiting resistant/ambivalent attachment tend to be either impulsive and tense or helpless and fearful. Their caregivers tend to have difficulties establishing boundaries and responding with appropriate consequences. A characteristic of parents of children in this group is their own struggle with separation. As a result, these parents have difficulty reading their children's cues and a low level of curiosity for their child's experience. The opening example (Jenny) in this chapter illustrates a resistant/ambivalent child and her mother struggling during separation.

Implications for teachers: the focus should be in providing experiences of separation and autonomy over those of anxious involvement. For instance, as much as it might feel helpful to allow the child to cling, seeking solutions where the child's self-esteem and autonomy can be highlighted are best, such as assigning the child a job during transition periods, one that is unique to the child. Recognizing that rigidity in these children is often a way for them to seek safety is very important to keep in mind when trying to understand the behavior and how we react to it. Playfulness and flexibility in responding to the resistant/ambivalent child is a must, as it relaxes the child's hypersensitivity and allows her to take small risks towards autonomy. Explicit naming and rewarding autonomous behaviors make the child feel thought-about even when physically distant from the teacher. Example: *"Good job Lilly, I can see from here you are helping Emma with that difficult puzzle!"*

The disorganized attached child

Children presenting with disorganize attachment tend to have histories of relational trauma characterized by highly inconsistent patterns of parenting in which the same person that is supposed to make them feel safe makes them feel scared. Many children in the foster care system fall into this category. There is no predictable pattern of response for these children. As the world tends to be perceived as unpredictable and dangerous, they tend to be ready to attack and present as highly anxious. The disorganized child "miscues" a lot, meaning that if the teacher looks at him in a stern manner or uses a serious tone, he immediately responds without trying to observe and then respond. Disorganized children tend to be described as highly hyperactive and often controlling, so they are often diagnosed as oppositional or with attention deficit hyperactivity disorder.

Classroom example: *Leo, age 3, is sitting in the corner playing with the large blocks next to Mia. Suddenly Mia starts crying; Leo has hit her in the head with a block because she got too close to him. He looks at his teacher with fear, stands up and begins to run around the room. His teacher tries to approach him but he becomes more agitated. He ends up in a corner of the room, hiding. It is difficult to figure out how to soothe and contain him.*

Implications for teachers: Paying attention to one's face and voice when speaking to these children proves very useful. It is important to remember that earning their trust and seeing through what tends to look as oppositional behavior are the two main challenges and priorities in working with the disorganized child. Assigning a clear place in the classroom for the child to "**organize his feelings**" will help the process of getting the child "**back online**" feeling safe enough to allow his teacher to help her. Sensory materials tend to help these children to calm down and regulate their emotions. Simple activities where they can use their bodies—such as pushing against the wall or playing with a toy like clay that helps them refocus their attention and release tension—usually prove effective. Basically, we *start with calming the body first, then trying to find the mind.*

Creating a secure base in the early education classroom: Mentalizing in action

How can one create a mentalizing environment in the early childhood classroom that promotes reflection and self-observation both in children and those who care for them? Contemporary attachment theory and the practices it informs focus on helping children and their parents regulate feelings and behaviors as well as integrate specific techniques which promote perspective-taking and overall executive function. The following are some strategies that might promote mentalizing and create a secure base in the early childhood classroom.

1.   **Respond with curiosity to behaviors; avoid attributions** (manipulative, controlling, etc.) before putting the child's behavior in the context of his developmental history, family and cultural environment. **Not knowing** (curiosity) and not understanding are very important attitudes to practice and model for children. For example: *"JJ what happened? (using facial expression) You were playing with Suzie nicely and now you have an angry face, hmmm . . .? I am a bit confused, should we try to figure it out? (playful tone)."*

2.   **Check and clarify:** Practice and model for kids *checking* regarding what you think they are thinking and feeling. Be explicit! For example: *"Lizzy you have a frown in your face, does that mean you are feeling bored or angry?"* Clarify when you feel a child is reacting to your posture, face or voice and feeling unsafe. For example: *"It might sound like I am speaking loud, and yes, I am not feeling very calm, but I am not angry with you."*

3.   **Model emotional regulation explicitly**: *Take a minute* to organize your feelings by checking and clarifying. Share with your students that you are experiencing *big feelings* and verbally describe what you are doing to calm down. For example: *"Lila, I think you thought Mrs. Anna was angry with you because she said you had to put the toy away and now you look angry and sad. How about we find a safe place and pretend to blow bubbles together to help your big feelings be a bit smaller?"*

4.   **Develop a language of emotional regulation:** Use phrases such as *big and small feelings*, naming repeated patterns of behavior and their impact, for

example, calling them: *"bumpy roads."* Speak about *stop and think moments*, times when you are inviting the child to pay attention to what is going on in that moment. In general, it is helpful to create a language of emotional regulation. Sharing the language with parents is very important so the child is receiving the same feedback from all the important adults in his life. For example: *"Liam I think you are going down a bumpy road right now by making that choice, is there any way I could help you to take a different road, what do you think? Let's stop and think for a minute."*

5. **Stop and rewind:** Practice *stopping, rewinding and telling "the story of what just happened."* Sequencing is useful in developing executive functioning, and children learn how to do it when they see the adults around them practicing it. It is a good way of getting everybody's thinking back online and away from "big feelings." For example: *"Jenny, let's stop and rewind before you got big feelings . . . shall we make a story of what happened?"*

6. **Encourage creativity and flexibility by modeling it**: The use of distraction, appropriate humor and playfulness fosters children's capacity to feel safe and resourceful in the face of stressful interpersonal situations. For example: Singing and moving are always ways to calm down and let our brain know that there is safety.

7. **Exhibit curiosity about families' values and cultural background**: Different families and cultures assign diverse meanings to behaviors around sleeping, eating, toilet training and friendships. All of these are tasks of great importance during the early years. Taking the time to be curious about the values and beliefs surrounding a child helps us be more mentalizing.

Brief conclusion

Finding the right balance between developing strategies to manage young children and taking the time to reflect before reacting to the behavior is a challenging task. We hope to have illustrated how an attachment lens can provide us with a new way to observe, explore and intervene in the context of challenging situations. An attachment focus is based on the belief that the wish to connect with others and the need to feel acknowledged and thought-about are core motivations for human beings. A mentalization approach seeks to respond to those needs and wishes both verbally and nonverbally in a way that promotes the child's and the parent's self-esteem and promotes their willingness to be active thinking and feeling partners with educators.

References

Ainsworth, M.D. (1978). *Patterns of attachment: A psychological study of the strange situation.* Hillsdale, NJ: Erlbaum.

Bartsch, K., & Wellman, H.M. (1995). *Children talk about the mind.* Oxford, UK: Oxford University Press.

Bowlby, J. (1969). *Attachment and loss* (Vol. 1, Attachment). London: Penguin.

Fonagy, P. (2001). *Attachment theory and psychoanalysis*. London: Other Press.

Gergely, G., Bekkering, H., & Kiraly, I. (2002). Rational imitation in preverbal infants. *Nature*, 415:755.

Goldberg, S. (2000). *Attachment and development*. London: Arnold Press.

Holmes, J. (1993). *John Bowlby and attachment theory*. London: Routledge.

Hopkins, J. (1990). The observed infant of attachment. *Journal of the Institute of Self Analysis*, 4(1):460–470.

Malberg, N.T. (2015). Activating mentalization in parents: An integrative framework. *Journal of Infant, Child and Adolescent Psychotherapy*, 14(3):232–245.

Malberg, N.T., Stafler, N., & Geater, E. (2012). Putting the pieces of the puzzle together: A mentalization-based approach to early intervention in primary schools. *Journal of Infant, Child and Adolescent Psychotherapy*, 11:190–204.

Novick, J., & Novick, K. (2010). *Emotional muscle: Strong parents, strong children*. USA: Xlibris.

Sroufe, L.A. (1983). Infant-caregiver attachment patterns of adaptation in pre-school: The roots of maladaptation and competence. In M. Permuter (Ed.), *Minnesota symposium of child psychology* (Vol. 16, pp. 41–81). Hoboken, NJ: John Wiley & Sons, Inc.

Stern, D. (1985). *The interpersonal world of the infant*. London: Basic Books.

PART III

Play in the classroom

5

PLAY IN THE EMOTIONAL AND COGNITIVE LIFE OF A PRESCHOOLER

Steve Tuber

Next to a parent or guardian, I can't think of a job more important to the emotional health of a young child than that of a preschool teacher. So much happens during this critical period of development that can have lifetime repercussions. A vital preschool teacher can truly be a godsend. What is the most essential ingredient insuring the vitality of such a teacher? Nothing is more central to a preschooler, and therefore nothing is more essential in the making of a viable preschool teacher, than to be skilled in the ability to enhance children's capacity to play.

Play is truly the elixir of a child's psychological and cognitive development. It is the prime means through which children can best understand the world around her and hence simultaneously the optimal way in which they can learn to best understand who they are and why they do what they do. In this chapter I will focus on why play is so essential to child development and then on what allows children's capacity to play to be most usefully developed. I will conclude then with some brief remarks about how to enhance children's play in the preschool classroom.

What is play and why is it useful?

I will define play as: all the activities of children that are spontaneous and self-generating, that are ends in themselves and that are unrelated to "lessons" or to the normal physiological needs of the child. I argue further that these spontaneous and self-generated activities enable children to conceptualize, to structure and to bring to tangible levels of activity the experiences and the feelings that define their identity.

Symbols and metaphors

We cannot speak about the nature of play without including two of its prime components: symbolism and metaphor. Young infants and toddlers manipulate objects and use the interaction between the objects and their bodies to make sense of things. What things can they put in their mouth, drop, bang or throw are the behaviors that dominate the "play" of the first six to 12 months of life. In the second year of life, learning is still almost entirely through sensory-motor activities: what can I run to, pull or build with, what objects are "crashable," soft, painful or fragile? By the start of the third year of life, however, brain development is such that objects can begin to "stand for" or symbolize other things. A doll figure can be a "mommy" and not simply something to grab or bang. Symbolizing frees up the child to move beyond the literal world around them. They can dress up to become anyone they like; they can build a fort while being a soldier; they can create an interaction among a wide variety of characters with impunity. It is this capacity to symbolize that makes play so psychologically essential to children and thus why the preschool age years are so central to children's emotional development: ages 3 to 5 are the crucible in which symbolic play lays the foundation for all subsequent development.

A close cousin of this emerging ability to symbolize, to make something stand for something else, is the ability to play metaphorically. That is, the baby dragon, for example, angry at her mommy dragon for not taking her to the park, can represent children's feelings about their real-life mom, *metaphorically*, without causing any harm to the real relationship between parents and their children. Acting out a "real life" interchange through the magic of metaphor and symbolization frees children to work on any or all aspects of their lives that they are struggling to make sense out of at their own pace and in a "space" that feels vibrant and real, yet is also safely just "pretend."

I am reminded of a moment in my younger son's life when he was a preschooler. He had a fascination with basketball and would play with a variety of basketball cards in which the player's name and body were displayed. The room where my children played had an old wooden floor with narrow slits between the thin planks of wood. My then 4-year-old would stand the cards in these slits and then "broadcast" a play by play of the cards as they played a game under his direction! In the midst of this play, I called to him to come upstairs and get ready for his bath. With barely a moment's break in the basketball commentary, he yelled out "in a minute daddy" and went right back to the "broadcast"!

What makes this moment relevant is that he was fully engrossed in a world he had created and yet this world stood side by side with the reality of his everyday life. He was not delusional – he knew he was *playing* – and thus could easily shift back to reality at the sound of my voice. Play is thus fully real in almost every sense of the word, yet it is also simultaneously "pretend." By being so close to reality, children can fully be engaged in mastering the themes, wishes, hopes and struggles that make up his real world yet do this under the safe guise that it is not *too real* and thus potentially emotionally threatening. Because play is metaphorical, it can be a world that is provocative and vivid. It is a world "as if" it was real, but it is that very slender but vital "as if" that makes it meaningful enough to stretch children emotionally and cognitively, but not enough to overwhelm them.

Playfulness thus provides the laboratory for children to master almost an infinite variety of experiences of the self in relation to other people and in relationship to different feelings. The more that the play can be maintained and not break apart, the greater children's emotional range becomes, the greater their tolerance of feelings both in and outside of them and the more multi-faceted their sense of self and others become. In large measure, this is due to the fact that the very nature of play is all about children taking different roles in the play. One minute they're the "mother," the next minute they're the "child;" the next minute they're the robber, a few moments later, they're being robbed. This fluently fluid shifting of roles also provides a host of precursors to the capacity to have empathy, the capacity to see the world from other people's points of view.

A viable preschool teacher recognizes the power of play and therefore uses her comments to enhance children's curiosity about what all the protagonists in the play might be thinking or feeling at a given moment without (and herein lies the art of being a skilled teacher) ending the play itself. For example, if children have identified almost literally with that mighty dragon that is scaring all the people in the household, the teacher can take on the voice of the people who are frightened by this dragon. They can also switch back and take on the voice of the hidden, yet frightened part of the angry dragon. Or perhaps they can take on the voice of the fully angry dragon. By being able to help children engage in what the different protagonists are thinking or feeling at any particular moment in the play, more-over, the playful teacher is also enhancing their *mentalization* skills. What are these mentalization skills? Mentalization is the ability we all have to a greater or lesser degree that allows us to see behavior (both our own and others') as related to a state of mind. We hit Johnny because of feelings and ideas we have inside about him or people like him, not simply because Johnny's behavior is confusing or unacceptable. Similarly, Johnny is sharing his toys well with us because of feelings he has inside about us, not simply because he was forced to share. Play allows children to practice tirelessly the ways in which behavior and feelings are linked. A primary job of the preschool teacher is thus to help in creating the mindset that children's play is above all else a safe and fun arena for developing these capacities for self-reflection.

The three prerequisites of play

Before we go into how preschool can provide an optimal arena for the develop-ment of children's capacity for play, we must describe three prerequisites of this capacity; two of these preconditions occur well before a teacher ever sees a child in preschool. One of the three does indeed fully emerge in preschool but all three can be markedly enhanced by the preschool experience, which validates why the tea-cher's role is so important to children's wellbeing.

Prerequisite #1: A predictable, stable environment

Research studies have shown that the average mother-infant pair has as many as 850,000 separate interactions over the first year of life. That is an enormous number of teachable moments! On the one hand, this large amount of interactions says that any one interaction has a minimal impact: thus parents can make an abundant number of "mistakes" in their attunement to their children (For the purposes of this paper I will use the term "parent" and "caregiver" interchangeably).

and still be overwhelmingly fine parents. On the other hand, this remarkable number of learning opportunities means that before children ever get to preschool they have become quite used to experiencing the world in certain repetitive ways. If their world as infants is one largely of attuned, predictable, stable parental responses, children derive perhaps the greatest gift a parent can ever bestow: the gift of reliability. This permits children the luxury of being able to increasingly take the parent's presence *for granted*, at first for brief periods of time.

Why is this such a big deal? Think about going on a first date as an adult. During the date you are self-consciously aware of what you're saying, how you look and if things are going well, not to mention how your "date" is faring across these same dimensions. It is most difficult to simply *be* one's self. Now think about how this vulnerability is magnified if you've never been on a date before. A young infant is in roughly the same position, although almost infinitely more dependent and hence more vulnerable. If they have to continually "check in" with the facial expressions and behaviors of their parent for fear that they will lose their attachment to them, it is far more difficult for them to just "be". They become preoccupied with, or disorganized by, their parent(s) and have to focus the bulk of their cognitive abilities on "reading" their parent's cues. This provides them with far fewer opportunities to check out their environment without a sense of vulnerability and/or brittleness pervading their explorations of the world.

In contrast, securely based children, well grounded in the reliable behavior of their caretaker, can afford to turn away from their parents for increasingly longer periods of time, knowing full well that when they feel the least bit of distress, they can turn back to them for caretaking. It becomes easy to see how this reliability becomes the stable platform for an interest in the world outside of their caretaker-infant unit and how this interest is a prerequisite for play. Securely attached babies can fully embrace the novelty of their environment if they know they have a totally reliable "fall back plan" should they get frightened and/or confused. The groundwork for play is thus helped immeasurably by this first prerequisite.

Prerequisite #2: The capacity to be alone

It is clear how crucial it is for parents to provide a stable, predictable and attuned environment for their baby if they are to help create playful children. But attunement in and of itself is not sufficient for this process to optimally occur. The next prerequisite is for children to feel increasingly comfortable in those moments, precious and rare at first, where they begin to look away from their parent(s) and toward the world around them. Can the infant take pleasure in exploring, mostly with eyes, hands and mouth at first, their environment? At first children are clumsy, trying to mouth everything they touch. Can they persevere when things are not easily sucked? Can they enjoy looking at their mobiles or other brightly colored objects? Can they let themselves experience new textures, sights and sounds? An unsung hero in this emerging capacity is their comfort in being alone. Being alone is very fleeting at first, maybe only a few seconds, before they look back and check in for grounding to their caregiver(s). If this turn back to parents is met with easy encouragement and availability, children will likely turn back toward the objects they were trying to manipulate. The feeling of being alone is thus increasingly one of comfort, ease and competence. Competence is especially key here. Being alone only feels acceptable if it is accompanied by feelings of being effective. If the infant's coordination is such that he cannot grasp the objects he is drawn to, as but one example, the feelings of frustration will quickly mount. Such frustrations will impel a quick wish to check back with parents and a retreat from the play he was first beginning. Thus, children develop feedback loops that can either propel them to further exploration or further retreat. The paradigms that are beginning to take hold are cyclical in nature: it is a process whereby feeling attuned to allows one to take the caretaker for granted. This, in turn, permits the feeling of being alone to be tolerable and leads toward an exploration of the world beyond the caretaker. Doing this with increasing competence brings more pleasure to the baby, increasing their wish for further exploration, enhancing the capacity to be alone.

Prerequisite #3: The development of curiosity

We now have the baby, perhaps as young as three months old or as old as the end of the first year of life, on a trajectory toward playfulness. Their being securely attached to their caretaker(s) allows them to feel comfortable with periods of aloneness, which then allows them to feel increasingly competent in trying to make sense of their world. Here we get to the third prerequisite for play, the development of *curiosity*. The infant is not born with a fully operational sense of curiosity. As we have just described, it takes months of attuned parenting to allow the child some degree of predictability about the world. The infant's cry is heard by their parent and attended to swiftly: the baby becomes increasingly assured that her needs will be met and embraces this now benevolent world. If "old" experiences are typically benign, the infant becomes increasingly "convinced" that new experiences will also be benign, that novelty in and of itself is a good thing, something to be embraced by children. We call this embrace *curiosity*. Children become increasingly interested in things because they are new. I cannot emphasize enough how critical this is to all future development. It would be impossible to account for the miraculous growth in cognitive and emotional development that occurs over the first five years of life without noting the role that curiosity plays. If children are limited solely to what is presented, their ongoing brain development would be severely restricted to only those events that they were familiar with already. Curiosity accounts for children's motivation to constantly test out the world, to assimilate new events into what they already know and to adapt pre-existing structures, beliefs and experiences to new ones. Curious children are scientists – forever investigating new combinations of experiences and discarding old "theories" about how the world works for new ones. A pacifier, as but one example, begins as a thing to suck. But it can easily become a thing to bang, an object to place in the mouth of others or something to throw. Each and every object touched, looked at or sucked becomes fodder for use in new combinations and each "experiment" yields further "data" for infants to make increasing sense out of this newer world. Curiosity is thus the engine for play. It is a hallmark of emotional health and the third precondition for a life of pleasurable learning that truly takes off in the preschool years of 2 to 5.

Back to play in preschool

This third prerequisite makes clear how central the role of a preschool teacher is to the development and enlarging of children's curiosity. Parental attunement and the making of a secure base from which to make sense of the world ideally happens long before teacher and child first meet. Feeling comfortable and competent with being alone also begins well before that first encounter. Even the development of curiosity has its precursors in the first two years of life. But the preschool years are absolutely crucial to enhancing these nascent capabilities, making a teacher's role so central in children's lives.

There is an enormous amount of research that speaks to the vast importance of play in children's development. Lieberman (1977) showed that there was a strong positive relationship between kindergarten children who were assessed as more playful and their ability to perform a task that measured divergent thinking, the ability to "think out of the box". Dorothy and Jerome Singer (1990) found that imaginative play in children was positively related to academic adjustment and greater cognitive flexibility.

Seja and Russ (1999) thought that children who were better able to have good quality fantasy play would be more adept at understanding emotions. They found that the quality of imaginative play in first and second grade children was positively correlated with children's ability to understand both their own emotions and the emotions of others.

Burstein and Meichenbaum (1979) reported that children who on their own initiative played with stress-related toys prior to surgery had less upset and anxiety after the surgery than did children who did not play with the toys, thus demonstrating how play can help a child master an intrinsically difficult situation.

Donahue and Tuber (1993) found that even in a sample of children struggling with the extremely stressful conditions of living in a homeless shelter, greater access to fantasy play and images was correlated with more adaptive functioning, as measured both by greater abilities to concentrate on cognitive tasks and better representations of self and others on emotional tasks.

How to enhance children's play

Given the critical importance of play, how does a preschool teacher create an optimal space from which to enhance children's playfulness? Certainly, the space itself must be conducive to play. Areas for "dress up", for playing with blocks, for drawing or painting, doll houses with figurines, puppets etc. are all necessary, but every teacher know that! Teachers also know that sometimes the very simplest of objects (large pots with wooden spoons, as but one example) are far more play enhancing than the most sophisticated of toy equipment.

But more crucial than the physical layout of the room and the toys available is the *attitude* the teachers have toward play and bring to the children under their care. A heralded pediatrician and child therapist named Donald Winnicott (Tuber, 2008) wrote beautifully and widely about how best to creatively enhance a child's capacity for playfulness. Although he wrote mostly for an audience of therapists and to a lesser extent to parents, his thoughts are central to a preschool teacher's work as well.

The mother-infant relationship, for Winnicott, is one whereby the mother provides sufficient but not omnipotent care. The baby needs an attuned mother, about whom we have already spoken. But the baby actually needs to experience moments where the mother's attunement is not perfect (omnipotent) so that the infant can have brief moments where they are "on their own". These moments begin the process of becoming one's own person, increasingly without having to check back with one's caretaker. By the time babies are finishing their first year of life, they can even begin to have moments where they can repudiate the parent (they learn to say "no"!) in the attempt to continue to do and play with what they want to play with. If caretakers can allow for this repudiation, then toddlers will eventually return to their caretakers, reaccepting the comfort they need and even showing gratitude to their caretaker for this working blend of separation and togetherness.

I stress that repudiation is an integral part of both the separation experience and the capacity to play because one of the greatest things about play is that it allows for the largely safe expression of all kinds of aggressive, even hateful feelings. If I go to my mom and mommy yells at me and says, "No, you can't use the TV remote as a javelin, go up to your room," I may at first be quite devastated. While going to my room, I may notice my dollhouse and take my doll figures out to play. I just might then have a monster come along and swipe the mommy figure and throw her to the moon! Crucially, nothing terrible happens! Indeed, I'm then perhaps mastering my feelings of devastation at my real mommy by my play with that mommy figure at the moment. I'm expanding internally what it's like to hate my mother while crucially both my mother and I are surviving. Once again, it is precisely because I am only "killing" my mommy *metaphorically* that my play is useful.

The metaphor is close enough to reality to provide a valid means of expressing my feelings, yet because it is *only pretend* neither my mother nor I are any worse for wear! Ideally, when I come out of the room after I've had my time out, I'm less likely to be as enraged at my mother as I was when I was banished to my room. This increases the chances that I will be contrite. If I am truly fortunate, my mother will also be calmed down enough so that the two of us can acknowledge the impasse and move beyond it. If I am still more fortunate, my mommy now shows that she can go back to being the loving person she was even though she was mad. I can then have the great luxury of learning once again that my mommy can tolerate my aggressive play without undue retaliation, allowing me to still feel lovable and valued even if moments before my parent and I were furious at one another.

Sadly, so much of the experience of a preschool teacher will be comprised of working with children where that benign level of negotiation over aggression has had limited success. If mothers cannot articulate why they were angry and/or reach some emotional resolution with their children, then children's experience becomes a more precarious mixture of feelings that are too readily felt as toxic, either in their experience of themselves or of their mother or both. If children cannot detoxify their experience through subsequent play or direct resolution, the now toxic self-experience is likely to rear its head repeatedly in the classroom. It may interfere with attention in school, it may interfere with friendships with their peers, indeed many of the symptoms of childhood that bring chaos to the classroom have much to do with children's capacity to manage and work through loving and hating feelings in their early years. The ability to manage loving and hating feelings, of course, is linked to the bi-directional nature of parent-child interaction. On the one hand, if children don't have the capacity to play very well, then one can readily realize how limited their resources are to cope with whatever difficult feelings arise, as they don't have a viable arena in which to symbolically work through the difficulties that create their maladaptive behavior. On the other hand, part of what makes teaching preschoolers so difficult with children who have a very limited capacity to play, is how likely it is that their mother or father or both may also have a diminished playfulness and hence a very limited capacity to understand the importance of play. These parents will make little sense out of one's explaining the vital importance of play, which in their eyes is at best frivolous, or at worst, dangerous. Work with parents is a topic beyond the scope of this chapter, but the informal assessment of the parent's playfulness is crucial as one tries to make sense of the student's capacity for play.

This to and fro between parents and children provide key parallels to the experiences of teacher and child in the classroom. Imagine a group of preschoolers playing in parallel in the "dress up" area. If all is going well, they can play and forget about the teacher for a while. Clearly, one's job at tha moment is to not jump in: "Oh, hello, remember me? I'm the teacher!" By waiting, the children will then, at some point, re-adapt to the teacher *if they need to*. The art of teaching preschoolers is thus often in recognizing a moment in the children's play where comments can amplify or clarify or call into benign question some aspect of the play without disrupting it. Usually this occurs in the context of managing one or more children who cannot at that moment tolerate the feelings evoked by the play and start to make demands on the other children that disrupt the flow of the play. As the teacher learns the differing needs and particular vulnerabilities of the students, he becomes increasingly adept at predicting which sort of feelings may get stirred up too strongly in what children, leading to a shift in the nature of the play or the participants to keep the play flowing smoothly.

It is certainly something teachers are not getting paid for, but a powerful part of the job is, then, an assessment of both parents' and childrens' capacity for playfulness. The more children feel comfortable in the world of play, the easier it is both child and teacher to enhance their creativity and to enlist the support of the children's parents in validating the importance of the child's play. Children who play easily and with spontaneity are far more likely to have parents who enjoy and tolerate play. I would urge every teacher to use the initial interviews with prospective parents even before children attend preschool, and certainly to use the "open school night" meeting with the parents, to keep a close eye out for signs that the parent's recognize the value of play. This may be especially true with kindergarten-age parents, who can often confuse this year as a year for the "three R's" as opposed to the culmination of the time in life when play is transcendent and must be cultivated to the fullest.

Back to the capacity for being alone

The capacity to maintain play in the classroom is, as we have described earlier, also tremendously affected by the capacity to be alone. It may be useful to think of the capacity to play as part of a continuum. At one end of this continuum are children who have minimal abilities to stay alone and play. Quite often these children can play if they have a teacher hovering and paying attention every moment. But as soon as they no longer have the teacher's attention, they can very easily get knocked off stride. This is quite typical of toddlers before the age of 2, but becomes increasingly of concern as they move toward the 3- to 5-year-old range. Children with fragile abilities to feel comfortable playing alone are constantly asking the teacher, in one form or another, to get involved in the minutiae of their play—serving as a prop, holding an action figure etc.— keeping one constantly involved for fear of losing connection. As a matter of fact, they're spending so much time directing the teacher's involvement that they may never really play in a spontaneous way, and that's because there's been a disruption in their basic capacity to be alone, which trumps what should be the increasingly autonomous nature of their symbolic capacities. Such children are often the thorn in the side of the preschool teacher, as they require a level of attention that can simply be impossible in a class with many other children. This is truly one of those times where the lack of caretaker stability invades the classroom, and it will take all of one's patience and skill to help set these children back on the developmental path of autonomy, creativity and curiosity.

The "good news" is that the preschooler is often resilient and malleable enough that the playful world of the classroom can truly compensate for much of what children might be lacking in play skills when they arrive at the door. The "bad news" however, is how sad and poignant it is to witness young children who are so limited in their capacity to play and symbolize that they remain overly concrete and literal and thus subject to a brittleness that puts their adjustment to the classroom at significant risk.

In the more optimal mid-range of the capacity to be alone are children that play readily and easily and can indeed lose themselves in play without fear across a wide range of feelings. Their brief/temporary loss of the capacity to be alone, or even to play in general, is relatively rare and situation specific – maybe they are struggling with a cold that day, a lack of sleep from the night before or a relatively recent disruption in the home. These children are often the "bright lights" in your classroom, regularly bringing a smile to one's face.

At the other end of this spectrum are children who desperately create an alone world because they constantly fear intrusion. Those are children with whom one has to be amazingly delicate, so as to not intrude on their play or even making a comment on their play because the slightest comment or gesture can leave them and their precarious capacity for play feeling violated. Importantly, while these children may indeed be engrossed in their behavior so that it looks like play, their manipulation of their play toys often has a rigid, repetitive quality that belies the spontaneity and creativity of true symbolic play. While these children may have the capacity to be alone, their play lacks curiosity. We can say that their play has a defensive quality; it serves primarily to shield them from novelty or surprise, rather than to set the stage for variety or spontaneity.

To go back to our first prerequisite for the capacity to play, we can now say that thinking about this spectrum of continuity of play in this manner is another way of saying that the nature of children's security of attachment can be derived through the assessment of their capacity to be alone and at play. One can make, I feel, a very easy parallel between intrusive, preoccupied parents with children who are constantly afraid you're going to intrude on their play; largely dismissive parents are paralleled by children who wants the teacher to be constantly be involved in their play; and secure parents are liable to be matched by children who can play by themselves for long periods of time and also tolerate their teacher's making comments on their play without it becoming disrupted. These first set of children need to keep the teacher out of their play, the second set of children need the teacher to be forever engaged in her play and the third set of children can much more readily create a balance between mutuality and privacy in their play. Still further, we can note that the first two sets of children will likely have difficulties negotiating their play with their peers, either because they fear the intrusion of a peer into their private and rigidly maintained world or need peers to conform to their play, without any give and take.

It is crucial to add here that children may differ profoundly in terms of what feelings disrupt their capacity to play. For some children, feelings of anger are most disruptive; for others, feelings of fear or anxiety and for still others, feelings of sadness are most dreaded. It can be most useful for the teacher to recognize these particular frailties in the classroom as a function of what most commonly disrupts children's play, thereby increasing an anticipation of breakdowns in play and even planning which children are best suited to play with one another, as their most vulnerable feelings are in synchrony with one another.

The world of social play

I have placed such an emphasis on the preschooler's capacity for play and what the prerequisites are to play that I have marginalized one of its most powerful contexts that teachers are immersed in every day. That is, in the preschool classroom, a significant part of children's days is in playing with others and not simply solitary play. This is not technically correct: the early preschooler largely plays in parallel with their peers. They may be sitting side by side at the sandbox, but the play is largely composed of two separate silos, with hardly a shred of interaction. This is so because the capacity to symbolize is still so new for the 2-year-old that it makes the give and take of a shared play highly stressful and fragile. Play at this age is more akin to the dreams a couple may have lying side by side together through the night; the dreams are remarkably vivid to the dreamer, but inherently personal and not to be shared at the moment.

Much as with the adult dreamer, I would say that the most creative processes for the very young (age two or under) occur when children are comfortably playing alone. That is when they can most likely get to symbolize deeply felt experience. If children are doing this comfortably, the experienced preschool teacher knows that he or she doesn't have to say or do anything the great majority of the time! Indeed, the teacher simply bears witness while the children play and master the dilemmas and pleasures of their inner lives. In this ideal situation, the teacher intervenes only if children are getting overwhelmed or bored by the play. It is at these moments that the behavior of the disrupted player can easily intrude upon the space of their peers.

Much as I described the progression and interaction among the capacity to be alone, to feel secure and to develop curiosity, children at first take these capacities into a solitary play space of their own creation. We must keep in mind the ego-centric thinking of the preschooler in this regard. That is, children's wishes and needs far outweigh the possible wishes and needs of those around them. The give and take of social play is at first unsettling and carries very little emotional relevance. Little by little, however, the play of other children is seen as interesting and not intrusive. Curiosity expands to slowly include the minds and feelings of peers. Others' ideas about play can interest children more than alienate them. Play begins to become additive and mutual. The input of others is appreciated and not warded off and play becomes cooperative and engaging rather than something to be avoided.

Once again, we need to go back to the three prerequisites of play in order to understand the progression to more social play. Children who are secure in their sense of self are likely the most able to engage in play with others, as they do not fear that their sense of autonomy will be compromised. Being curious about others is an easy transition, as the world is also expected to be benevolent. Curiosity about things then extends to being curious about others', including their ideas about playing. At the other end of the spectrum of felt benevolence, children who are preoccupied with their teacher's presence in order to be able to play will have a hard time adjusting to the far less accommodating play interests of a peer. The teacher will likely find themselves repeatedly having to "referee" these children's tolerance of the play of others and having to model cooperative play. Children who play in a "silo" out of a fear of intrusion, of course, will likely reject the entreaties of others to engage in mutual play. Here the teacher's role is one of delicately enlarging children's play, often by doing the exact sort of hovering and adult-child interaction that the preoccupied child yearns for from the teacher. As more isolated children become increasingly comfortable with their teacher playing with them, one can slowly start to enlarge their world still further by including a peer (often a particularly easy going or mature peer) as part of a threesome with the teacher and the fearful child.

Conclusion

Children, at their most secure, can be masters of play. They are often able to use their teacher and the preschool classroom to symbolically work on and master the complexity of the world around them. Through the use of play figures, art materials and "dress up", they can reveal their pleasures and their conflicts and, just as compellingly, reveal *how* they think and feel and not just *what* they think and feel. Play is as valuable to children as breathing. It is an achievement that depends on crucial prerequisites formed before children ever get to the preschool classroom. It is simultaneously a naturally evolving part of the human psyche that the preschool teacher can play an enormous role in shaping and cultivating. I truly don't believe there is any position more valuable than to be a play cultivator and I hope that this short paper underscores my appreciation of the work of a preschool teacher and provides perhaps some novel ways to think about what they do and how it may be enhanced.

References

Burstein, S., & Meichenbaum, D. (1979). The work of worrying in children undergoing surgery. *Journal of Abnormal Child Psychology*, 7:121–132.

Donahue, P., & Tuber, S. (1993). Rorschach adaptive fantasy images and coping in children under severe environmental stress. *Journal of Personality Assessment*, 60:421–434.

Lieberman, J.N. (1977). *Playfulness: Its relationship to imagination and creativity*. New York: Academic Press.

Seja, A.L., & Russ, S.W. (1999). Children's fantasy play and emotional understanding. *Journal of Clinical Child Psychology*, 28:269–277.

Singer, D. & Singer, J. (1990). *The house of make-believe: Children's play and the developing imagination*. Cambridge, MA: Harvard University Press.

Tuber, S. (2008). *Attachment, play and authenticity: A Winnicott primer*. Lanham, MD: Rowman & Littlefield.

6

BEING A PLAYFUL TEACHER

Peter Blake

A teacher who appreciates the value of play and playfulness not only enhances a child's cognitive and social skills, they also enable the child to learn about their inner world and the inner world of others. This capacity to place one's self in the mind of another begins when the small child begins to imagine and play. This is referred to by psychologists as "mindfulness." This capacity is seen as being crucial for mental health and intellectual development. As Tuber (2015) notes, in imaginative play a child is not only having fun making up stories but is also learning how experiences involve a process not just content., This is vital for problem solving, both in relationships and in real life situations. In playing a child also gets to know who he or she is. It is that personal and that profound. Play is fundamental to the development of a sense of self and a teacher, especially in the early years, is a particularly important contributor to this development.

Donald Winnicott, a paediatrician and child psychoanalyst, is an author who has written extensively about the personal nature of play (Winnicott, 1971). He stresses play as an important bridge between the inner and outer world, the personal and the objective. Winnicott suggests that in their imaginative play the child has a sense of controlling or even creating the world. He notes that it is important not to disillusion the child too quickly of this belief that makes the world feel personal to the child. That is, from the child's perspective there is a lot of "me" in the world. Too quickly letting the child know the "objective" reality, taking away the pretend, can overload the child with too much "not me." This weakens their fragile developing sense of self. Of course, a child needs to eventually learn they did not make the world, but this needs to be done gradually. Some children may feel their inner world, their feelings and thoughts, are too big, too strong, too powerful, too out of control and attempt to manage this by emphasising their knowledge and control over the outside world. They will be really keen to objectively know everything. If this tendency becomes too strong they may start to become obsessional – trying to control and know everything in the outside world to counteract their feelings of inner instability.

This needing to know may be appealing to a teacher. A teacher is rightly excited by a child's willingness to learn, but there is the danger that if this desire to learn is not tempered by play and playfulness the child is then full of facts but won't know who they are. This is a vague concept, 2 plus 2 = 4 is much easier. But the teachers' own playfulness, in his/her actions and attitudes, is a crucial element in the child's future mental health. This playfulness is manifest in a joy of wondering, of NOT knowing and of exploring uncertainty. It does not mean the teacher is always happy and funny, but rather is allowing for spontaneity and is showing the children he/she is enjoying the discovery of their own mind.

Both in the playground and classroom a teacher's observation of a child's capacity to play, and the quality of that play, is invaluable. Also, in being playful in their interactions with their students, they provide a most powerful model of spontaneity, creativity and fun. In internalising these interactions, the children are given a legacy of how to relate to the outside world and to themselves. This enables them to feel their experiences as personally authentic and a source of exploration and growth.

While not a child psychotherapist, the teacher's observations of play over weeks and months put him or her in a strong position to contribute significantly to understanding the child's emotional development. If observed closely, a child's play not only informs the teacher about what interests the child and their cognitive and creative capacities, but it can also give them a window into what may be happening emotionally for the child. Children express themselves through their play. They will not sit down and tell you their problem, but they will communicate via their play.

To understand this communication, it can be helpful for a teacher to consider certain elements of the play and also how they can use play to deal with common developmental issues. The different types of play include such things as:

- Emotionally alive play
- Boring and repetitive play
- Unassociated play
- Driven play
- The duration and intensity of play
- The sequence of play
- The structure of play
- The content of play

Types of play

Emotionally alive play

The first question the teacher should ask himself or herself is can the child play. This may seem a fairly simple question, but what one is looking for is emotionally alive play. This is play that has an enjoyable energy. It contains spontaneous moments. It is reasonably coherent with a sense of a narrative – that it has a beginning, middle and end. It has "made up" moments rather than mindlessly copying a pattern of Lego blocks. It has a speed or pace that feels just right for the particular activity – not too fast or too slow. At a group or class level a teacher can promote this spontaneity by offering such activities as making up a class story. In this situation a teacher can provide the structure for a story, for example, about "living on the moon." The children can then be asked to imagine the various happenings on the moon. With an individual child, if they are struggling with being imaginative, a teacher could "lead" such a child by sharing their own imagination through a story and then gently encouraging the child to enter into some pretend state. In doing this a teacher needs to get in touch with their own inner child – to be comfortable with their own "inner childishness."

One way to assess the emotional utility of play is to think about the types of play that are not emotionally alive and how a teacher can help a child begin to play. In doing this the teacher is being psychotherapeutic. As Winnicott (1971) states, the aim of psychotherapy is to help someone play.

Boring and repetitive play

Boring and repetitive play is probably the clearest example of play that is emotionally dead. The play may have a structure (indeed, too much structure) and energy but it is just played over and over again in the same precise way. Observing such play can be especially mind numbing. There are no variations in its repetitions and this kills any sense of curiosity. You know exactly what is going to happen next. Of course, this may be the purpose of the play for the child. They know exactly what is going to happen. This play is often observed when the child has been overwhelmed by uncertainty in a particular situation and this is their attempt to take control of the trauma of fear and unknowing. This type of play stifles any opportunities for the children to get to know themselves – to experience a new thought or feeling. Everything must be controlled. This play can be the result of a severe trauma, as in fleeing a country, or it may be a reaction to uncertainty in the home setting, as in the parents divorcing, or a death in the family, and so on. In this situation a teacher needs to break this repetition by suggesting a new activity or at least a new variation in the play. This needs to be done gently and gradually, for too much variation can alarm the child. If a child is playing with toy cars and continually lining them up or driving them around in circles the teacher could enter the play and select a car that does something different- it starts to fly or goes off the track and starts exploring other "streets." The teacher needs to do this with a sense of fun, even silliness! This is a powerful model for the child that being out of control can be enjoyed rather than being a worrying state of mind.

Unassociated play

A lack of freedom, or being emotionally stuck, can be witnessed in unassociated play. By unassociated I mean the child rarely elaborates on a piece of play. A child can do a drawing but is unable to tell you anything about it.

Cars, animals, or people may be moved around, but that is where it seems to end. The people may go to a farm, or the animals may be left out in the cold, but then nothing else happens. Or the animals may fight, but when you ask what they are fighting about, the answer is, "They are just fighting." Such play can have verbs but few adverbs or adjectives. The frequent use of computer games can be related to this problem of unassociated play. If the game is strongly determined by the software, that is the choices are determined by the pre-set algorithms, then the child's play is not personal or creative. In unassociated play the teacher needs to 'lend' the child their mind. If a child does a drawing but is unable to talk about it, then the teacher can start making up a story about the drawing. This playfulness in the teacher is a model to the child that their creation, their drawing, sparks off new ideas, an expansion of their teacher's mind.

Driven play

In driven play, a child engages in an activity or talks with great speed to such a degree that there is no space to wonder. Everything feels too fast. The pace of play is disturbed. One activity or idea is immediately followed by another. There never seem to be moments of wondering what will happen next. Children diagnosed with hyperactivity commonly engage in such play. This sort of play is normally accompanied by a great deal of physical activity. While this can sometimes feel like a physical release, it often does not feel cathartic, but rather there is no let-up in this driven activity.

This activity can feel too excitable, as if it is too much for the child's physical system. Usually underlying such over-excitement is anxiety. While the child may be enjoying this excitement, the teacher can often get a feeling that such enjoyment is on a knife's edge, with a sense that this will end in tears. Children often "show" their anxiety through movement, reflecting a limited capacity to hold such anxiety in their minds. This is like the small baby who can only show distress through becoming physically agitated. In the presence of such over-excitement the teacher may need to step in by stopping the play, so as to contain this emotional/physical spill. They need to act as the "brakes" for this driven play. Ideally this can be accompanied by such comments as, "I think you're going too fast today," or "I think your excited feelings are getting a bit too big today and you need to stop that play now."

Broken play

Broken play is play that is constantly being broken off and not completed. The child can be happily engaged in a story, activity or drawing and suddenly stops and looks for something else to do. From an emotional perspective such behaviour can suggest the play is making the child anxious and he/she needs to move away from it. In play children uses displacement to distance themselves from something that may be worrying them. So, when the play is suddenly halted, the anxiety behind the play may be too great. It begins to break through in the child's conscious mind – the pretend in the play breaks down. If a child is often unable to complete a piece of play, then anxiety must be considered. In this regard it is important to note what the child was doing before the play was abandoned as this can help to understand what may be worrying them. For example, did the play involve someone being left out or behind, like all the horses are placed in an enclosure and one remains outside? Or does the child stop playing when some angry figure is introduced? Terminating the play at these points can indicate the child may be struggling with overwhelming feelings of being excluded or feeling frightened by aggression. Sometimes the play can prematurely stop if the child is unable to bear the experience of anything ending as a result of experiencing too many painful endings in their life. At school this can manifest in difficult behaviour around endings, such as the end of playtime or lunch or the end of school. When the teacher is aware of this type of play they can help the child by gently noting when the play was broken off and then helping them to continue. For instance, in the previous example, the teacher may note to the child that the left-out horse is upset and then move it in with the other horses, or note that an angry figure has been introduced but then suggest that the angry figure was able to calm down and wasn't so scary anymore.

Fixated play

Fixated play involves a child always engaging in the same sort of play and seems unable to move on to anything else. It is the opposite of broken play. Being fixated on a particular form of play is suggesting this play is carrying a great deal of emotional significance. A 4-year-old child I once observed only ever wanted to play with the toy scissors and cutting paper. He would do this for over twenty minutes. Then he would spend a great deal of time gluing or sellotaping the paper back together. When this was accomplished he would start cutting again. This exclusion of other forms of play suggests the child was very concerned about things separating and the need for them to be back together. Significantly, this little boy's mother had just had a new baby and was worried about his clinginess. Attachment issues are often an underlying dynamic behind troubling behaviour in small children. But it was this boy's near obsession with cutting and pasting that strongly indicated he was struggling with separation anxieties. A demonstration of the teacher's playfulness can be helpful in these circumstances. A teacher can enter the play and voice the worries behind the fixated activity. For instance, in the scissor play just described, the teacher can speak as the paper and how it doesn't like being cut apart, it doesn't like being separated. Naming this worry in this playful way tells the child the worry about separation can be named albeit in a safe, projected form onto the paper. It is important for the teacher to closely monitor the child's reaction to this. If the child does not seem too disturbed by these playful comments, it is best to leave it open and say no more. This will allow the child to play with it. However, if the comments worry the child, then a supportive reparative suggestion that the paper loves it when it can be stuck together again may be helpful. But if this reassuring comment is made too quickly it can communicate to the child that even the teacher can't tolerate worries about separation. So, judging what is bearable for the child is crucial in this situation. In talking as the paper, it is best expressed in a high-pitched "silly" voice to let the child know that the teacher is only playing (Blake, 2011).

Aspects of play

Intensity of play

The intensity of a piece of play can also alert an observer to its emotional significance. For instance, a child may be peacefully playing and then suddenly becomes excited, loud, and fast. It is as if some feature of the play has triggered a strong reaction. For instance, a little girl was telling a story about her version of Jack and the Beanstalk. She related this story with a lively energy, but when she got to the part when the Beanstalk was being cut down, she suddenly became very excited and loud, exclaiming, "It's going to fall, it's going to fall. It's going to crash to the ground. It's going to make a really, really big hole."

This was said with speed and her body became agitated. Such an intensification of play needs to be noted and thought about. While this little girl looked as if she was very excited, the theme of something being chopped down and causing damage may indicate that she has anxiety over destructiveness, either she is worried about causing damage or being damaged. In these circumstances, the teacher can 'play' with this theme by first noting the intensity to the child, e.g. "You're really thinking about the fall and the big crash." Just acknowledging the importance of these thoughts and feelings may be enough (child therapists, such as Alvarez (2012), refer to this as working at a descriptive level). If the child seems especially worried about the falling, the teacher can contain this concern by saying something like, "I think the crash to the ground will be alright, it won't really hurt the ground." However, in reassuring the child it is important not to do this too quickly, for this can give a message to the child that the teacher is really worried as well and can't tolerate this worry even for a second. So, a slight pause and giving this reassurance in an unhurried manner can be the most helpful approach.

Selective play

If a child has a number of toys or activities in front of him/her, a feature to be noted is what activity the child chooses. Does the child pick up a doll and start feeding it? Are small cars chosen so they can be used for racing, repaired or used to crash into each other? Do they select the strongest or biggest animals? Such selections are not a matter of chance. If there is a free choice, emotional factors can determine the child's selected activity. The child who feeds the doll may not only be copying its mother, but could also be exploring the issue of dependency and attachment – selecting cars to race can indicate issues of competition and a possible worry of not being good enough. Selecting the big animals may be a way of managing feelings of being small and vulnerable. None of these selections are necessarily indicating there is something troubling the child, rather they help the observer, be he or she a teacher or a psychologist, to consider what may be pre-occupying the child's mind and in so doing help them to deepen the understanding of the child. With this understanding the teacher could play with this theme. If the child's play involved competition then the teacher could talk about how lovely it is to win but also how it can be sad to lose.

The sequence of play

Child therapists take great notice of the sequence of a child's play. Certain dynamic forces may be determining why a child goes from one activity to the next. This may be difficult for teachers to observe in the hustle and bustle of a classroom or a playground. But sometimes these sequences or associations can be striking. An example of such a sequence was a bright 4-year-old girl who was describing a monster she saw on television. She said she was scared because the monster could squash and eat up anything. Then in the next breath, she said her little sister was a good runner. Why was the monster story followed by the reference to her little sister? In her overt behaviour she was kind and loving to her sister, but this sequence in the story could be suggesting she may also feel her sister is a monster who eats up all the attention, or she herself has monstrous jealous feelings towards her sister – that she wants to squash and eat her up. This is not suggesting great pathology but rather how the girl's mind may be operating. If this sequence was noted by the teacher (the teacher has to be aware of this possibility in the back of her/his mind – not an easy thing to do in a busy classroom) then they could give space for these feelings by underlining or emphasising the feeling by commenting on how the monster really, really wanted to squash and eat things up. It would NOT be helpful to suggest the monster is like her sibling or herself as this could certainly close down her thinking on this whole area. It is important for the teacher to recognize that this is an issue for the child but to leave it open so the child can process this in their own time. Understanding that a child like this may be struggling with feelings of jealousy could help the teacher make sense of why she gets upset if she can't sit in the front row when the teacher is reading a story. The teacher could then be sensitive to making sure she is not placed in the back row too many times – to not expose her to too many jealousy-provoking situations.

Content of play

Observing the actual content of a child's play is probably the most obvious way of understanding what is going on inside their mind. This may be difficult for a teacher who has certain required agendas or schedules to fulfil. Finding the space and time to observe the child in a free play situation may be rare. But listening to children's stories in such activities as show and tell, or what they may tell you about their weekend, or what they draw or make in craft are all opportunities to think about the content of their play – a chance to see what themes are noticed over the weeks and months. Obviously, stories or activities representing anger and violence are very different to those concerning caring and cooperation. For example, over the months a teacher may hear a child talk about a new robot that smashes everything before it. Then to hear stories of watching big boys hurt each other playing football, and observing drawings of army men and watching the child play goodie and baddies in the playground. These observations over different times and settings enable a teacher to be in a strong position of putting these different observations together. In so doing, the teacher can get to know the child in a much deeper psychological way. If the play can be understood, the teacher is in a much better position to manage the behaviour more effectively. In this case, the teacher may become aware that issues concerning aggression and harm are very prominent in this child's mind. If this is so, the teacher could 'play' with these observations by introducing play that deals with these issues. For example, he/she may suggest playing games or telling stories about being an ambulance person who wants to and can fix up people if they are hurt; or to imagine a machine or robot that fixes things up if they are smashed. Or the teacher could direct the child to more creative, reparative activities, e.g. craft activities of creating or repairing things.

Observing in the classroom

Although thinking about a child's play can be considered to be a window into their mind, other school activities can be used to gain insight into their inner world. Melanie Klein was one of the earliest child psychoanalysts who believed children expressed their thoughts and feelings not only in their play but also in a wide range of behaviours (Klein, 1929). She felt that children's relationship to their early caregivers was expressed in their relationship to objects in the world around them. While some feel this is reading too much into things, it can be helpful to play with this idea. For example, how a child holds his/her pen can be an expression of how they feel about personal relationships. One example would be gripping the pen very tightly so it would never fall out. This could be expressing concerns of not feeling secure in their attachments. Of course, holding a pen loosely so it is always dropping could be manifesting similar concerns.

Here opposite behaviour may have a similar meaning. Or how a child writes or draws on a piece of paper can have relational meaning, that is, the relationship between the pen and paper can be representing how the child may feel in relationships. The child may really dig the pencil into the paper, either aggressively or desperately, so it is heavily marked. Is this child representing their feeling about relationships? Are they aggressive or desperate? Do you really have to impress upon another your presence so you will be noticed? Or are relationships uncertain and uncomfortable with worries about 'impressing' too much? Does the pen very gently brush against the paper? When I teach child therapists a technique, I suggest that, when they are watching a child engaging in some activity, they try to imagine what it would be like to be the object with which the child is engaging? Be the pen. Would you feel securely held or squashed to death, or worried you could be dropped at any moment? Or be the paper. Would you feel dug into, or would you feel the pen barely touched you? This 'being the object' can apply to anything – be the chair, are you sat upon firmly, aggressively, tentatively? If a teacher notices a particular theme, such as a child holding on tightly to everything, he/she can playfully comment, "that pen is *really* held in your hand." This comment communicates to the child that their teacher understands what issues may be worrying them. Generally, it is better to put these thoughts in a positive manner i.e. the pen is being held rather than the more anxiety orientated comment, "You're really worried the pen is going to fall or be dropped." Commenting on the need of being held usually is better able to be heard by a child than naming the anxiety. Often the child only hears the 'anxious' words and this can be disturbing to them (Alvarez, 2012).

It is important to play with this way of observing and thinking. Just because the child holds the pen firmly does not mean he/she is anxiously attached, but he/she could be! To understand and read a child's inner world one must be open to these possibilities. Clearly a judgement should not be based on one example but rather it needs to be built up on impressions over time and in different settings. Unfortunately reading a child's mind cannot be achieved by using some objective checklist.

It is also important for a teacher to be aware that learning is not solely a cognitive exercise. A child's emotions will affect their learning. I saw a very intelligent 10-year-old who had a terrible childhood, being in and out of children's homes and foster families for most of his life. This lack of continuity in his background manifested itself in his learning difficulties. He was consistently unable to remember the correct sequence of the days of the week, despite being very clever in other areas. Even such things as basic arithmetic can demonstrate this link between learning and emotions. Some children who have very strong feelings of jealousy and have difficulty sharing can really struggle to understand division and fractions, while others who have experienced a great deal of loss in their history cannot deal with subtraction. Even such things as writing can be influenced by emotional dynamics. Joining up letters in discursive writing may be difficult when the child has a background of family disturbance in which family members have found it difficult 'coming together' in a peaceful way. A child who may feel small and vulnerable could struggle with managing capital letters, for such 'big' letters may be quite frightening to the smaller letters. Even in these more formal academic activities there can be opportunities for the teacher to be playful. In teaching division, a teacher may say that there are four chocolates and two children, how many chocolates will each child receive. But then say (in an exaggerated hammed up voice), "Oh no, I don't want to share, I want all the chocolates for myself."

Thinking about teaching and learning from this emotional perspective can be both exciting and confusing. A teacher would probably go mad if they considered all these emotional factors in the child's play and in the classroom situation.

However, being open to the various possible meanings of play and learning situations can add a depth of understanding of the child, which in turn leads to greater sensitivity in their management. These emotional elements need to be kept in mind, although perhaps at the back of the mind. Over the weeks and months of observing and interacting with a child, these emotional possibilities of meaning can be played with. Even if such thoughts are incorrect, a child will be aware of the teacher not only being a source of knowledge and authority but someone who is interested in who they really are.

Having a playful attitude

A teacher may spend more waking time with a child than do their parents. As such he/she is a very powerful model on how the students think and feel. If the teacher displays a playful attitude in class this gives the child the message that playing and being playful are valued activities. This is not suggesting teachers just play all the time. Rather it is the teacher demonstrating his/her joy in playing around with ideas. For example, a teacher may say that two plus two equals four, but then say, "Now I wonder what four things I might buy at the shop, or if I had four holidays where I would go." Or even when reading a story, the teacher has the opportunity to 'play' with the different characters that are on the page. By wondering about how they are feeling, this also helps the children develop their emotional vocabulary. Are the story characters sad, miserable, unhappy, depressed, or down in the dumps? The teacher who 'wonders' a lot is showing the class that she/he enjoys exploring the contents of his/her mind. All this will help stimulate the children's imagination, which is just another way of saying it will help them know who they are, or in psychological jargon it will help them develop a strong sense of self and expand their capacity for mindfulness.

Consulting with parents

Teachers also consult and influence parents. Stressing the importance of play and playfulness to parents is an important message. Helping to educate them on the value of play and giving suggestions that promote play at home is one way teachers can promote the mental health of their students. Parents can be advised on the value of having set, reliable play times at home. They need to be advised that such play will help reduce their child's stress levels (Sunderland, 2006). This may be 30 or 40 minutes in which one parent plays with the child in an imaginative way. This should be child-led with the parent describing a child's play but not suggesting themes or story lines, unless the child is unable to start without some initial prompting. Within this play there should be no limitations on what can be expressed (Magagna, 2014). Stories can involve love, anger, fear, jealousy etc. In this regard there can be a danger of not staying with any negative feelings that may arise in the stories. Too quickly "cheering up" a child or a character in a story can send a message to the child that anger or sadness or fear is not acceptable. The parent needs to acknowledge painful feelings before offering reassurance and resolution. Teachers can also advise parents of the value of sharing the parents' imaginative ideas with their children. Telling "silly" humorous stories is a parental skill that should be highly valued.

The therapeutic value of play

While this chapter has focused on the role of play and teacher playfulness, play can also be thought about as a direct therapeutic intervention both for teachers and parents. As children communicate and "think" through their play, play can be designed to help them work through issues that may be troubling them. Externalising an internal problem by playing it out in a concrete way can give the child a sense of mastery and this can often reduce or even eliminate emotional problems. Probably the most dramatic example of this was with a mother who was distressed over her 3-year-old daughter refusing to poo. In her discussions with the psychologist, she came up with the idea of cutting one end of her stockings so that the stocking had two open ends. She then invited the daughter to push a tennis ball through the stocking from one end to other. Her daughter loved this game and played it many times. Within two days of this play the poo problems had disappeared.

Emotionally designed play

Play and loss

One of the most common emotional issues for small children is attachment. Being fearful of losing Mummy or Daddy is behind a great number of behavioural problems at this age. One way of playing this out and working through these concerns is the game of peek-a-boo. It is a rare baby who does not enjoy this game. In peek-a-boo, the child is exposed to the anxiety of the loss of the parent but then quickly reassured the parent/face will return. This game is like inoculating a child with a small dose of anxiety so as to help them gradually be able to cope with small periods of loss. For a toddler or a slightly older child playing the game of hide and seek fulfils the same function. This may either be with an object that is hidden, or a parent or child hides and has to be found. Another version of this is putting a ball or object through a closed tunnel or slide and seeing it come out at the other end, just like the little poo girl. In the classroom, the teacher has the opportunity to introduce playful activities involving loss. When reading a book to the class a game can be made out of finding small characters, such as a bird in the tree. Some books are designed for this purpose. For older children books like, "Where's Wally," in which a small character has been lost in the crowd, fulfil a similar purpose of playing with the anxieties of loss and loneliness. The teacher could introduce different "treasure hunts" for the class. Hiding an object in a particular area exposes the children to loss and abandonment but also to the reassuring experience of being found.

Themes of loss, separation, and return can also be discerned in activities such as playing with a yoyo (something been thrown away, which then comes back), throwing or kicking a ball back and forth, bouncing on a trampoline, being on a see-saw and going back and forth on a swing. Playing simple memory games in the classroom is the mental equivalent of being lost and found.

Play and regulation

For children who have temper tantrums or emotionally "lose it," games concerning regulation can be considered. Hose play can be great fun and helpful in this regard. Plying with the nozzle of the hose, so its flow of water can be controlled, can be an externalisation of the child's struggle for internal regulation. Even bath play, where water can be channelled, damned or have its flow regulated, may be explored as a therapeutic play activity.

Any other games or activities concerning regulation may provide the child with the opportunity to "play" with their concerns. Activities such as playing musical instruments – controlling or regulating the speeds of a sound – regulating the air out of a balloon, and playing with gears and brakes on a bike, can be a helpful metaphor or symbol for the child. Obviously, a teacher can introduce regulation games in the classroom. For example, getting the class to make a noise of ten, then a noise of seven, then five and so on. Or getting the class to say something very fast, then slower and slower. All such activities help externalise and play with this theme of regulation – a developmental task all small children are still struggling with, as their developing feelings can feel very powerful and out of control or disregulated.

Play and fragmentation

Related to the concerns about regulation is the issue of the child feeling fragmented and disintegrated – he/she seems to be all over the place. This feeling of not feeling "whole" is common in small children as they are still forming their personality – putting the bits of themselves together. Activities that involve integration and containment can be helpful in this situation. The common activity of a jigsaw puzzle can assist a child feel that pieces can be put back together – unlike Humpty Dumpty. Even helping a child bake a cake has the same integrating element. The egg, flour, milk and sugar are magically mixed together and eventually form a delicious treat. Even adults like to do this! Any activity in which bits are put together – Lego, simple construction tasks etc. can be used to address this common developmental task. Indeed Anna Freud, an early child psychoanalyst was very keen on teaching children how to knit. The teacher can play with this theme in numerous ways. Getting the class to make a simple collage, either individually or as a class, allows students to play with integration. Getting each student to write their initial in glue, then to sprinkle glitter over it can literally show the student how tiny fragmented bits can be held together.

With all of these play activities, it is crucial that the child is enjoying it and is happy to play it over and over again. If the child doesn't want to be involved, this is suggesting that the play is not distancing the anxieties far enough away. The aim is to expose the child to the anxieties and for them to gain a sense of mastery. Being unwilling to play is indicating that the activity is still too emotionally unsafe.

Reading

While games and play activity are a wonderfully concrete expression of inner world issues, these concerns can also be safely explored by reading stories that deal with children's emotional difficulties. As with play, it can be helpful to encourage parents to read to their children appropriately selected stories that engage an issue or theme that is troubling their child. There are many books now written dealing with issues such as parents' divorce, sibling rivalry, sadness, anger, bullying and so on (Fox 1995; Coon 2004). There is now a movement called Bibliotherapy that uses literature for therapeutic purposes. Many classic books such as the Dr. Seuss series, also deal with a wide variety of children's anxieties. As with play, it is best if these stories are safely displaced o to made up creatures or animals rather than directly portraying children and their families. The sillier and more displaced the stories the better. A teacher can also apply these ideas about reading to the selection of books that they read to the class. This is not only engaging them in the practice of reading, it is also exploring with them, in the safety of the class group, what emotional issues they are confronting in their day-to-day development.

Conclusion

This chapter has suggested that closely observing and understanding a child's play is a hugely valuable asset in the skills of being a teacher. Teaching small children involves helping them cognitively, socially and emotionally. Valuing the communication of play enables the teacher to emotionally attune to each child. Appreciating how play can also be used therapeutically further equips the teacher to be a better consultant to parents as well as enriching his/her interactions with the different personalities in his/her class. The old saying, "All work and no play, makes Jack a dull boy," may not only be referring to a cognitive dullness but also to children's dullness in knowing who they are and inhibiting their joy in discovering their own personality. In this sense, both the work and play of a teacher is a potent mix in promoting the mental well-being of their students. It also enables the teacher and students to have a fun time – an essential ingredient for learning and life.

References

Alvarez, A. (2012). *The thinking heart: Three levels of psychoanalytic therapy with disturbed children*. London: Routledge.
Blake, P. (2011). *Child and adolescent psychotherapy*. London: Karnac Books.

Coon, C. (2004). *Books to grow with: A guide to using the best children's fiction for everyday issues and tough challenges*. Portland, OR: Lutra Press.

Fox, J. (1995). *Books that help children*. Sydney: MBF Publications.

Klein, M. (1929). Personification in the play of children. *International Journal of Psychoanalysis*, 10:193–204.

Magagna, J. (2014). *Being present for your nursery aged child*. London: Karnac Books.

Sunderland, M. (2006). *The science of parenting*. London: DK Publishing.

Tuber, S. (2015). Psychological mindedness in the face of a learning disability: The utility of play. *Journal of Infant, Child, and Adolescent Psychotherapy*, 14:288–293.

Winnicott, D. (1971). *Playing and reality*. New York: Penguin.

7

MINE! NO, MINE!

Interaction in children's play

Jill Bellinson

Two 3-year-olds are playing next to each other, building with Duplo blocks. There is one bin in front of them, and they are each taking out the pieces they want and adding the blocks to the structure they are building. Carrie is building a train, adding cars to make it as long as she can and driving her train to see how it works after each addition. Joshua wants his train to be shorter, with a tall tower of blocks on each car. They both reach into the bin at the same time and pull out the same red car, then create a tug-of-war as they each pull on it and scream "Mine!"

Every early education teacher sees interactions like this every day, multiple times. Preschool children play comfortably next to each other all the time, in easy rhythm until they argue over a disputed object, at which point the play often turns hostile. Each child wants the object and neither gives up, as they get louder in their insistence and more physical in their squabble. Most teachers understand that they can postpone the battle if they provide enough duplicate toys so that every child can have his own or structure children to play with different sets of toys rather than pull from the same bin, and most teachers hope to intervene before the inevitable consequence—one child ends up in tears and the other has to be scolded for hitting.

And this sequence is repeated daily.

But let's look further at this, and try to understand what this sort of play means and whether there might be more effective ways to intervene. In fact, bickering and even physical fighting is normal in young children, serves an important function, and communicates significant information that teachers need to know about children's lives.

First, a look at the development of play (First, 1994; Freud, 1946; Lyons-Ruth, 2006; Peller, 1954; Slade & Wolf, 1994). Babies' first play uses their own bodies in interaction with the world. They learn about the world they live in by practicing. They play peek-a-boo to discover that Mommy can disappear and reliably reappear, and they eventually come to understand that Mommy is still there even when they can't see her. They play Catch-Me-If-You-Can to practice their own mobility and to understand that if they stray from their secure base someone will notice, care, and seek them out. The delight they feel when they are seen or caught makes it play; the repetitive occurrence makes it practice; the understanding they develop makes it learning.

Toddlers begin to add objects to their play, which still relies on themselves and their bodies in interaction with the world. They put on Mommy's shoes and "become" her; they carry Daddy's briefcase and "go to work"; they doctor their babysitters, feed their teddy bears, and rock their baby dolls to sleep. They pretend to be the parent, the doctor, the truckdriver, the princess—using toys and dress-up materials to accessorize their play. Once again, they experience pleasure as they pretend and they practice as they repeat the play over and over. As they do this, they learn what it feels like to be a caregiving parent, a sequined fairy queen, a hard-working bricklayer.

Later still, children can identify with their play objects and use them as stand-ins for themselves. So, dollhouse figures can rock their babies to sleep, teddy bears can serve tea to each other, action figures can go off to work.

In each of these developmental stages of play, children are enjoying themselves, practicing life skills, and learning about the ways of their world. Even structured games, which typically spark children's interest when they later enter structured schools, are ways children can learn about themselves and their worlds through the safe world of pretend (Bellinson, 2002).

Along the way, children's connection to others changes, as well. Babies are largely oblivious to others, except as they have to climb over them to crawl to their own destination. They need others—adults primarily, at this stage—to feed and clothe them, to understand their needs and feelings, and to respond when they're ready to play. But they're not yet aware that these others have existences apart from their own.

Over time, children can play in parallel to others, sitting next to their peers but not yet interacting with them. Adults can guide interaction at this point—structuring turn-taking or leading group songs and dances—but young children don't spontaneously interact except briefly in passing. Eight-year-olds can typically join together successfully, playing competitive games in teams, jointly defining elaborate battle scenes between soldiers or super-heroes, enacting long and intricate dramas between interacting Barbies. In the intervening years between toddlerhood and middle school, children gradually learn to accommodate others, in play and in real life.

The scene described at the beginning of this chapter was an early example of this accommodation, a common one in which children playing in parallel find each other, often in conflict. It's important for early education teachers to understand that this conflict is itself an important developmental step. In play, children are working out their competing needs, learning about others' response to their demands, and practicing their budding ability to collaborate. If teachers intervene too quickly or insistently, they may hinder this exploration. If they solve too many disagreements, they may actually impede the development of the children's ability to resolve their own disagreements.

Conflict itself is part of the practice toward mastery that children gain from play, and it is a necessary developmental step on the way to maturity. If they didn't ever disagree with others, they would never understand the feeling of conflict. If they didn't argue, they would never experience the strength of their power to demand or the pain of another's competing needs. These are mild and fleeting feelings when children are little, if children can be permitted to feel and then let go of them in the safety of the classroom. The practice they get in experiencing the conflict, surviving it, and slowly letting go of the feeling will serve them well as they grow. The conflict itself, though not as pleasurable as pretending or building, contains the practice of play and the model for learning real-life skills.

Teachers know that some children are involved in conflicts far more than others. Every classroom has a child who seems to be conflicting with others repeatedly throughout the day, who will likely be the one screaming when the sound level in the room rises and who will probably be the aggressor if anyone is observed hitting or pushing. And every classroom has a child who seems to be the chronically aggrieved one, whose toys are grabbed away most frequently and who is most often in tears. Our hearts go out to the child who gets hit, and our anger spreads toward the habitual hitter, but it's important for us to recognize that these experiences, too, are normal developmental sequences and vital life experiences, and anything the teacher does to circumvent the process may thwart development and make the situation worse rather than better.

But, of course, teachers also want their classrooms to run smoothly and without conflict. They want children to enjoy coming to school, and they have to keep their classrooms safe for all children, so they do have to work to resolve at least some of the conflicts that arise in the room, and they do have to try to minimize the physical aggression between children. How can they do that, without derailing the developmental process?

Understanding the issues

Let's try to think about what quarreling children might be feeling. We've talked throughout this book (Tuber, Malberg, Sapountzis . . .) about the need to mentalize (Fonagy et al., 1991) children's states of mind, so that they can feel understood and so that they can develop their own ability to predict their feelings and control their behavior. What states of mind might lead to conflictual behavior in young children?

Consider Carrie and Joshua, the 3-year-olds in the opening example; what might they be feeling? In the simplest terms, they each desired the red car and were annoyed at anyone or anything standing in the way of that wish. This may be a straightforward case of two conflicting needs—both want the Duplo piece and only one can have it (The fact that there may be another red car in the bin is irrelevant here. Each wants THAT red car). In this uncomplicated instance, there may be no meaning beyond their both grabbing the car at the same time and experiencing the developmental progression from parallel play into interactive play.

Battles often have meaning beyond those simple terms, as well. Joshua may come from a home where his older siblings get all the goodies, so he has learned he has to grab if wants to claim anything for himself. Carrie may come from a home where there has never been enough money for toys, so school represents her only opportunity to touch Duplo blocks. Or they may both come from comfortable homes, but recently their parents have been arguing a lot, or a family member was diagnosed with a serious disease, or a beloved grandparent died; that is, one or both of them may have been unusually stressed at home, and that stress may appear in the classroom in what seems to be acute needs or excessive demands.

Regardless of which of these—and many more—possibilities might apply to Carrie and Joshua, it is important for teachers to understand that conflictual behavior, like most behavior, comes from a state of mind that the child experiences, and the conflict can only be truly resolved when the teacher understands, acknowledges, and resolves that state of mind. A child who feels deprived, continually or in this particular instance, can only let go of the red car when she no longer feels needy. A child who is anxious about stress at home can only let go of the red car when the stress at home abates or when the teachers recognize his stress and help to soothe him.

It's even possible that this particular red car is imbued with special meaning for one of the children. It was the car that a beloved teacher was playing with before she went on maternity leave, or it's the one with the cracked bumper just like the crack in grandpa's car, or it's the toy that was on the table the day Mommy left for the first time. No other car will do in this case, not even a different red car, and there will be no way to distract that child with puzzles or circle time. That child is soothing himself with the red car and may have to hold that car all day if he is to be able to participate in school activities.

These children will relinquish the red car when the teacher requires it, and use inside voices and apologize on command, but they can't let go of the need or the conflict itself unless a caregiver helps them with their underlying feelings. It's only by detecting the meaning of the conflict for the children involved—the meaning of this particular conflict, even for children who are frequently involved in conflict—that a teacher can resolve it in a way that it doesn't last for hours or escalate into a bigger commotion, and in a way that can aid in the development of successful interpersonal relationships.

It takes two to tangle

When a teacher does intervene to resolve a conflict between two or more children, it is vital that she recognize and frame the difficulty as a two- (or more-) person dispute. It is never one child aggressing against another, no matter how much it may appear to be. If it were—Maryann grabbed a block away from Jennifer who had been building peacefully by herself—there would be no incident. Jennifer would calmly give the block to Maryann and pick up a different one. We, the adults, may wish Jennifer would stick up for herself and refuse to cede the block so easily, but there would be no squabble and the pair would not stir the teachers to even notice their interaction.

The truth is that both children are grabbing and screaming when we get to the scene, and—no matter what it might look like—we have no way of knowing how it began. Maybe Jennifer grabbed the block from Maryann when we weren't looking, and Maryann was simply demanding it back. That can be true even when Maryann is the usual suspect who is involved in disputes all day every day; she may be the aggrieved party this time, or even many times, but we didn't see it. Maybe Jennifer taunted Maryann with the block, knowing Maryann would reach for it and then get punished when the teachers noticed her grabbing. Maybe both girls had been calling for the teachers to help them with their project but not getting their attention, so they felt abandoned and stressed, and expressed their needs toward each other rather than toward the oblivious teacher.

Commonly, two particular children are involved in conflicts on a daily basis. One is always the one who shouts and hits, the other always the one who cries when he is "injured." In fact, this is almost never as it seems. A child who is truly and repeatedly injured by another will not play near him. Even when both love puzzles, a child who is afraid of another will find a way to stay far away and involved with other children and other toys. If one specific preschooler is repeatedly being hit or pushed or bitten by a specific other, it can only be that both children are seeking each other out—which suggests that the "victim" is not so innocent after all. In families, a younger sibling tends to know how to get an older child into trouble with parents, and it often involves getting hit and starting to cry, which immediately grabs parents' attention and gets the older child punished. In classroom families, children learn that as well, as they compete for the in-loco-parentis attention of their teachers. Parents and teachers rarely see the beginning of these interactions; they tend to be involved elsewhere until the noise level rises or someone screams or cries. Any adult who intervenes at the end point in support of one child over the other will reinforce the behavior so it is sure to happen again.

Helpful, mentalizing interventions

So how should an adult intervene?

First, explore whether intervention is even necessary. Given that conflict is an expectable and even useful part of normal development, this may be a conflict that can be left alone. Once a teacher understands that it is not important for her to quickly stop squabbling, he may discover that these little squabbles work themselves out without him. In fact, removing the teachers from these spats often results in fewer spats, since children can't get attention by raising their voices. Even hitting often lessens when teachers don't act to stop and punish every episode.

If intervention is judged to be necessary, it should be as little as possible. "Let's be sure to use inside voices" spoken to the whole room or, "You two are getting a little loud; can you find a way to speak more quietly?" spoken softly and just to the squabblers can often break up a disagreement—and may be all that is needed for one or both to move on to a different pursuit. If this happens, a teacher only prolongs the conflict if she tries to talk things through or insist on apologies.

Toddlers will need to be treated differently from preschoolers, of course. Two 1-year-olds can be distracted from their dispute, but 4-year-olds may be more insistent in their demands; at the same time, 4-year-olds can be more capable of working through their conflicts on their own.

It is important to always reframe the issue as a two-person disagreement. Both children want the same magic wand; each of them wants to build a city in the same location; one likes to build the blocks higher and one likes to knock them down. Their needs are mutually exclusive, they feel them simultaneously and with the same intensity. Young children can't experience a sophisticated level of empathy, so the fact that the other has a conflicting wish won't be felt as relevant. And someone who is emotionally triggered—whether because of the agitation of the current dispute or because of some ongoing life stresses—will be unable to use logic or language.

So, a teacher has to be the one to consider the stressors involved for each child and identify the competing needs and feelings of the two. "Carrie, you and Joshua both want that red car." "Jennifer, you want that block and Maryann doesn't want you to have it." "Stefan, you want to build your road there and Roberto, you want your city there without a road through it." And he could even add, "and we all had a scary time this morning when we had a fire drill, so it might feel extra important today." In each of these examples, an understanding teacher is framing the dispute as a two-person disagreement in which each child has a viewpoint that he acknowledges. He also shows them that he recognizes that stress can provoke tempers and increase conflict. And he does all this with a kindness and understanding that validates both children's experiences without blame or shame.

The next step is one that has been called reticence (Steele et al., 2015) or scaffolding (Bruner, 1966). It involves holding back from saying or doing anything that the child might be able to do for himself and offering only as much help as he or she needs. This is probably the hardest for teachers to implement, since it often feels important, when voices rise or arms flail, to do something to keep the room peaceful and safe, and teachers think of themselves as playing an important role in training children in how to behave. So, their tendency is to intervene quickly, speak firmly to the apparent aggressor ("We don't hit in this room") and tenderly to the apparent victim ("Let me see where you got hurt and hold you until you feel better"), and press the children to "use words" to express themselves. But this approach is rarely successful. In the moment, the injured party may receive some comfort but also significant reinforcement, guaranteeing that it will happen again, so she can have the teacher's lap to herself. And words are not available to children in those moments. Preschoolers are still developing language skills, so their vocabularies are limited in the best of times, and we all lose our ability to articulate when we are stressed. A teacher can provide words—"You're both mad" or "Say,

'Don't do that' instead of hitting" or "Tell Maryann 'Ouch, that hurt'"—but she can't expect that children will be able to call on their own words in those moments of upset.

After soothing, a teacher can ask the children what they think the best solution would be, and the answers might surprise him. Consider this example: two 4-year-old boys are playing with Legos, an activity these fast friends often shared, but focused this time on the human figures rather than the building blocks. Kevin has collected all the heads, separated from the figures, and connected them to each other in a chain; Kenny has all bodies stacked into a long, high tower of bottoms. They have been playing comfortably for quite some time when the sound level starts to rise. They begin yelling—"you can't . . . " "I need . . . " "Stop!" "No" "NO!" and Kenny begins to cry. I approached them to try to defuse the argument. I notice the unbalanced distribution of pieces, and ask what the problem is. Kenny says, in a hurt and angry tone, "He has all the heads." Imagining I can fix this for the boys, I take the toys and give each child 1/2 the heads and 1/2 the bodies. And they both start to cry!

Only when I really stopped to question the boys about their experience could I understand their conflict and work to resolve it. Each child wanted the pieces he was holding, but the child with the bodies wanted one head—only one head—to complete his tower. When I helped him express that (after spending considerable time helping to calm the children down when I had made them both cry), Kenny could ask his playmate for a single head. Kevin agreed, as long as he could have a single body for the bottom of his head-stack, and they joined together to discuss which head went with the bodies and which bodies went best with the heads. This shows clearly how important it is to hold back from stepping in too quickly or too directly, to reframe the conflict as two children each wanting something the other has, and to support the children resolving the conflict in ways that best suit them. This was not a case of one child grabbing or one child refusing, regardless of how it appeared, and it could not be resolved with the textbook solution of splitting toys equally between the children.

It is also important to recognize that if adults short-circuit children's conflict, if they jump in to resolve it quickly and without allowing the children to feel it fully and deeply, they communicate that disagreement—any disagreement—is unacceptable. If adults are worried about children's squabbles, the message transmitted is that children's squabbles must be very wrong and very scary. This can make children feel that they have done something so terrible that even the grown-ups are afraid, and it can cause them to fear their own wishes and needs. Then they feel very bad about themselves, since of course they frequently have disagreeing opinions, or they may feel that they have done something shameful. This is the very opposite of what teachers and parents hope to convey to their youngsters.

So, the path that best supports emotional growth and developmental progress is one in which adults appreciate conflict as a normative part of life, productive practice of life skills a child will need later in life, and part of the child's growing model of interpersonal relationships. Adults should expect that children will conflict as they develop the ability to play together. They should hold back from resolving the conflict too quickly or too fully, waiting for children to fully feel the dispute, consider their options, and think about solutions they would want themselves. As they practice this, they become able to design resolutions themselves.

Some examples:

Roberto is yelling loudly at Stefan and kicking his blocks across the room. Stefan screams back and knocks over Roberto's structures. A teacher approaches and asks about the difficulty. Each angrily describes the other's destructive behavior—kicking and knocking the other's blocks. The teacher asks why, and slowly, with a great deal of help, Stefan says he is building the "longest road on earth and to Mars" and is trying to building it across the room. Roberto says his city is already built, and he needs it to be placed right where Stefan wants his road. A perfect model of real-life politics! The teacher has many ideas about what they could do, but refrains from offering. Each child offers potential solutions—you could make a space in your city for my road to pass through; you could build your road around my city—none satisfying. Eventually one of them notices an arched block and suggests a bridge, and the two boys begin to construct it together, discussing what to name the bridge and who will be allowed to pass over it on the way to Mars.

Evelyn and Bobbie are arguing about whether the dinosaurs are friendly or mean, and the argument itself turns mean. They scream and poke each other with their dinosaurs to underscore their points, and soon even the "friendly" dinosaurs are inflicting real pain. A teacher asks them to quiet down, since their loud screams are disturbing the other children. They each try to involve the teacher in resolving their difficulty: "He says . . . " "She wants . . . " The teacher listens for a moment, then interrupts. "It sounds like you have a disagreement," she says. "You'll have to figure out how to make this work." And she walks away. A few minutes later, she notices the room has become very quiet, and she returns to wonder how they resolved their dispute.

Alicia wants to cook an elaborate meal in the kitchen area, but Jeremiah and Chris are monsters who want to roar and knock the dishes off the table. They scream loudly at each other for ruining their games as they look back and forth to the teachers, who are far from the action, watchful but not stepping in. Finally, Alicia says, in a very different tone of voice, "Wait, I think this is where we're supposed to settle this ourselves." Jeremiah and Chris become silent. They look at each other for a moment, then turn away from the kitchen and roar toward the block area instead.

Conflict tends to be fleeting for young children. It follows them closely as they explore their world, especially their interpersonal world, and find themselves at odds with others. In their play they practice feeling conflict, surviving conflict, and occasionally resolving conflict, just as they have practiced other life skills in peek-a-boo, dress-up, and doctor. If adults can see conflict in the same way—as developmentally appropriate, productive practice, and likely to be short-lived—they can help children reframe their difficulties and develop the ability to understand and resolve them. Most of all, adults need to be slow to intervene, allowing children to experience everyday disputes—even if they're sometimes expressed physically—and to work to find their own creative resolutions. And if they do intervene, it should be in a mentalizing way—teachers should identify and validate the states of mind of the participants, all participants.

Biting anger

Biting is a very specific example of conflict expression, and one that worries many teachers and parents unnecessarily. It appears to be seriously aggressive—it causes bruises more often than any other kind of inter-child assault—and often seems to grow from zero to sixty so fast that it feels unpredictable and uncontrollable. But it isn't. Biting, with very few exceptions, is a common form of expression in pre-verbal children. It is a way for them to say "THAT MAKES ME REALLY ANGRY"—biting mad, literally—when they don't have the vocabulary to do so. Or when they have the words in a calm state but lose them (as we all do) when they are riled. Biting almost always disappears when children develop stronger language skills.

For those who are too young to have strong enough language skills, or who are multilingual and therefore speak later than monolingual children, simply waiting a few months is the simple cure. Speech and language therapy may be needed for children who are pre-verbal because of a developmental delay. In either case, biting will cease as language skills grow.

In the short term, teachers can watch the biting child carefully to note exactly when and where biting is most likely to occur. While it probably feels unpredictable, there are usually specific situations that raise the likelihood of a particular child biting. Maybe she is most irritable when she hasn't had a snack or is approaching rest time. Maybe the loud noise of large groups running onto the playground frightens him. Maybe settling into a new activity or out of a preferred activity leaves her most vulnerable. Once the likely triggers are identified—mentalized—teachers can take reparative action (providing earlier snacks or naps; holding a child back until everyone else has run outside; giving longer and clearer notices of transitions) and can stand close to the biter at those moments to help keep him from getting frustrated. As in all conflicts, a teacher can provide the words that a child can't find at those moments, to help her feel understood and to begin to develop the words for herself.

Constant conflict

There are a few exceptions and special examples of the idea that conflict is normative and developmentally necessary for children, times when there are complicating factors that need to be taken into account if the classroom is ever to calm down.

First, trauma in the early lives of children alters their experience of conflict. If a child grows up in a home where relatives are constantly fighting and striking each other, he will incorporate this idea into his understanding of the world. He may experience conflict as terrifying—Daddy yelled at Mommy and then hit her and Mommy died and Daddy disappeared forever, so loud voices in the classroom might lead this little boy to tremble and hide. Or to lash out to protect himself. Alternatively, traumatized children may experience fighting as a normal way of resolving disputes, possibly the only way; Mommy hits me when I don't sit still and Daddy hits Mommy when dinner isn't ready on time, so I hit Jeremiah when he takes my place in line. Teachers should beware when they intervene with children who have experienced this level of trauma, lest they instill shame and fear. These children love their parents, however neglectful or abusive. So, if a teacher suggests that hitting is a bad way to resolve a dispute, she is suggesting that this child's parents are bad. And if she inquires about the situation at home, she risks making the child worry about the consequences—often terrifying—of revealing family secrets. So, helping children with traumatizing or abusive home lives is a very precarious process; teachers must be careful how they approach these children even though they may be the ones who are most frequently involved in classroom disputes.

A second type of constant conflict occurs when the classroom system itself is in conflict. If co-teachers have been disagreeing with each other, if teachers have been frustrated with their headmaster, if the school has been at odds with its higher administrators, classrooms will reveal these stresses. Just as home difficulties enter the classroom when stressed children act out, so school system difficulties can be revealed in children's actions. If many of the children are frequently arguing, if the whole class seems to be unable to settle down, if every activity is met with challenges—it may be the teachers, not the children, who need to resolve their conflicts.

Teacher issues

Teaching is an emotional profession, and preschool teaching is the most emotional. Devoted teachers love their children and the work they do, and they take the role very seriously. So, of course, they are impacted by feelings about what happens in the classroom. Just as a stressed teacher will stress her students, so stressed children will cause their teacher pain. Teachers will feel frustrated when there is conflict and difficulty in the room, just as they feel delight when everything runs smoothly. These feelings are expectable—any teacher who didn't feel them wouldn't be very good at his job—but they also can interfere with the work. So, it is important for teachers to follow their feelings closely, to be aware when they feel sadness or pity or annoyance or disappointment. Not so they can stop those feelings (we can never stop a feeling) but so they can decide how to act in the face of the feeling. If a teacher has had a crying child in his lap all morning, it might be useful for a different teacher to hold that child in the afternoon. If a teacher is at her wits' end trying to keep a child from biting, it could be necessary for her to take a long break at rest hour. And if a child pushes one teacher's buttons, it would be important for a different teacher to deal with that child as much as possible.

Conclusion

In summary, conflict is a normal part of children's lives, occurring in the development of their ability to interact collaboratively and productively with others. It is also a useful part of childhood, in that it serves as a model for disputes and dispute resolution later in life, when we hope children will be able to engage in working and loving relationships which can survive the disagreements that are sure to occur.

Caregivers of young children can help them best by being patient with and accepting of their squabbles, rather than giving the message that conflict is unacceptable and wrong. If they do intervene, it should be minimally, at the developmental level of the children involved, and equal for all disputing parties. Children themselves should be helped to do as much of the resolution as possible, which might mean that they develop a solution that would be unacceptable to a teacher but which works to meet their own needs.

Most of all, teachers and parents should try to be aware of the states of mind of everyone involved in the dispute, themselves included. Children express their needs and difficulties through their behavior, including their interactions with others, and those needs and difficulties must be resolved for the dispute to be fully and enduringly resolved.

References

Bellinson, J. (2002). *Children's use of board games in psychotherapy*. Northvale, NJ: Jason Aronson.

Bruner, J. (1966). *Studies in cognitive growth*. New York: Wiley.

First, E. (1994). The leaving game, or I'll play you and you play me: The emergence of dramatic role play in 2-year-olds. In A. Slade & D.P. Wolf (Eds.), *Children at play: Clinical and developmental approaches to meaning and representation* (pp. 111–132). New York: Oxford University Press.

Fonagy, P., Steele, M., Steele, H., Moran, G., & Higgitt, A. (1991). The capacity for understanding mental states: The reflective self in parent and child and its significance for security of attachment. *Infant Mental Health Journal*, 12:201–218.

Freud, A. (1946). *The psychoanalytic treatment of children*. London: Imago.

Lyons-Ruth, K. (2006). Play, precariousness, and the negotiation of shared meaning: A developmental perspective on child psychotherapy. *Journal of Infant, Child and Adolescent Psychotherapy*, 5(2):142–159.

Peller, L.E. (1954). Libidinal phases, ego development, and play. *Psychoanalytic Study of the Child*, 9:178–198.

Slade, A., & Wolf, D.P. (Eds.). (1994). *Children at play: Clinical and developmental approaches to meaning and representation*. New York: Oxford University Press.

Steele, M., Murphy, A., & Steele, H. (2015). The art and science of observation: Reflective functioning and therapeutic action. *Journal of Infant, Child, and Adolescent Psychotherapy*, 14(3):216–223.

PART IV

Techniques of play

8

ART-MAKING EXPERIENCES FOR YOUNG CHILDREN AFFECTED BY TRAUMA

Ann-Marie Mott

One of the continual wonders in my work with young children is watching their open curiosity in the world around them. Social and physical phenomena are equally fascinating for them. Since I am an art teacher, I offer experiences with the basic properties of art materials, clay, paint, drawing, blocks, collage and puppets, in their early childhood classrooms. All their senses are engaged as they observe, touch, hear and smell the particular art material before them. I never cease to wonder at the spontaneity and intuitive freshness of their creations. Visual, motoric and verbal exchanges naturally occur as children work together at the art table. While manipulating the material, they reveal their familiarity, interest and ability with the art experience at that particular moment in their lives. During these times of exploration and discovery with the offered material, we teachers have the opportunity to observe and learn from each young child's unique expressive ability. Each art experience can offer an entrance into a child's emotional, cognitive and physical worlds. The invisible becomes visible through the child's physical and verbal actions with the material. The fleeting nature of feelings and thoughts are made stable through their visual marks, shapes and forms. These visual images are children's first recorded or "written" language.

While making art, children often reveal significant events that are occurring in their home lives. The results of their actions bring forth associations or reminders of recent events. I witness and feel the impact of particular times in their family lives that they are trying to make sense of. Through their actions and verbalizations, they express strong feelings about their own and their family's joyful, puzzling or painful life experiences. It might be about an exciting birthday celebration, holiday, or the expectation of the birth of a sibling. At other times they might reveal more painful or frightening events such as a personal or family illness, injury, divorce, death or a social or environmental disaster. While we can easily share and relate to joyful occasions within the young child's daily life, we are usually challenged and fearful of our ability to provide the necessary support during traumatic experiences. We hope to provide the care and comfort to our young children who do not have the emotional and cognitive maturity to make sense of our inescapable human vulnerability and mortality. Fortunately, their developing minds make them more able to change and adapt to new ways of living in the world than we adults.

We know that the sooner we respond to a traumatic event, our supportive and caring responses become more effective for children's recovery. A safe and caring classroom environment filled with open-ended sensorial materials encourages active expressive and communicative play. When adults try to shield and prevent children from expressing their pain, severe consequences can emerge, such as aggressive, rejecting and isolating social behaviors that can persist through a lifetime. While art therapy is often recommended for children who are experiencing emotional and physical traumas, we often do not have the developmental knowledge about the young child's art-making that will make a positive therapeutic experience possible. How can a child's scribbles with crayons, messy piles of clay and puddles of paint relieve the intensity of the young child's fears, grief and anger when traumatic events occur?

What is unique about art is the integration of feeling and thought. When teachers are aware of the cognitive and emotional processes involved when making art, they can offer motivating art experiences that encourage young children to bring to consciousness personal thoughts and feelings that may arise when they are confronted with painful events in their lives. Art allows the child to externalize fearful and angry emotions and thoughts, necessary for healing after a traumatic event. Their artistic communications enable us to develop strategies that will help the child to understand and feel some measure of control of the feelings experienced.

Developmental guidelines

As we observe and guide children's exploratory and playful behaviors with the art materials, we keep in mind developmental guidelines (see Burton, 1980; Lord & Smith, 1973; Lowenfeld 1947; Piaget, 1962; Werner, 1948) of the young child's cognitive growth and competence with the art material. The following is a summary based on Nancy Smith and Lois Lord's (1973) descriptions of children's developmental stages in art. Each stage of development becomes the foundation that enables and furthers the development of cognitive artistic thinking for the next phase. During the earliest years, babies' and toddlers' motions with the material result in marks and circular lines or scribbles in their drawings, muddy puddles in their painting, and scattered or randomly placed piles in their clay, collage, or block work. These beginning explorations offer visual feedback from which children realize that they can deliberately control the material and make similar or different kinds of actions and visualizations. The children's developing control of the material enables them to repeat and vary arrangements of lines and shapes on the paper or clay surface. After many months of these conscious and intuitive manipulations, children begin to create organized and elaborate designs from their visual vocabulary of lines, dots, and shapes. It is fascinating to watch children at this stage, as one deliberate action seems to inspire the next action and its placement on the surface being worked on. I often wish that this stage of incredibly colorful and elaborated non-representational compositions lasted longer. However, this fascinating artistic growth proceeds as young children begin to see similarities between their combined lines and shapes and what they see in the world around them. They begin to name these configurations. Soon they are able to deliberately match what they perceive in the world around them with their visual vocabulary of lines, shapes, (circles, squares, rectangles and triangles) and dots, and to combine them into recognizable people, animals, vehicles, buildings and plants.

Children's expressive artwork can offer windows into their proud and joyful anticipations and accomplishments along with the problems, difficulties, and traumas encountered at home or in the society at large. During the course of a year in an early childhood classroom, I see children who remain in one stage for a prolonged amount to time, others who regress to an earlier stage during difficult times in their lives, and some who easily move from one stage to another as they communicate visually and verbally the joys and pains felt in their experiences in the world around them. Likely you can recognize similar stages in your own classrooms.

Art experiences in the early childhood classroom

Separation

When I enter the 3- or 4-year-old classrooms at the beginning of the school year, I witness how children are separating from their parent and caregiver at the beginning of the school day. This is a developmental challenge for every young child. At this time, children and their new teachers are actively engaged with developing trusting relationships with teachers and their peers within a safe and predictable environment. They also need to feel a sense of independence and initiative when they make choices in their work with materials and with other children. Some children seem to easily make this transition from home to school. However, weeks or months may go by before they are able to express their feelings about their deceptively easy separation. Other children may need considerable time before they can develop trusting relationships with their teachers and playmates. Often, the presence of inviting art materials can ease this phasing-in period for the child who keenly feels the loss of the familiar adult. The teacher may be sitting at a nearby art table when the child arrives and offer the child new crayons, special drawing pencils or Cray-Pas. The child may enjoy feeling and seeing the results of his or her actions on the paper. Another child may express their sadness and anger by refusing the material or by making dark rapid scribbles with it. One preschool teacher recalled an upset young 4-year-old who asked for help while trying to draw her mother who had just departed. The teacher replied, "Yes, I can help you. Can you tell me what part of your mother's body you want to draw first?" The reply was the head, and the child proceeded do draw a face and then the rest of the figure.

Instead of the teacher drawing the mother, the teacher supported the child's developing autonomy by asking the child how to begin the drawing. The teacher had observed that this child had an emerging awareness of the shapes and lines necessary for early figure drawing. The child was able to feel confident and competent in her ability to physically and symbolically create and retain her mother's image and presence. Similarly, any of the other art materials could have been offered, especially ones that the child prefers. Every child has unique interests and needs. Thus, children may desire a particular sensory material such as clay, paint or collage to be their soothing material or transitional object to manipulate during trying times. This teacher knew which children needed her help and support during separation or at other difficult times during the school day and could act accordingly.

At times, the child may reject the teacher's comforting strategies and continue to express strong feelings of sadness, fear or anger. At these times, the child may need considerable time and adequate space in order to feel relief from these intense feelings. Finding a separate and quiet, less stimulating space may help, along with the teacher's patient comforting presence. If a parent or caregiver is reachable, a telephone call may calm the child. When some measure of relief is felt, art making and storytelling may ensue.

During the separation process, creating stories with child- or adult-created animal or people puppets can be an engaging and helpful strategy for all involved: the child, parent or caregiver, and teacher. The puppets can take on the roles of these people through dialogue about saying goodbye and promises of return. If the child is reluctant to verbally respond, the teacher or caregiver can take on the role of the child. Through these dramatic play interactions, puppets allow children to transfer their deeply-felt feelings from their primary world of family to a "secondary" imaginative playful scenario of dramatic possibilities within the separation event. All participants become involved with the healing properties of story-telling and the resulting resolutions within the improvised plots. In the words of Maurice Sendak, fantasy, "is the best means children have for taming wild things" . . . emotions that "are an ordinary part of children's lives – fear, anger, hate and frustration" (in Cott, 2017, p. 120; 27). As in his book, *Where the Wild Things Are* a puppet can bravely tame the "wild" scary beasts of felt emotions and achieve feelings of mastery and competence.

Another example of how art can help children resolve the inevitable feelings that arise in relation to separation occurred during a painting experience in a 3-year-old classroom. One child, Ava, painted rectangles and then covered them with dark grey and white streaks over the entire paper space during ten minutes of concentrated work. When her teacher commented about how she changed her painting, the child spoke about her bedtime, "It's a shadow. Sometimes when I sleep a shadow comes over the wall." The teacher responded, "Where is the shadow?" The child replied, "At the wall. Up high up in the sky where Arthur (her brother)'s bed is. But the shadow was watching. I'm going to make another painting." During this painting experience, a child on the opposite side of the table was painting a representation of several family members. Stimulated by her friend's subject, Ava began her first representational painting, simple images of her family: her father, mother, brother and herself. While painting four circles with attached lines and dots, she quietly talked to herself, "Arthur, Mommy, Papa . . . " When her painting was finished, her teacher said, "Look how different this painting is."

This interactive exchange between the teacher and child supported the child's growing ability to express her feelings and thoughts through the languages of art and speech. The teacher's question brought Ava's intuitive fears of the dark and isolation to conscious thought. Even though the first painting was non-representational, in the second phase of finding out about line, color and shape, the child was able to control and choose the dark colors on the paper. This control reinforced her feelings of autonomy as well as her sense of trust as she willingly responded to her teacher's questions and interest. Given the young child's emerging competency with our spoken language, it is probable that these verbal articulations emerged because of the stimulating expressive qualities of the painting experience and the teacher's thoughtful questions. Her second, representational, painting is an example of Vygotsky's (1926) research of how children learn from each other. Social interactions can provide a proximal zone of development that enables a child to move on to another more complex stage of learning. Moreover, Ava's choice of subject may have been motivated by the desire to bring forth feelings of security that family images provided.

Birth of a sibling

A major emotional event in the young child's family life is the birth of a sibling. At this time, the child has to learn how to accept his parents' attention and ministrations with the cries and needs of a helpless infant. The children often have conflicting desires between imitating and regressing to former immature behaviors and feeling proud of the more advanced abilities that they have acquired. In the school environment, children have the opportunity to attain feelings of competency and power with the materials and in their relations with their friends and teachers. While manipulating the sensory materials of art, inner feelings of loss, anger, jealousy and rivalry can be safely expressed by vigorously pounding and squeezing the clay into various shapes, building precarious vertical structures with blocks, pounding nails into a piece of wood at the woodworking table or pouring bold areas of paint over their previously made imagery. While drawing, they might depict themselves as the largest member of their family and the sibling the smallest and least developed symbolically. During this period of adjustment, some children may regress to earlier stages of behavior such as continually making muddy, watery paintings, fast, dark scribbles with crayons and pencils, crashing block buildings or aggressive loud banging actions with the clay. A teacher's kind empathic responses to these behaviors along with clear firm limits and alternative options can eventually offer children feelings of safety and control over these powerful emotions.

Sibling and parent relationships

While children usually adjust to their growing knowledge that the sibling is going to be a permanent presence, rivalry and tensions will continue to erupt even if the adjustment appears relatively easy. When asked by the teacher to draw herself, Sophie, a young 4-year-old drew herself first and then made same size drawings of her Mommy and Daddy. At the bottom of the page, she made a very small figure for her 2-year-old brother. A younger sibling also might suffer from comparative differences in physical and cognitive abilities. Daniel, a year younger than his physically aggressive 5-year-old brother, constantly makes superheroes and bad guys when working with clay or crayons. He even called his colors "bad guy colors." While parents and teachers can be upset by the intensity of the emotions expressed during sibling rivalries, superhero play and recreations enable the child to feel powerful and victorious when otherwise feeling little and vulnerable during family disagreements and fights. Similarly, stories about parental disapproval and disciplinary actions also emerge during children's symbolic artwork and play. Three-year-old Robert dictated this story about his drawing. "This is me and Daddy. Daddy is angry and I'm going to cry. I wanted to play games on my iPad while I'm waiting for dinner." After expressing his strong feelings of shame and guilt after disobeying his father, he was able to leave the art table and pursue another play choice.

Illness and death

Inevitably during their young years, children become ill and witness sick family members, friends or pets. At these times, they may experience feelings of help-lessness and fear about the pain and changes in physical and emotional behaviors that are being felt or observed. Again, offering art materials to either the sick or concerned child helps relieve and brings to consciousness feelings and thoughts about physical or mental illness. The act of making lines and shapes often stimulates verbalizations about the illness being experienced of witnessed. When children are able to make simple images of people, animals and objects in their environment, they may depict the frightening event. A 4-year-old child who recently had a tonsillectomy created herself in clay on the rolling cart that brought her into the operating room. This visualization allowed her to reflect back on this scary event and communicate to others how she was making sense of what she experienced.

Learning about death for young children is a challenging cognitive process that develops over the years from infancy through the end of early childhood. Before they are able to understand the finality of death during the middle years of child-hood, they may regard the disappearance of a familiar adult as a departure, some-one who may eventually return. The severity of feelings of abandonment and loss depend on the age of the child, his/her unique personality and the closeness of the relationship. Again, comforting and nurturing adults need to provide a stable secure environment with open-ended materials that encourage dramatic symbolic play.

After attending her aunt's funeral, 5-year-old Yuko recreated her visit to the funeral parlor in the block area. She laid one of the wooden female figures on a block within one of the rooms of the building's funeral parlor. The next week she recreated the graveyard in the block area and drew and pasted a drawing of a gravestone on one of the blocks. She was willing to discuss her creative work with her friends and teachers when asked about her building. Her feelings of trust, independence and initiative that emerged during this endeavor were the result of being in a classroom that supported children's inquiry into and developing knowledge about the "big events" that occur in their physical and social world. During her block work, Yuko reinforced her understanding of herself as a person who has control and the ability to make sense of this difficult and painful family event.

The uncontrollable, unpredictability of natural forces such as hurricanes, floods, droughts, earthquakes along with human-caused disasters such as war, pollution, poverty and homelessness can cause considerable emotional havoc and trauma within the lives of families who are directly or indirectly affected. A month after school began, a 4-year-old child was enrolled in a New Jersey nursery school after his family moved from Hurricane Katrina's disastrous effects in New Orleans. In one child's words, "Nigel came to our class because he had a hurricane." Although the children had discussed their fears and thoughts about the hurricane before he arrived, his presence made this event more immediate and personal. When he left the school to return to his home in New Orleans, the teachers decided that each child would draw a picture for a book about "Nigel and the Hurricane." Teachers wrote children's stories under their drawings. One child dictated, "The hurricane made the waters come up soooo high" Another child said, "After Nigel left, we dug holes on the playground and pretended to go to New Orleans." At the end of the book is a note from the teachers about their hope that "the children will learn the importance of raising their voices in a meaningful way about social issues in their world." Scholastic published the book and all the proceeds of the book were given to the child's family for rebuilding their lost home. This book was a communal interdependent effort that was viewed and read again and again by the entire school and nearby community. The children's early drawings were visual symbols, a language that stabilized fleeting events in time and space for others to share and empathize with. Each child gained new scientific and social political understandings about hurricanes and their effect on people. Their artwork became a means for enacting democratic processes within the life of a classroom and school.

After the September 11, 2001 World Trade Center tragedy, children and their families were deeply affected by the horror and violence of this attack in New York City. In the Bank Street School for Children where I was working as the lower school coordinator and art teacher, I witnessed how children 3 through 13 years, teachers, families and administrators reacted. The younger children were able to use the materials of art as a means for coping with the horrifying scenes that they either imagined or saw from pictures in the media: print, films and TV. The block area especially offered children the opportunity to create towers and then invent devices for the trapped inhabitants to escape. They made slides that reached to the upper floors of the Trade Towers as well as parachutes for safe landings. Some became superheroes with physical powers that allowed them to cope and master their fears of being as little and powerless as the people within and around the towers. Teachers in the upper age classes recounted how their attempts to have children verbalize their feelings and thoughts at the early morning meeting were met with silence and a deep reluctance or inability to talk about what had just happened the day before. When they suggested drawing or painting about it, children were willing to visually depict their visions of the destruction of these buildings and the people within. I remember being surprised about this reluctance since these older children are highly articulate in their daily verbal interactions with their teachers and peers. I am reminded of Robert Coles (1967) writing about his decision as a young doctor to pursue training in child psychiatry. Stymied by verbally unresponsive child patients, he sought the advice of two older pediatricians. They suggested that he try drawing with these children and learning from those experiences.

> . . . as I sat with children, asked them to draw or paint, and afterward talked with them about their work – we were, that way, getting close to their mind's life, its worries and expectations and yearnings, its memories of the past and hopes for the future. Such meetings eventually became part of an abiding interest in children's artwork as an expression of their emotional world and their intellectual life.
>
> *(p. 8)*

Toni Gross, a teacher of young children 2 through 5 years, wrote of her experience after the Twin Towers were destroyed in an article in *Young Children* (2002). Even though the school was located in distant California, many of the children were aware of the horror and terror of this event and worried they might be the victims of a similar attack. The teacher had been influenced by the Art Workshop course with Naomi Pile at Bank Street College of Education and by Sylvia Ashton-Warner's book, *Teacher* (1963). Paraphrasing Ashton-Warner (1963), Gross and Clemens (2002) wrote that these teachers deeply believed in the power of art materials "as an antidote to the violence in their lives" (p. 44). Gross and Clemens recount how children drew, painted and sculpted with clay their versions of this event.

Many educators and parents wish to protect their children from the terrifying events that are daily communicated through our various media. As a result, children learn that their awareness of frightening events should not be shared with others. However, when given the opportunity to express their feelings of fear and powerlessness with open-ended materials, we teachers learn how much children know about the violence within our society. Children are able to work through their understandings, feel control and work through their changing perceptions of the disaster. In all of these aforementioned schools, teachers and children were willing to express and communicate these important feelings through their art making. They respectfully looked, listened and learned from each other's unique version of the traumatic event. Instead of burying their fears and feeling unresolved pain and tension, children felt safe and powerful in their growing ability to express and work through their inquiry about threatening circumstances in their lives.

Importance of teacher's role during the art-making experience

In order for the art experience to become a growth and healing experience for the child as in the previous examples, the teacher needs to understand that each child's art is a unique personal experience that involves a gestalt of cognitive, emotional and physical abilities. The teacher becomes a guide who supports each child's individual interests and need to make meaning in the surrounding society and world.

As Gross and Clemens (2002) note in relation to their work with children subsequent to the September 11 tragedy, such efforts not only are helpful to the child who illustrates a difficult experience, but also invite other children to express their own difficult and perhaps yet unformulated experiences. "Children have to know that their most important and painful concerns can be expressed, played out and discussed in the classroom (p. 50). When teachers ask about the story that goes along with an artistic expression, writing down the words helps to document and validate the experience. "Rather than banning play or art containing violence, adults should help children use these activities to work out an understanding, regain control, and reach some resolution on the violence they see" (p. 47). As an example, these teachers offer the instance of a young girl who initially is quarrelsome and tearful in relation to her classmates' expression of feelings, but then expresses her scary feelings in a painting of a fiery inferno. On a subsequent occasion, the same child begins to make and knock down her own towers after watching her classmates engage in such activities.

The teacher as artist

I deeply believe that it is never too late to enjoy the "joie de faire" of art-making and feeling competent as an artist. When teachers discover "the artist within," they undergo a transformational change. Just as teachers expect all of their students to become proficient readers, writers and mathematicians, teachers can encourage and develop their own and children's inherent visual abilities. In order for this to happen, teachers need opportunities to work with art materials themselves in order to understand the pleasures and problems that emerge when children make art. As they discover their abilities with the art material in their hands, adults inevitably discover the therapeutic nature of expressive creative work.

Teaching and experiencing art with teachers of young children

My experiences with teaching both children and adults may be helpful for teachers who would like to provide therapeutic art experiences for the children in their care. I have been fortunate to work with colleagues at the Bank School for Children, in workshops for teachers in their nursery school classrooms at private and public schools and in the Graduate School at Bank Street. Since the 1980's I have been teaching art to children during their school day and, once a week each semester in the Art Workshop, a graduate school course. At Bank Street, we teachers were strongly influenced by our mentors who were previous instructors of the Art Workshop graduate school course: Lois Lord (1996) and Naomi Pile (1990). Their art teaching and writings include many lively anecdotes that illustrate how art gives children a means to express feelings they do not wish to or are not able to verbally articulate. Their articles and books in the bibliography can provide considerable support and fresh ideas for teachers who wish to pursue developmental art experiences within their classrooms.

Art workshop suggestions

If you are a teacher who would like to include the visual arts in your daily curriculum, you might consider including these two important components within your early childhood classroom.

- Developmental examples of your children's artwork
- Providing time for yourself at home or in the classroom to directly work with art materials

Throughout the years we have learned from teachers' feedback that children's developmental stages in their work with materials is one of the most compelling insights they acquire. Teachers are fascinated by how their children gradually learn how to make artistic symbols during their art experiences. They are amazed how children's artistry becomes more complex and differentiated as they grow and learn. Familiarity with developmental stages helps them realize the importance of age-appropriate motivations that children can readily relate to when making their visual imagery. When teachers work with the materials themselves, they often exclaim how they can now understand the problem-solving and learning that children can achieve during art experiences. They see that when teachers offer children continuous in-depth art experiences during their years at school, all children can become competent and confident visual artists. Often, they wish that they had been as fortunate as the children in our nursery and elementary school who have had multiple hours of art-making within their daily curriculum studies. Fortunately, when given the opportunity to make open-ended explorations with the materials, teachers can eventually feel and know the pleasure and confidence derived from their creative endeavors. Whether they work with the materials themselves or just witness the fascinating results of children's spontaneous artwork, teachers will find that observing and responding to children's art is a deeply rewarding artful experience!

The collection and presentation of developmental examples of young children's artwork

During the process of collecting and ordering children's artwork, teachers have the opportunity to witness and assess children's artistic journey throughout the school year. Teachers can place each child's drawings, collages and paintings within a "portfolio." This can be easily made by folding a large sheet of sturdy paper in half with the child's name on the cover. Photographs of children's three-dimensional work with clay, construction and wood can also be stored in the portfolio or in each child's computer record or folder. The contents can be shared in a parent/teacher conference or in a written report as a record of the child's artistic growth over the school year. Displays of young children's drawings, paintings, collages and three-dimensional clay, wood and constructions can be gathered and displayed on bulletin boards or counters in the classroom and halls. These "art shows" communicate how the teacher and school value children's art-making abilities.

The portfolio is also an invaluable resource if the teacher has to make either an oral or written report of the child's progress during the school year for parents, therapists or other teachers. Stories that the teacher elicited from the child during and after the art experience can be either written on the back of the art paper or on a separate piece of paper. These stories offer invaluable information that can be shared and reflected on. They may include children's psychological interpretations of the events perceived and felt in the world around them. These visual and verbal records can provide the evidence needed when children's anxieties and traumas need to be communicated and addressed to parents, teachers and therapists.

Responding to children's art

Teachers often praise children's art by exclamations, such as "how beautiful; it's wonderful; I love it; good job," etc. While it is important to communicate your pleasure and approval of children's artwork, children soon realize that their teacher offers these general praises to everyone all the time. Sometimes a child will say to a teacher that "You say that every time you look at my work." Instead, you can ask a simple question, such as, "Can you tell me about your drawing (painting, clay work, collage or construction)?" This simple question often enables children to articulate painful events and feelings that are happening in their lives. Usually children are forthcoming about their actions and thoughts about their art. At other times, you may quietly just observe the child making art. The child will be aware of your interest and may talk about the actions and thoughts that are emerging. However, some children may be reluctant to verbalize their responses to their art. Since art making is a visual and not a verbal language, the child's reluctance needs to be respected. When teachers insist that children verbalize their thinking about each one of their creations, children may refuse to reply or may make up a story that will please the teacher.

In order to bring to consciousness children's intuitive artistic efforts, the teacher can respond to the specific visual qualities within each artwork. You can think about what visual qualities are present in the child's art – such as line, color, shape, texture, pattern and movement. When teachers use the language of art, children know that their teacher has seen what is special about their efforts. Moreover, by avoiding value judgments, such as "I like, I love it," children do not feel their work has to please the teacher. Children realize that they can express the pleasures and joys of their artistic discoveries along with artwork that expresses fearful and angry feelings. Teachers can practice responding to what the child has done, such as, "I notice your long and short lines," "Look how you made little and big shapes" or "I see such bright colors all around your paper." If the artwork is three-dimensional, a teacher might say, "Look how strong and sturdy you made your clay shapes," or "I notice how you glued the wood pieces together so they won't fall apart." When I'm asked by an insistent child, "I want to know if you like it," I respond, "What is important is that you like it!" Usually children accept this response, especially if you talk briefly about what you notice that is special and unique about the child's work.

Importance of exploration in artistic development

The question, "What is it?" is often asked when an adult notices that a young child has finished their artwork. Many parents, teachers and friends are unaware that young children under four may not be able to make representational symbols of the world around them. When adults see the nonrepresentational imagery, they expect that it's the child's immature attempt to make a person or object. This belief is further reinforced when the child attempts to please the adult by saying it's a house, a boat or a family member. Sometimes children accompany their art-making with verbal utterances. It's usually their physical actions with the art tool that brings forth their articulated associations and memories. For example, a rapidly painted line across the paper may trigger a memory of a fast car ride on a highway. When young children begin their art, they are usually motivated to explore the possibilities of the material and how their actions can impact the material in their hands. If they are offered continuous supportive art experiences they gradually discover that they can control their actions with the art material, make conscious choices about how they will use their colors, lines and shapes and eventually realize that this visually graphic vocabulary can be assembled together to make people, animals, vehicles, buildings and plants in the world around them. Usually by the end of their third year, they make this symbolic discovery, depending on their experience with the art material and their physical, emotional and cognitive individual predisposition to the art experience.

References

Ashton-Warner, S. (1963). *Teacher*. London: Secker & Warburg.
Burton, J. (1980). Developing minds: Visual events. *School Arts*, 80(3):58–64.

Coles, R. (1967). *Children of crisis* (Vol. 1: A study of courage and fear). Boston, MA: Atlantic-Little, Brown.

Cott, J. (2017). *There's a mystery there: The primal vision of Maurice Sendak*. New York: Doubleday.

Gross, T., & Clemens, S.G. (2002). Painting a tragedy: Young children process the events of September 11. *Young Children*, 57(3):44–51.

Lord, L. (1996). *Collage and construction in school: Preschool/junior high*. New York: Bank Street College of Education.

Lord, L., & Smith, N. (1973). *Experience and painting*. New York: Bank Street College of Education.

Lowenfeld, V. (1947). *Creative and mental growth*. New York: Macmilllan.

Piaget, J. (1962). *Play, dreams, and imitation in childhood*. New York: Norton.

Pile, N. (1990). *Art experiences for young children*. Acton, MA: Copley Publishing Group.

Vygotsky, L.S. (1926). *Educational psychology*. Boca Raton, FL: St. Lucie Press.

Werner, H. (1948). *Comparative psychology of mental development*. New York: International Universities Press.

9

YOUNG CHILDREN'S MUSICALITY

Relating with rhythm

Sophie Alcock

Introduction

All of life moves, and musicality is emotive movement: feelings in motion. Musicality is more than music; it also includes dance, drama, poetry, and play. Musicality is a language of emotion expressed, heard, and felt in play and when young children communicate and connect in the rhythm of play. Musicality pervades their play as rhythmic movement that becomes meaningful. Events presented throughout this chapter illustrate how musicality, in early childhood care and education (ECCE) settings, can include teachers and children playing, dancing, chanting, singing, rocking, and playing instruments.

Teachers who understand musicality as emotion can relate, recognize, reflect, and respond – in tune with children. When we respond reflectively and engage with children's spontaneous musicality we become aware of ourselves relating and connecting with children. We become tuned-in to children. Attuned and aware teachers can create conditions that contribute to children and teachers connecting, with themselves and with each other, as individuals and within groups, in ECCE settings.

This chapter explores how teachers can create conditions to support children and teachers coming together, feeling and expressing emotions through musicality and play. Events illuminate connections between musicality, play, and teacher awareness. I also explore how teachers can enhance the healing qualities in play through reflectively observing themselves, while responsively interacting with children playing, musically.

Musicality: Movement, rhythm, playing, and teaching

Awareness includes observing and sensing rhythm and movement in and with our bodies. Movement and rhythm are central to the musicality we observe and intuitively feel when watching young children play. Movement with rhythm, in its many forms, is the heart of musicality.

Event 1: Moving

This first anecdotal event serves as a reminder for teachers of young children's desire and need to move.

> After my five-year-old son had been at school for a year I asked him what he'd found most difficult. "Sitting still" he said loudly with a confidently critical edge. His teacher was concerned about his lack of progress in reading and writing. I was concerned about his lack of interest in academic learning generally. Chris was more concerned about moving his body; sitting still in a chair or on a mat, inside a school room felt physically frustrating.

Twenty years later I continue to be fascinated at how the reading, writing, and other controlled learning activities didn't seem to bother Chris the way sitting still did. Chris's comment was so apt; movement does underpin all of life and feelings of aliveness. That boy has become a jazz musician; he improvises while playing with the movement of sounds, feeling and listening to the movement and rhythm in sounds and silences that make up music. Movement underpins this musicality.

Event 2: Baby dancing rhythmically with teacher-dad

This dancing baby event illustrates musicality in action and as a relational process. Here Jack, the teacher-father, securely holds baby Bill, and gently dances with him, while chanting. He is sensitively aware of and in-tune with baby Bill, who at just 12 months old, loves to dance, with and without music. Jack observes; he sees and hears Bill's enthusiasm for rhythmic moving and dancing with music.

> Bill's body rocks with rhythm as he dances with his dad. Jack listens and responds musically with his body and voice, tuning into baby Bill's musical body language. When Jack chants a suggestive question: "dansa dansa Bill?" this baby responds with his entire body and soul, shrugging his shoulders smoothly, twisting his torso excitedly from side to side, answering his dad. Jack scoops Bill up and dances to recorded music, with Bill in his arms. Bill connects with his dad and with himself, feeling feelings with and in his dancing, moving, held, body.
>
> On other occasions Jack offers Bill objects such as ribbon rattles to wave and shake while dancing. Bill swings his arms and turns his wrists, moving his body rhythmically in new and old ways, while sitting on the floor, or in his buggy, or in his father's rocking arms.

Dancing together, Jack and baby Bill exude loving, caring energy.

Jack the father, teaches baby Bill to dance and move with feeling by observing and tuning into the shared bodily-felt feelings of rhythmic movement that also support Bill's (and Jack's) musical ways of being. With joy in physical movement and enhanced control of his moving body, Bill becomes increasingly open to experiencing, expressing, representing, feeling, and just being himself in languages of dance and movement, before he has learned to speak with words.

Having access to multiple languages for experiencing and representing feelings expands the range of ways in which Bill learns to feel and to think, to be and to become, to communicate and connect. I hope his teachers will continue to support Bill's musical openness when speech also kicks in.

This is an example of how teachers can draw on musicality in everyday teaching.

Dance, movement, rhythm, and music add richness beyond words to how we relate together in this world (Beebe, Knoblauch, Rustin, & Sorter, 2003; Beebe & Lachmann, 1998; Malloch & Trevarthen, 2009; Trevarthen, 2002; Stern, 2010a).

Musicality: Teaching

Nina is training to become an early childhood teacher. In the following three related events Nina casually observes and notices children's interests. She initiates and responds to children's interests. She responds in musical ways, in tune and in the moment. Nina supports children's musicality with her own musicality.

Event 3a: Swinging and singing in rhythmic containment

This event begins with three children sitting snugly inside rubber tyre swings waiting for someone to swing them. Nina approaches.

> Nina is now outside at the swings, pushing children who can't swing themselves. Instead of talking the actions she sings them, improvising words and tunes "Can Liam see the big tree? . . . I can see the big tree . . . , swinging up and swinging down . . . high and low . . . " As the swinging winds down, Nina moves away and goes inside.

Swinging integrates musicality with up, down, high, and low movements. Teachers are responsible for noticing and responding to children's interests and Nina does respond and extend the swinging to include singing. She enhances the rhythm in swinging. Chanting is another option. Perhaps singing/swinging allows these 3- to 4-year-old children to feel their younger infant selves, securely contained in the rubber tyre swings, rocking back and forth listening to soothing singing sounds.

Event 3b: Becoming a musical teacher

This next event involves more intentional teaching, as a teacher-led, planned music session, where musicality mediates group togetherness. Unlike some music sessions I've observed, this session is not rigidly rule-filled. It is enjoyable and playful.

> Nina walks towards the music corner where she had earlier set up a musical circle space, created from the range of child-sized percussion instruments that she'd taken down from the adjoining shelves; a few tambourines, small hand drums, maracas, wooden blocks and small wooden xylophones invite players. In setting up this music space Nina has made the instruments more readily available, and given the children space to play together. About five children drift towards Nina, who sits on the floor surrounded by the inviting instruments. These children and Nina begin hammering out rhythms in time with a recorded children's song. After a few minutes Nina picks up a ukulele; she stops the recorded music and asks the children: "What do the wheels on the bus do?"
>
> This is a cue for the group of now six children, led by Nina, to begin singing and playing a familiar song together: "the wheels on the bus go round and round, round and round, round and round (sung twice) all day long . . . " After a few verses Nina again stops. She asks the children: "what else does the bus do?" "It keeps on going" says a child, prompting the next verse: "The wheels on the bus keep on going, keep on going, keep on going." Other children add that the bus also: "goes straight ahead, straight ahead, straight ahead" ... and attachment themes of coming and going emerge when . . . "the mummies on the bus get on and off, on and off, on and off . . . "

Nina's flexible style and her responsiveness supported the spontaneity that pervaded this small group of children coming together in a planned music session. Nina sat with the children. She asked meaningful questions that drew them into the music song, prompting the children to think and feel, so that together they co-created, sang and played meaningful verses for an old song. Teacher Nina listened to individual children's feelings and words calmly and warmly; she made sure that they were all included in the shared group song. Nina gave the children voice.

The group tone changed with the children becoming more animated, engaged and alive when Nina invited them to create lyrics, to begin thinking and playing with possible story lines around the actions of the wheels, the bus and the mummies. I observed and felt their energy as they enthusiastically co-created and re-created new words for an old song. The repetitively sung and chanted chorus lines both grounded and gave meaning to this spontaneously improvised, playfully produced group musical story. Without a reflectively observant teacher initiating and sustaining this music session the musicality would likely not happen.

Teachers learn more about children by reflectively observing, and being in-the-moment when playing with them. We feel their spontaneous energy. It moves us. Watching, listening, engaging, and observing children playing opens us towards understanding and enjoying children. Reflectively observing how children's bodies and voices move and sing can also open us to being more responsively in tune with ourselves, with our inner child, as well as with the children we observe while playing and teaching.

This whole sequence reminded me of Winnicott's (1974), lines: "in playing and perhaps only in playing, the child or adult is free to be creative" (p. 62).

Event 3c: Listening to children; managing conflict

Comforting and nurturing children and listening to children's stories are everyday occurrences in ECCE settings and in this next event. Eric is just 3 years old and this is his first morning here. Nina knows that Eric loves drumming; his father and uncle are drummers. Drums are part of his home life and they're also part of this early childhood setting.

> Nina now attempts to teach the children about sounds as high and low, loud and soft and fast and slow. She starts singing a verse more quickly, conveying the image of a fast bus that "keeps on going". The children respond by beating their instruments and chanting loudly, as well as quickly. They seem unable to separate the concepts of loud and fast. Nina models and asks them to listen, but these suggestions simply challenge the group's more spontaneous musical dynamics.
>
> Eric, absorbed in loud and fast drumming hits Bob, seated "too close" beside him. Nina comforts a bewildered Bob with hugs and more singing, and at this point the play begins to disintegrate. As Nina's attention shifts to Bob and Eric the other children drift away towards other play areas.

So, for Eric the drum was a transition object, with the act of drumming creating a secure felt transitional space (Winnicott, 1974). Drumming helped Eric feel secure in this unfamiliar early childhood centre. When Bob came too close, Eric lashed out, pushing Bob away and out of his secure drumming space.

Nina sat with both Bob and Eric, calmly supporting both children to explain and to feel their feelings around hurting, hitting, and feeling safe. She had allowed these children to be playfully free within the boundaries of the music session. A little chaos is part of the freedom in play and in musicality; play is never totally predictable; each child's experience is unique. Teachers need to understand how what happens in homes and neighbourhoods, outside the ECCE setting, impacts children's and teachers' ways of being, knowing, and playing musicality.

Musicality: Managing children's stress

ECCE settings can be stressful places with feelings filling the air. Musicality in its many forms – moving, singing, dancing, listening – can transform the atmosphere, easing tensions that can so quickly spread across groups of children and teachers. Singing words, humming tunes, rocking bodies, and gentle touch can soothe both children and teachers, while supporting them to also feel feelings.

Event 4: Lullabies easing and connecting children

Lullabies, sung or hummed with feeling and touch, can calm crying babies and ease the contagious stress that so easily pervades ECCE settings when children cry and are tired or sad. Quietly sung, with rhythmically rocking holding arms, lullabies exemplify musicality in combining feelings, sound, and movement, as in the following event.

> Teacher Sue sings softly, holding, rocking and soothing tired Sam to sleep. She gently strokes and rhythmically pats him: "Lay down now, and rest, may your slumber be blessed! Lay down now, and rest, may your slumber be blessed!" Sue randomly hums and sings the words.
>
> As Sue's body moves, Sam also moves, reciprocally responding to her strokes and rhythmically rocking movements. Musicality connects Sue and Sam physically and psychically. Soothing and healing become attuned processes and so Sam dozes to sleep, feeling securely held. Musicality works in such magical connecting ways.
>
> "You shall have a fishy in a little dishy, you shall have a fishy when the boat comes in; dance to your daddy, my little laddie, dance to your daddy my little man."

Lullabies sung here include: "Rock-a-bye baby," "Dance to your daddy my little laddie; dance to your daddy my little one," "Moe moe pepe" ("Go to sleep baby" in Māori) and the Brahms lullaby. Teachers can improvise words and tunes spontaneously and responsively with and to children, as well drawing on known lullabies. Teachers can also use quiet music with gentle rocking, humming, and whispered singing to soothe upset children and to sing tired children asleep. Lullabies are sung, whispered, hummed, and chanted in all cultures as ways of gently soothing babies to sleep and easing stress.

Musicality: Easing teachers' music stress

Teachers may be shy about singing, feeling they can't sing in tune. Singing with different tunes doesn't usually upset young children. But teachers may have internalised feelings of musical inadequacy from early experiences of being criticised, when singing in school, in choirs, or when learning musical instruments. The voice is a sensitively responsive and intimate musical instrument. Negative judgements can silence singing before finding our musical voices, which, coming from the heart of our bodies, may feel quite vulnerable to criticism. ECCE teachers too need to sensitively encourage young children's singing voices.

If singing feels too difficult, teachers can also hum sounds while rocking, moving, dancing, or clapping, inviting and sharing musical ways of being together with children. Humming or singing, while breathing air in and out, opens our bodies and hearts to feeling our feelings. Thus, musicality opens up hearts, minds, and bodies to connecting with self and others with feeling, thereby nurturing emotional wellbeing, tunefully.

Musicality: The rhythm of music sessions

Music sessions develop rhythmic patterns that are like stories, with beginnings and endings, conveyed in the rhythm of the session. Aware teachers respond to musical cues from children and themselves to co-create sessions accordingly. The following three related events illustrate the changing rhythms, teacher responsiveness and non-responsiveness, and the contagious playfulness of teachers and children in a relaxed teacher-led music session.

Event 5a: Teacher responsiveness, spontaneous gestures, and missed cues

Teacher-led musical mat-time sessions with a mixed-aged group of about fifteen 1- to 5-year-olds with four teachers is a regular morning routine in this early childhood centre. Despite, or perhaps because the routine is so regular, the teachers miss Cleo's cue.

> Teacher Kat, seated on a low stool, strums her guitar, the signal calling children to this daily music session. The other teachers sit on the floor in a circle with the children.

CLEO: (4 years): "Now can we do um Puff the Magic Dragon with no words and just the actions?" [to teacher Kat who's still strumming her guitar]
TEACHER KAT: "Puff the Magic Dragon [she bends down and faces Cleo] doesn't have any actions."

> The nearby teachers laugh quietly, trying not to let children see or hear their laughter.

CLEO: "No but, can we do Puff the Magic Dragon?"
TEACHER KAT: "Yeah, we'll do Kentucky first"

(Alcock, 2016, p. 122).

Cleo asked for actions. She made a *spontaneous gesture* (Winnicott, 1987), used her initiative, and bravely asked the teacher for music with movement. But the teacher did not pick up on Cleo's gesture. The teachers did not hear Cleo's possible meanings. They laughed at her request for a song which had words and didn't have actions, in that setting. They were careful not to laugh directly at Cleo. But they could have also listened to Cleo and explored her request. Given encouragement Cleo might have created her own musical actions, or the teachers could have invented actions on the spot. Importantly, Cleo felt free to spontaneously ask and assert her desires, despite not being heard. She quietly accepted their lack of response. The group did sing Puff later and Cleo did move her body, rocking from side to side while sitting and singing and listening. Listening to children is a skill that sometimes requires teachers to reflect on possible meanings, but the important point in this event is that Cleo asked for something. She asked and the teachers did not hear her. They were otherwise engaged in the regularity of their teacher-led morning music session.

Event 5b: Children and teachers dancing together and blurring boundaries

In this event teachers moving and singing playfully together with children seems to blur boundaries between dancing bodies. Playfulness and joy spread across the moving dancing group.

> Children and teachers all stand in a rough circle and the song starts, teacher Kat playing the tune, while the other teachers sing the words.

> TEACHERS: "We're going to Kentucky, we're going to a fair to see a senorita with flowers in her hair."

> The children and teachers shake and wriggle their hips consciously purposely bumping nearby each other's bottoms, as they dance the sung actions.

> TEACHERS AND STUDENTS: "Well shake it baby shake it, shake it all you can . . . Shake it like a milkshake, until we all go Bang!"

> Cleo and Bob bump each other's bottoms and bodies with energy. This song dance calls for physical contact, like soft rough 'n tumble play with laughter. Their bodies seem to joke and they pull teacher Ann into their play, holding her legs tightly, their bodies clinging to hers.
> And with the "Bang" they all suddenly sit down on the floor.
> *(Alcock, 2016, p. 122).*

These teachers were as playful as the children they played with. They laughed loudly while dancing exuberantly with the children. The actions described in the sung song words became amplified by the loud dancing, with words adding narrative depth to these playful movements. Dancing, moving, and singing connected the group, seemingly also dissolving the usual boundaries that exist between bodies. In this sense music brings people together.

This music session exemplifies how boundaries and separations between individuals, and between external and internal, subject and object, are not clear and distinct. Rhythm, gestures, sung words, and touch blurred boundaries between dancers. Children and teachers moved chaotically as a group of individuals, expressing externally their internal feelings and thoughts, and connected by feelings, sounds, and rhythm. In this event the ever-changing and always emergent movement that was visible in the dance, yet invisibly felt and heard in the music, mediated and connected individuals together in group activity (Zinchenko, 2001).

While I have frequently observed teachers having fun dancing together with children in ECCE settings, the energetic exuberance of these young teachers stood out. Their bodies exuded both wild playfulness and soothing calmness in their dancing ways of moving, with each other and with the children. Moving and dancing together with others can support all teachers to relax in their bodies, to let go of shyness, to move more freely and with feeling. Music, movement and dance are all ways in which teachers can communicate and connect emotionally and physically with themselves, each other and children

Event 5c: Circles creating belonging

The music session flows naturally into its planned wind-down phase with everyone sitting in a large loose circle on the mat. Circles connect groups and by including every child's name the teachers affirm each child as a person, as valued members, connected to and part of this group.

> Cleo and Bob let go of teacher Ann and sway gently when the song changes to "Puff the Magic Dragon."
>
> Teacher Mary sits on floor with three children half lying over her lap. Bree (4 years) has a teddy bear, which she dances with, holding it as a "partner" for the Wibbly Wobbly song. The teachers lead and go around the circle addressing and including every child's name in the repetitive wibbly wobbly song.

TEACHER AND STUDENTS: "Wibbly wobbly woo an elephant sat on you.
And wibbly wobbly below, an elephant sat on Cleo.
Wibbly wobbly wob, an elephant sat on Bob.
And wibbly wobbly wee, an elephant sat on Bree.
Wibbly wobbly weena an elephant sat on Nina.
And wibbly wobbly Wema, an elephant sat on Emma . . . "

> The children move in wobbly ways.
>
> One child starts shaking her head from side to side, hair swinging, others follow, catching the idea and imitating her.
>
> The session ends with morning tea-time, hand washing rituals
>
> *(Alcock, 2016, p. 123–124).*

The flexibility in this untidy circle matched the relaxed and open ways in which the teachers led the music session. Children and teachers moved their upper bodies, swaying with the sung music, lying on and over each other, connected very physically and relaxingly, safely held together as a group by music and movement in a community of named individuals. It was enjoyable, playful, and not overly controlled. Thus mistakes, or simply different ways of singing, sitting, moving, responding, and just being were accepted. This flexibility typifies playful attitudes and ways of being that are such a contrast with those play-deprived teaching styles that follow rules narrowly and rigidly. Playfulness can bring flexibility and creativity to music sessions by freeing-up teachers and children's ways of relating and connecting.

Musicality: Playing and singing names

Names acquire subjectively felt meanings, contributing to children's developing feelings about themselves. In the previous event (5c), the teachers initiated and did most of the singing, thereby ensuring that each child heard their name sung by the group. The emotional tone in singing names intensified children's feelings of belonging. Their bodies linked together, connecting them in a grounding circle. Children smiled and laughed on hearing their names sung and matched with nonsense rhyming words. This playfulness further added to the group cohesiveness.

Event 6: Name play – rhythm and poetic chanting

In my observations name play is a fairly frequent 4-year old teasing, joking phe-nomenon. The following spontaneous musical name-play event erupts within a small group of waiting children, seated around a table. When the oldest child, Anna, begins playing with name sounds, the others respond by spontaneously cocreating a rhythmic poem of sorts.

OLAF: "Tom, you've moved".
ANNA: "You know what Tom's really called? He's called Lom, Olaf's really called Lollaf".
OLAF: "Sammy's really called Spammy".
SAMMY: "No Wammy".
PETA: "Eeta, no Weeta and Dolly's called Polly, no Wally. Byman [Simon]
POPE: . My name is called Geeta".
SAMMY: "My name is Wammy". [repeats 3x, to everyone]
OLAF: "I'm Lollaf".
ANNA: "I'm Panna".
TOM: "Tom's name is called crrrrrrr . . . "[moving chair a lot, while making sounds, rather than words]
SAMMY: "My name is called Andewope, I'm Andewope".
TOM: "I'm Gwandelope".
SAMMY: "I'm Ropeerope".
TOM: "I'm Hairyhair".
SAMMY: "I'm Photograph".
TOM: "I'm Motograph".
ANNA: "And my name is Wupwupglee."

(Alcock, 2016, p. 120)

These children speak quickly and chaotically, tuning in to each other, matching their moving shifting bodies as together they co-create poetic nonsense rhymes out of their own names. This name play exudes pulse, tone, and narrative. The children improvise experimentally with sounds, rhyme, and rhythm, while their teachers are busily occupied, managing more serious aspects of this eating together routine. Teachers are not always needed or wanted in children's play.

In playing from their seats the children have fun creatively and can tolerate the waiting. Words, including names, offer great possibilities for creative play, particularly for children constrained physically by chairs and tables, waiting for routines to pass.

While names are important for young children developing their sense of self - their identities - names are also just words. Names are not the actual person, but a symbol, apart. Name word-play may mediate children developing awareness of themselves as both individually apart, separate and alone, yet also connected to and with others. In playing with their individual word-names these children were actively co-creating connectedness and feelings of belonging as an individual within a peer group.

Musicality: Pretend play in musical performance

In playing children make sense and meaning of their everyday worlds. Pretend play is always grounded in meaning for the playing children, though others might not understand those meanings. Given time, space, and freedom, children can re-create culture in weird and wonderfully dramatic play performances, full of musicality expressed in movement, rhythm, and narrative.

Event 7: Play as musical performance

This event exemplifies how children's spontaneously rhythmic play can emerge in unplanned dramatic ways that resemble modern opera, with sentences chanted, rather than being merely spoken. The children here play with big questions of birth, life, and death. They draw on elements of fire, water, earth, and related symbols, to express these themes dramatically and metaphorically.

> Alan directs the teacher by loudly chanting: "Into the pond." [sandpit]
> Teacher Sue walks compliantly towards and sits down in the sandpit; children begin putting handfuls of sand on her body.
> She runs out of the sandpit: "I don't like it all over me."
> Ben holding a shovel full of sand responds: "We'll put it on your feet so you'll die."

TEACHER SUE: "Okay, if you just put it on my feet . . . I'll just roll these up" [she rolls up her pants. The children bury her feet in wet sand.]
TEACHER SUE: "Oh it's cold, oh it's freezing."
JO: "You're dead now."

TEACHER SUE: "Am I dead?"

JO: "Yeah."

TEACHER SUE: "What do I do now then? I suppose lie down."

ALAN: "It's not funny." [to another child who's laughing]

Teacher Sue lies down in the sandpit, they bury her feet again.

JO: "Now you're going to grow into a tree."

TEACHER SUE: "Am I growing into a tree?"

JO: "Yeap."

Ben sing-chants: "Put her in the fire. Put her in the fire. Put her in the fire." [wood to fire?]

[Teacher Sue sing-chants in a matching tune:] "Help, Jackie save me." (Jackie, another child, comes to teacher Sue's rescue . . .)

Here teacher Sue enhances the possibilities in the children's dramatic play by improvising her designated role in their drama. As the power balance between the children and teacher shifts and changes Sue allows herself to be imaginatively directed by the children. She tunes into and connects with them, fitting into their rules of play and adding reflective strategies, while still being the teacher. Sue repeats and reflects phrases checking out meanings. She matches children's actions with turn-taking (Stern, 2010b).

Mythic themes of birth, death, and rebirth with associated emotions underpin this play adding to its emotional tone. Significantly, the ending was not planned; it evolved as the children together, performed and played with emotional themes in empowering and dramatic ways, as in a story, a play, or an operatic performance. In replaying elements of fairy-tales, myths, legends, and stories heard, they had fun. Collaborating together in play these children asserted power over the giant teacher with this playful performance reversing the usual powerless small child position.

Event 8: Replaying Kapa haka performance

Stories and musical traditions permeate children's play as children re-create culture with musicality in play. For example, New Zealand Māori *Kapa haka* performing arts integrate music with movement in ritualistic patterns that also convey primal emotions in powerful ways. Kapa haka uses the whole body as an instrument combining traditional action songs and chants with rhythmic dance movements, postures and facial expressions. The dance includes aggressive war dances, fierce faces, and weapons including *tiaha*, as well as more gentle line dancing with swinging balls of flax *poi*. The power of the group amplifies the vitality of individual performers as rhythm rules the dramatic and musical kapa haka performances.

The cultural significance of the following event, where Eli plays kapa haka, was unnoticed by all but one teacher in this setting.

Eli stamps his feet and a long-handled child-sized spade, rhythmically on the ground. The stamps of his feet and the pretend tiaha match Eli's haka-like chanting voice, adding volume to his dance-like performance.

Over several weeks I notice Eli playing kapa haka for some time on most days, often with pretend tiaha. He uses a long-handled spade to deliberately make waving, pointing, and poking movements, just like a tiaha. Another toddler, William, often joins in. Almost synchronously, they bang spades on the ground and stamp their feet, making fierce warlike shouts, exuding energetic vitality. They play their bodies like instruments. Though these two toddlers can hardly communicate with words, they use symbolic actions and sounds fluently.

Eli isn't yet 2 years old and hardly uses words, but he plays with symbols. In playing at kapa haka Eli is developing aspects of his Māori identity, influenced and motivated by experiences at home. Together with his adoring dad, Eli has watched kapa haka on TV and in live performances. His dad too loves and values these warlike ritualistic dance song performances. So, Eli's kapa haka play creates strong emotional connections between his family life and his early childhood centre life, like a transitional object (Winnicott, 1974). In playing kapa haka Eli feels himself at home with dad, despite being elsewhere. Playing opens up spaces for being and belonging. Pākeha (European) children such as William become part of this play, very possibly attracted by Eli's enthusiasm and energy. It is likely that William is also internalising something of the expressively rhythmic kapa haka movements while enjoying the freedom that is integral to the flow of play.

Teachers allowed the play, with at least one teacher noticing and commenting: "He loves kapa haka, his dad teaches it and Eli watches kapa haka on TV at home." But they did not respond, despite kapa haka being a dominant interest and preoccupation for Eli. In not responding to Eli's kapa haka play, these teachers missed opportunities to support Eli's developing identity and sense of belonging, in the ECCE setting. The teachers missed important opportunities for getting to know this very young child, within his cultural milieu.

It was other children, including William, who responded by engaging in the play and seemingly mirroring Eli's sounds and movements. Mirroring involves responding to and with a person by imitating and reflecting back their actions, like a mirror. Actions here include the sounds, gestures and movements that Eli made. Mirroring supports children to see, hear, and feel their own actions in relation to others. Teachers and children can come to know each other through mirroring processes. Mirroring is a powerful reflective strategy that teachers can use for connecting with children, while also supporting their interests and sense-making through musicality in play.

Musicality: In non-musical activity

Young children in the 3- to 5-year-old age range seem to naturally gravitate towards small cluster groups of fewer than five or six children, when given the freedom to do so. Smaller groups feel safer. They can provide sufficient space for all children to feel included and to actively contribute within the group. Musicality emerges spontaneously in the play of children who feel safely secure within small groups, with opportunities to be playfully creative together.

Event 8: Children creating musicality

A fluctuating group of between three and six children are involved in the following shopping card game. The teacher creates the conditions for this play by setting the game up; she checks occasionally also joining in at times, but at this stage of play the children are managing the game without her presence.

ZIZI: "Can anybody help find the honey?"
TOM: "I know which one is the honey, that one." [points to a card]
ZIZI: "I'm way ahead of you."
ZIZI: "Open up your heart and look inside". [singing]
TOM: "Open up your cards and look inside, look inside". [singing response]
ZIZI: "Frank's turn, Frank's turn, Frank's turn, Frank's turn".

[Tom joins in the last round, chanting, singing]

TOM AND ZIZI: "Frank's turn, Frank's turn, Frank's turn, Frank's turn."

> Zizi claps her hands over her head while dancing and chanting; Jack and Tom jump up and down, and Tom eventually climbs onto the table, positioning himself powerfully above the others.

The sung words and the tune add to the emotional tone as these children spontaneously sing of opening up hearts, cards, and selves in this play within a game. When Zizi sings the words of a fairly well-known children's song, "Open up your heart and look inside," Tom's spontaneously sung response refocuses that song on the groups game, "Open up your cards and look inside, look inside". The children's playfully rhythmic reciprocity adds to the joyful energy, sustaining and holding the game together for thirty minutes. Towards the end the oldest two, Zizi and Tom assume leading – teaching – roles singing the rules and roles of the game.

Movement as action proceeds words (Vygotsky, 1986). Movement added feeling to the chanted and sung song words with emotion, in motion, in action (Malloch & Trevarthen, 2009; Trevarthen, 2002).

The teacher did not take over this game by becoming a rigid controller. She watched from a distance, trusting the children to manage themselves and each other. Teachers can enhance the musicality in children's play, without taking over. Teachers can also plan environments and activities to support children coming together in small groups.

This is the art in teaching; trusting and giving children space, being attuned, initiating, and following their interests in play, and also knowing when and how to join in, to play together, and with musicality.

Conclusion: Musicality in play

Throughout this chapter I have drawn on events to convey different uses and interpretations of musicality for ECCE teachers working with young children. Themes that stand out in the diversity that is musicality include: the energy, movement, and rhythm that underpin musicality and play; the feelings of belonging and togetherness, and the creativity that musicality can generate; the importance of teacher's being tuned in and aware. Awareness includes teachers observing and listening to children reflectively with feeling, trusting and giving children space to play and to be, initiating planned musical activities and also being spontaneously joyfully playful with children. Achieving this balance between calm reflectives watching and warm open connecting with children can be challenging. It takes a teaching team who support each other while also supporting their children to feel securely free and able to play. Teachers can draw on musicality as a language of emotion, to make teaching meaningful and feelingful, to heal hurts, to create joy, and to support children being and becoming themselves, alive to living.

References

Alcock, S. J. (2016). *Young children playing: Relational approaches to emotional learning in early childhood settings* (Vol. 12). Singapore: Springer Singapore.

Beebe, B., Knoblauch, S., Rustin, J., & Sorter, D. (2003). Introduction: A systems view. *Psychoanalytic Dialogues*, 13(6):743–775. doi:10.1080/10481881309348767

Beebe, B., & Lachmann, F. M. (1998). Co-constructing inner and relational processes: Self- and mutual regulation in infant research and adult treatment. *Psychoanalytic Psychology*, 15(4):480–516. doi:10.1037/0736-9735.15.4.480

Malloch, S., & Trevarthen, C. (2009). *Communicative musicality: Exploring the basis of human companionship*. Oxford; New York: Oxford University Press.

Stern, D. (2010a). *Forms of vitality: Exploring dynamic experience in psychology, the arts, psychotherapy, and development*. Oxford: Oxford University Press.

Stern, D. (2010b). The issue of vitality. *Nordic Journal of Music Therapy*, 19(2):88–102. doi:10.1080/08098131.2010.497634

Trevarthen, C. (2002). Origins of musical identity: Evidence from infancy for musical social awareness. In R. MacDonald, D. Hargreaves, & D. Miell (Eds.), *Musical Identities* (pp. 21–38). Oxford: Oxford University Press.

Vygotsky, L. S. (1986). *Thought and language*. Cambridge, MA: MIT Press.

Winnicott, D. W. (1974). *Playing and reality*. Harmondsworth: Penguin.

Winnicott, D. W. (1987). *The spontaneous gesture*. London; Cambridge, MA: Harvard University Press.

Zinchenko, V. P. (2001). External and internal: Another comment on the issue. In S. Chaiklin (Ed.), *The theory and practice of cultural historical psychology* (pp. 135–147). Aarhus, Denmark: Aarhus University Press.

10

PROMOTING IDENTITY DEVELOPMENT THROUGH MEMORY NARRATIVES

Elaine Reese and Tia Neha

Parents in cultures around the world talk about past experiences, from long ago and from recent times, with their children. In turn, children actively engage in these reminiscing conversations throughout early childhood and beyond. By the time children enter school, these early memory narratives with parents are related to children's developing self-concepts. In this chapter, we will describe the memory narratives that parents share with their preschool children. We focus on New Zealand Māori whānau (families) because their oral narratives are particularly detailed. We will discuss the implications of parent-child reminiscing for teachers' practice in early childhood and primary school classrooms (see Neale & Pino-Pasternak, 2016 for a review). In particular, we will draw upon positive features of these parent-child conversations that teachers may want to incorporate into their classrooms to promote young children's learning and identity development. The following excerpt from one of these conversations introduces some of these positive features:

MOTHER: You, know the reason why you're called Rangi it is because . . .

CHILD: Because Koro Rangi got dead and I can remember you, make me remember 'bout Koro Rangi.

MOTHER: That's right. So, you've got a very special name 'cause you're named after your great granddad, eh, who died in the war. Also, at your birth, when you were born you popped out of mum, you came and lay on my puku and I introduced myself to you and said, "Hello Rangi, I'm your mum." And dad said, "Kia ora Rangi, I'm your dad." And it was awesome. But do you remember anything else about your birth? Remember how I told you that you took ages to come. What was so awesome though was that when you did finally come out you were a beautiful little boy and you had a very beautiful little face and you—

CHILD: And now—

MOTHER: And you didn't cry, you didn't cry at all. Did you know that?

CHILD: No.

MOTHER: You know how sometimes you see movies and as soon as the baby is born and the baby cries out? You didn't even cry out, you just lay on mummy and had a look at us as if to say, "Hey you guys, who are you?" In this excerpt from a conversation between mother and child about the day her son was born, the mother passes on important knowledge to the child about his identity in relation to his ancestors and parents, and how warmly he was welcomed into this world. Clearly the child has heard this story before, as evidenced by his knowledge of the reason for his name, along with his comment "I can remember you make me remember 'bout Koro Rangi." Family stories about a child's birth mark the child's entry into the family, and are a rich source of identity information for the child (see Reese, 1996; Snow, 1990). In this chapter, we will explore the way in which parent-child conversations cover a range of past events, both from recent and more distant times, and are related to children's developing sense of self.

People in cultures around the world talk together about past events. The twin practices of reminiscing about shared past events together, and recounting unshared past events to others, occur across cultures (see Reese, 2013a; 2013b; Wang, 2013 for reviews). In New Zealand Māori culture, talk about the past is elevated to an art form. A plethora of oratorical forms exists in traditional Māori culture (e.g., Bishop, 2005; Dyall, Kepa, Hayman & Kerse, 2013; Rewi, 2010). Because of the richness of oral narratives in Māori culture, our focus in this chapter is on the memory narratives that Māori children tell with their parents and other adults. We explore the positive features of these narratives and discuss their implications for children's developing self-understanding and identity. We end by offering ideas for teachers who wish to incorporate past event narratives into the classroom.

Reminiscing around the globe: A brief history

In the past 25 years, researchers have become interested in the stories that adults and children tell about the past together. This interest originated from two sources at around the same time: the first was from the study of children's language (Brown, 1973), and the second was from the study of everyday memory phenomena (Neisser, 1978). Early case studies showed that children talk about the past almost as soon as they begin to talk (Eisenberg, 1985; Sachs, 1983, Reese, 1999). When children start talking about the past, parents across cultures begin to expand on these utterances (Eisenberg, 1985; Hudson, 1990).

At around the same time, memory researchers noticed that parents differ in the way they talk about the past with young children (see Hudson, 1990; Fivush & Fromhoff, 1988; Nelson, 1993). Some parents are highly elaborative in their responses to children's early references about the past, providing many details and praising children's rudimentary responses. Other parents are less elaborative, and structure these conversations more like testing situations, in which the parent has the answer and it is up to the child to discover it. It will be no surprise to teachers that this less elaborative approach is largely unsuccessful in engaging young children in conversation.

From the 1990s, a veritable explosion of research mapped the territory of parent-child reminiscing with children of different ages, across time, and from different cultures. The short version of the story (see Fivush, Haden, & Reese, 2006; Salmon & Reese, 2016 for longer versions) is that parents who adopt an elaborative reminiscing style have children who go on to possess richer memories as well as advanced language, narrative, and socioemotional skills. These socioemotional skills include their burgeoning self-concept and self-esteem (Bird & Reese, 2006; Reese, Bird, & Tripp, 2007), social problem-solving and self-regulation skills (Leyva, Berrocal, & Nolivos, 2014; Leyva & Nolivos, 2015), and emotion understanding (van Bergen, Salmon, Dadds, & Allen, 2009). These socioemotional skills are crucial for children's successful functioning in early years' classrooms (see Sirotkin, Denham, Bassett, & Zinsser, 2013). The emotional aspect of parents' elaborative reminiscing appears to be particularly important for children's memory and socioemotional skills. Talk about the past is rarely neutral; events that are neutral are not often remembered, much less retold (Reese, 1999). Children's understanding of emotions and their ability to control their own behavior grows when parents discuss the emotional aspects of past events – especially negative past events – from the child's point of view, with a thorough exploration of the causes and consequences of emotions (e.g., Leyva & Nolivos, 2015; see Salmon & Reese, 2016). In the longer term, elaborative conversations about the past in early childhood are linked to adolescents' identity development (Reese, Jack, & White, 2010).

Cultures differ in the frequency and elaboration with which parents discuss the past with their children. In particular, parents in East Asian cultures discuss the child's personal past less frequently, less elaboratively, and for different reasons compared to European American parents (see Wang, 2013 for a review). However, parents within East Asian cultures who reminisce in relatively more elaborative ways still have children with more developed self-concepts compared to their less elaborative counterparts (Wang, Doan, & Song, 2010). So, although there are cultural differences, elaborative reminiscing, particularly about past negative events, spells positive socioemotional development for children across cultures. Yet this research is almost exclusively with parents and young children, not teachers (but see Coffman, Ornstein, McCall, & Curran, 2008 for research on teachers' memory-related talk).

We turn now to an overview of early childhood education in New Zealand in order to frame our work with New Zealand Māori parents and children, which we believe provides the best illustration of reminiscing for teachers to adapt for the classroom.

Early childhood education in New Zealand

Te Whāriki (the New Zealand Early Childhood curriculum) has woven sociocultural Māori and Western concepts into a pioneering document written in Te

Reo Māori and English, which are New Zealand's official languages along with New Zealand Sign Language (Ministry of Education, 1996, 2017; Orange, 2015). Te Whāriki views learning as arising from children's active participation in meaningful activities in an environment of social interactions and warm relationships which are emulated from the family/whānau to the classroom and back to the whānau context. The holistic concepts of Te Whāriki and related child-initiated activities are captured in "learning stories," the primary mode of assessment in the New Zealand early childhood curriculum (Carr & Lee, 2012). Teachers write narratives of children's learning experiences, accompanied by photos and compiled in a portfolio. Teachers may later use children's learning stories as a springboard for reminiscing with the children (see Reese, Gunn, Bateman, & Carr, 2019). The children's portfolios are also shared with family/whānau, which could elicit further past event narratives between parent and child about the child's experiences at school.

Reminiscing in New Zealand Māori Whānau

Given the elaborated nature of oral narrative forms in Māori culture, it is not surprising that New Zealand Māori adults have earlier memories than either New Zealand Chinese or New Zealand European adults (MacDonald, Uesiliana, & Hayne, 2000). This Māori memory advantage spurred our interest in the early reminiscing environment for Māori children. For instance, Māori mothers are less elaborative than European mothers when discussing everyday past events with their children, such as a museum visit, but are more elaborative than European mothers when discussing the child's birth story (Reese, Hayne, & MacDonald, 2008). In particular, Māori mothers referred more often to emotions experienced during the event and to the time of the event in relation to other events in the whānau history. In the birth story at the opening of the chapter, note that the mother focuses on how Rangi "didn't cry, didn't cry at all" and how mother and child situate the birth in relation to the child's great-grandfather who died in "the war." Given the importance of elaborative reminiscing for children's socioemotional development, we undertook a study of reminiscing with young children in Māori whanau (families) that we outline here because we believe it offers early years' teachers a "best-practice" model to emulate (see Reese & Neha, 2015; Reese, Taumoepeau, & Neha, 2014 for more details). Nearly all of the families spoke primarily English in the home, with only six families speaking Te Reo (Māori language). After establishing trust in a series of home visits, Tia Neha invited mothers from over 40 Māori families to record discussions of a range of past events with their preschool children: about shared positive events (e.g., going to a special playground), culturally significant events (e.g., collecting pounamu (greenstone) from ancestral land), the child's birth story, and a shared negative event (e.g., a misbehavior, such as the child drawing on a cupboard).

We coded the conversations for instances of maternal *elaborations* (utterances containing new information), *repetitions* (mothers' repetitions of their own previous question or statement), *confirmations* (confirming the child's response), and *linking* (establishing a link to another past or future event) (see Table 10.1 for examples). We also coded the conversations for children's engagement in the form of conversational placeholders (*I don't know*), yes-no responses, and memory provisions.

The findings. We will not detail all of our findings to date here, but will instead highlight those findings we believe are most relevant for early years' teachers. The first finding is that all the types of conversations we requested – about everyday events, birth stories, cultural rituals, and misbehavior – were important in different ways for children's memory and school readiness, as well as their self-regulation (see Neha, Taumoepeau, Schaughency, Robertson, & Reese, 2016; Reese & Neha, 2015). Thus, we recommend that parents and teachers reminisce with children about many different kinds of events. We offer more specific recommendations in the next section.

The second main finding is that within the conversations, both mothers' elaborations and their repetitions were important for children's development. Recall that maternal repetitions here refer to mothers' repetitions of their own previous utterance, not to their repetitions of the child's utterance. The latter instead functions as a confirmation of the child's response. This finding is in contrast to prior research with European samples showing that repetitions were not linked positively to children's development (e.g., Farrant & Reese, 2000). Thus, whereas elaborations appear to be a positive feature of reminiscing conversations for all cultures studied so far, repetitions may function differently across cultures. Repetitions may be a positive feature of reminiscing in cultures with an oral memory tradition, such as Māori culture (Jenkins & Harte, 2011) or West African cultures (see Champion, McCabe, & Colinet, 2003). Thus, teachers may wish to employ the repetitive feature of reminiscing with children from cultures with a rich oral memory tradition. Children from all cultures should benefit from teachers' use of elaborative reminiscing.

The stories. In the following (see Table 10.2), we illustrate these positive features of reminiscing with examples from the everyday, cultural ritual, and misbehavior conversations in our sample (M refers to mother and C to child throughout). The

TABLE 10.1 Examples of mother and child reminiscing codes (from Reese & Neha, 2015)

Code	Example
Maternal elaborations	*We went to Gisborne to a tangi.* *Which one's your favorite karakia?* *Do you remember them doing the haka (performing arts)?*
Maternal repetitions	*What about the haka?* (after mother said, *Do you remember them doing the haka?*)
Maternal confirmations	*Yeah, that's right. Tom used to chase you* (after child said, *Tom chasing me*)
Maternal linking	*If we go and get another haircut, what kind of haircut are you going to have?*
Children's memory provisions	*She was dead in that box and you kissed her.*

TABLE 10.2 Reminiscing about everyday events

Getting a haircut	*Positive features of the conversation*
M: Tama, do you remember when you got your hair cut? The first time you got your hair cut? C: Um when I was five M: Yeah just before you were five you went and got your hair cut didn't you? How did you feel when, after you got your hair cut? C: Not that great M: Why? C: [quietly] because it was not my hair I thought she was gonna snip my head off M: You thought she was gonna snip your head off. Cause that was your first haircut wasn't it? How did you feel when you had your second haircut?	The child immediately supplies some memory information and the mother confirms and expands, then asks an open-ended elaborative question about the child's emotions. The mother then asks for more detail about why he felt "not that great," to which the child responds eloquently and the mother validates and explains.
C: Great M: Great cool. And you know how you had really long hair? C: Yeah M: What did it feel like in the wind? After you got your haircut C: Kinda blow me back M: Kinda blew you back. When you had long hair? C: It always used to go psshh M: Always used to go in your face. C: Yeah M: So when you got your hair cut how did it feel? C: Great M: Great	To ameliorate the negative emotion, the mother turns the conversation to the more positive past event of the child's second haircut. The mother continues to ask open-ended elaborative questions for more detail about the event and associated emotions, and the positive consequences of that first haircut.
C: I love bananas, kiwi M: You love bananas and kiwifruit. You love food don't you my boy. Mmm. So um if we go and get your hair cut another haircut, what's, if we go and get another haircut what kind of haircut are you going to have? C: Um chop this off M: Your rat's tail? C: Yeah M: Oh	The child momentarily goes off-topic. The mother validates the child's love of fruit but skillfully returns to the haircut conversation by bringing up a future haircut. Again she uses an open-ended elaborative question to get the conversation back on track.
C: Cause people say I'm a girl M: Not really. I like it cause then we can um we'll always know how long your hair would've been if we kept it growing it long. And how are you gonna have the top bit? C: huh M: Are you gonna have spikes? C: Yep	The child has definite ideas about what this future haircut will entail. We get the sense that there would have been ongoing negotiations between this mother and child before this next haircut!
M: Yeah. Do you like spikes? C: Yep. Now that's all please	The mother allows the child to terminate the conversation when he's had enough.

everyday and misbehavior conversations may be particularly relevant for teachers. First, for the everyday story, a popular topic in many cultures between parent and child is a discussion of the child's first haircut (see Fivush, Reese, & Booker, 2019; Salmon & Reese, 2016). Note how the mother uses open-ended elaborative questions throughout and confirms the child's responses, with a special emphasis on accepting the child's emotions.

Second, for the cultural event story (see Table 10.3), a mother and daughter talk about planting native trees at the marae (meeting house). Notice the mother's skillful teaching in this example of the names of native trees and grasses, again through the use of open-ended elaborative questions and confirmations of the child's responses.

The final example (see Table 10.4) is from a misbehavior conversation in which a mother and daughter discuss the child's tantrum at the supermarket. This example is notable for the mother's exploration and positive resolution of the child's

TABLE 10.3 Reminiscing about cultural rituals

Planting native trees	Positive features of the conversation
M: Hey do you remember when we went to Taupiri marae? C: Da da M: What did we do out there? C: Um we planted plants M: We did plant plants. Do you remember what tree it was that you and Aroha planted? C: No M: It was the Kowhai C: It was the big plant M: A big plant? C: Yep M: Can you kind of describe what it looked like to me? C: It was yellow M: It was yellow, good girl. What else? You planted, oh do you remember planting heaps of trees down the driveway C: Yes, I remember doing that. Um we put holes in there M: Yeah C: And we stuck them in M: And we stuck the what in? C: Um the um, the trees in M: The trees in. The trees were called the Mahoe, eh? C: Mahoe	After orienting the child to the event, the parent asks an open-ended elaborative question. The child supplies a memory, and the parent confirms that memory and then asks a series of open-ended elaborative questions, encouraging the child to provide more detail with each turn. In the process, the child is learning the names and features of native trees.
M: And then there was some . . . Mahoe C: Papoe (wordplay) M: Not true. And there was some Kahikatea C: Kahikatea	When the child playfully supplies a rhyming word that is not an actual tree name, the parent quickly corrects the child and continues.

TABLE 10.4 Reminiscing about child's misbehavior

Tantrum at the supermarket	*Positive features of the conversation*
P: Yep. We're talking about when um we were in Pak 'n Save. And remember when I wanted you to buy me something [sic; you wanted me to buy you something] and I said no. And you got angry. Can you remember that?	
C: No no. And I was hungry	The child initially denies the event, or
P: Yeah and I think you wanted to buy some lollies or something or some chocolate and I said no	perhaps the emotion of anger, instead asserting that she was hungry. The mother accepts that she was hungry, and validates
C: And some ice cream	the child's memory of the banned item
P: No. Oh it might have been ice cream eh. And remember what happened when you got angry? What happened?	being ice cream, but then asks again about the child's emotion of anger through an open-ended elaborative question. The child
C: I, I wouldn't stand up	then supplies the rest of the memory,
P: Yeah that's right you wouldn't stand up. Can you remember what mummy done? When you wouldn't stand up? You can't remember?	which the mother accepts and elaborates upon.
C: I think you sat down with me	
P: You think I sat down with you. I think I did too	
C: And you hugged me I think	
P: And I hugged you didn't I? Can you remember what else we did? Do you remember what else we were doing when mummy was sitting with you?	
C: Hugged me	
P: Hug you. What else? Anything else?	
C: Um kiss me	
P: Kiss you. Cover you in kisses. Can you mum, remember what mum was saying to you?	Here the mother accepts the child's perspective on the event and remarks on the child's memory.
C: Stand up	
P: Did I?	
C: Maybe	
P: Oh, maybe. Wow, you remember that?	
C: I think	
P: Yeah. Do you like it when Mummy does that with you? Does it make you feel better? Oh, Mummy must try that more often then, eh?	Finally, the mother brings the discussion to a positive resolution of the tantrum, and a solution for future instances of inappropriate behavior, which the child
C: You try again	seems to endorse.
P: Yeah	
C: When I, when I be naughty	
P: Yeah, I do it again, eh?	

negative emotion of anger. Throughout the conversation, the mother validates the child's perspective on the event.

Across all of the conversations, note the features that support children's responding. In successful and smooth reminiscing conversations, there is a balance between the adult's and child's contributions; there is acknowledgement and respect for the other's perspective; there is validation and exploration of the child's emotions; there are links to other past and future events. These sensitive strategies are known to be more frequent in dyads where the child is securely attached to the mother (Laible, 2004; Newcombe & Reese, 2004). We speculate that these sensitive strategies when discussing significant personal experiences help to further strengthen the attachment bond between child and parent, and between child and teacher. In collaborative reminiscing, the adult guides the conversation with just the right amount of steering (primarily through open-ended elaborative questions) but does not monologue, even when discussing an event that occurred before the child is capable of conscious remembering (e.g., the child's birth). The adult follows up on the child's responses and initiations and expands upon them. All of these features of reminiscing are positively linked to children's socioemotional development, and in particular to their self-concept and self-regulation (see Salmon & Reese, 2016).

Implications for teachers' reminiscing

How can teachers incorporate these positive features of reminiscing from the home into the classroom? We suggest that teachers may find reminiscing an especially useful tool for exploring children's negative emotions, and for conflict resolution, particularly in instances when children have misbehaved (see Reese, Taumoepeau, & Neha, 2014). Here the adult helps to scaffold the child's language and behavior whilst keeping the child's integrity, spiritual well-being, autonomy, and emotions in check – a practice in Māori culture called poipoia (Tangahaere-Royal, 1997). Poipoia serves as an anchor for the child's well-being and as a way to support the child's identity and emotional development (Ritchie & Rau, 2010). We propose that this practice would be useful for teachers to adopt with children from other cultures. When discussing negative emotions and behavior, however, it is important to wait until the heat of the moment has passed to broach the conversation. Children (or adults!) are not effective problem-solvers when still in the grip of strong negative emotions.

There will be other past events besides highly charged negative events that teachers could discuss with children. Shared positive events, such as special visitors (the local fire brigade) or a field trip are good options because they offer common ground and enable the teacher to delve into the emotions everyone experienced during the event. Unshared events, such as positive experiences from the child's home life, are also good topics because the child needs to become independent in telling others about something they didn't experience. These unshared events are most likely already coming up naturally in early years' classrooms in the course of mat time, circle time, and sharing time. As teachers know, children are more than willing to share their home experiences. Note that although preschool children are still acquiring an understanding of others' minds, even at age 3 they know the difference between shared and unshared events and are sometimes more willing to engage in conversations about unshared events because they know you weren't there (Reese & Brown, 2000). We urge teachers to be creative in selecting events about which to reminisce. Remember that the most successful conversations may occur when teachers sensitively follow in on the past events for which the child initiates the talk. These references to the past will occur throughout the course of the day, at mealtimes, during inside and outside play, and during dramatic play. Young children bring up past events frequently (Reese, 1999), so becoming attuned to their mentions of the past, however mundane they seem, is the first step to having rich, collaborative reminiscing conversations.

It is also important for teachers to be creative in their strategies for keeping the conversation going. We have used puppets in our research on children's retelling of stories from picture books (Reese, Sparks, & Suggate, 2012); we speculate that teachers could also use puppets as a way to engage reluctant or less verbal children in discussing shared events. Perhaps children could tell their stories of shared past events to a puppet, with an adult playing the part of the puppet. Other resources (e.g., the outside environment, felt boards, building blocks, collage, puzzles, and board games) could also be useful activities in prompting children's longer event narratives. Children are more likely to discuss past events whilst engaged in other activities (see Gross & Hayne, 1998; Peterson & McCabe, 1983/2013). In New Zealand and in some European countries, early childhood teachers create portfolios of "learning stories" as a form of assessment in which they document children's learning with a written story, accompanied by a photo (Carr & Lee, 2012). For instance, for a child who is learning how to get along with other children, the learning story might depict a time when the child collaborated with two other children in creating a block tower. Discussions of learning stories at school and at home are argued to shape children's identity, both as a person and as a learner. These learning stories also provide a perfect springboard for teachers to revisit significant past events in the child's life and to have extended reminiscing conversations about shared experiences (Carr & Lee, 2012; Reese, Gunn, Bateman, & Carr, 2019).

As alluded to throughout this chapter, the times and places for reminiscing are virtually unlimited. Reminiscing conversations can be slipped in during transitions, mealtimes, outside play, and cleanup time. We believe that once teachers become aware of the power of reminiscing, they will be able to use it mindfully as an enjoyable opportunity for enriching children's oral language and socioemotional development, and for strengthening the bond between teacher and child.

An important caveat is that the special role of repetitions may be unique to Māori culture, or specific to cultures with a rich oral memory tradition. Adults' repetitions of their own questions or statements tend to be "conversation-stoppers" for children in other cultures. Elaborations, praise, and linking strategies, however, appear to engage children positively in all cultures studied to date.

A challenge for teachers will be in negotiating reminiscing conversations with multiple children simultaneously. Our work and the research to date with parents focuses on dyadic reminiscing, and we encourage teachers to reminisce with individual children whenever possible. We believe that group reminiscing could also work, however, with a few accommodations. We speculate that the daily circle time/mat time/news time could be used to discuss shared group events (positive and negative) and to engage in problem-solving and conflict resolution. As much as is possible in these group conversations, we recommend following in and expanding upon each child's contributions for maximum effect.

Conclusions

New Zealand's Te Whāriki curriculum positions itself at the heart of quality early childhood education based on respectful relationships and effective early childhood teaching. A central part of the curriculum is for relationships between teachers and children, and between family members and teachers, to be established through conversation and discussion. We offer reminiscing as a promising tool for early years' teachers to enhance children's oral language, memory, and socioemotional skills, and to strengthen relationships at school and at home. We acknowledge the many other kinds of important conversations that take place in the classroom while reading books, during playtime, and during instruction. We believe, however, that reminiscing can be woven seamlessly into these other interactions once teachers are aware of its benefits. We look forward to future conversations with teachers about their work implementing reminiscing in their classrooms.

References

Bird, A., & Reese, E. (2006). Emotional reminiscing and the development of an auto-biographical self. *Developmental Psychology*, 42:613–626.

Bishop, R. (2005). Freeing ourselves from neocolonial domination in research: A Kaupapa Māori approach to creating knowledge. In N. K. Denzin & Y.S. Lincoln (Eds.), *The SAGE handbook of qualitative research* (3rd ed.). Thousand Oaks, CA: SAGE.

Brown, R. (1973). *A first language: The early stages*. Cambridge, MA: Harvard University Press.

Carr, M., & Lee, W. (2012). *Learning stories: Constructing learner identities in early education*. London: Sage.

Champion, T. B., McCabe, A., & Colinet, Y. (2003). The whole world could hear: The structure of Haitian-American children's narratives. *Imagination, Cognition and Personality*, 22:381–400.

Coffman, J. L., Ornstein, P. A., McCall, L. E., & Curran, P. J. (2008). Linking teachers' memory-relevant language and the development of children's memory skills. *Developmental Psychology*, 44:1640–1654.

Dyall, L., Skipper, T. K., Kepa, M., Hayman, K., & Kerse, N. (2013). Navigation: Process of building relationships with kaumatua (Māori leaders). *The New Zealand Medical Journal*, 126:65–74.

Eisenberg, A. R. (1985). Learning to describe past experiences in conversation. *Discourse Processes*, 8:177–204.

Farrant, K., & Reese, E. (2000). Maternal style and children's participation in reminiscing: Stepping stones in autobiographical memory development. *Journal of Cognition and Development*, 1:193–225.

Fivush, R., & Fromhoff, F. A. (1988). Style and structure in mother-child conversations about the past. *Discourse Processes*, 11:337–355.

Fivush, R., Haden, C.A., & Reese, E. (2006). Elaborating on elaborations: The role of maternal reminiscing style in cognitive and socioemotional development. *Child Development*, 77:1568–1588.

Fivush, R., Reese, E., & Booker, J. A. (2019 in press). Developmental foundations of the narrative author in early mother-child reminiscing. In D. McAdams, R. Shiner and J. Tackett (Eds.), *Handbook on personality development* (pp. 399–417). New York: Guilford Press.

Gross, J., & Hayne, H. (1998). Drawing facilitates children's verbal reports of emotionally laden events. *Journal of Experimental Psychology: Applied*, 4:163–179.

Hudson, J. A. (1990). The emergence of autobiographical memory in mother-child conversation. In R. Fivush & J. A. Hudson (1990). *Knowing and remembering in young children* (Vol. 3, pp. 166–196). Boston, MA: Cambridge University Press.

Jenkins, K., & Harte, H. M. (2011). *Traditional Māori parenting: An historical review of literature of traditional Māori child rearing practices in pre-European times*. Auckland, NZ: Te Kahui Mana Ririki.

Laible, D. (2004). Mother-child discourse in two contexts: Links with child temperament, attachment security, and socioemotional competence. *Developmental Psychology*, 40:979–992.

Leyva, D., Berrocal, M., & Nolivos, V. (2014). Spanish-speaking parent–child emotional narratives and children's social skills. *Journal of Cognition and Development*, 15:22–42.

Leyva, D., & Nolivos, V. (2015). Chilean family reminiscing about emotions and its relation to children's self-regulation skills. *Early Education and Development*, 26:770–791.

MacDonald, S., Uesiliana, K., & Hayne, H. (2000). Cross-cultural and gender differences in childhood amnesia. *Memory*, 8:365–376.

Ministry of Education. (1996, 2017). *Te Whāriki: He Whāriki Mātauranga mo ngā Mokopuna o Aotearoa: Early childhood curriculum*. Wellington, NZ: Learning Media.

Neale, D., & Pino-Pasternak, D. (2016). A review of reminiscing in early childhood settings and links to sustained shared thinking. *Educational Psychology Review*, 29(3):641–665. doi:10.1007/s10648–10016–9376–0

Neha, T., Taumoepeau, M., Schaughency, E., Robertson, S.J., & Reese, E. (2016). *Parent-child conversations support Māori children's school readiness*. Manuscript in preparation.

Neisser, U. (1978). Memory: What are the important questions? In M. M. Gruneberg, P. E. Morris, & R. N. Sykes (Eds.), *Practical aspects of memory* (pp. 3–24). London: Academic Press.

Nelson, K. (1993). The psychological and social origins of autobiographical memory. *Psychological Science*, 4:7–14.

Newcombe, R., & Reese, E. (2004). Evaluations and orientations in mother-child reminiscing as a function of attachment security: A longitudinal investigation. *International Journal of Behavioral Development*, 28:230–245.

Orange, C. (2015). *The treaty of Waitangi*. Wellington: Bridget Williams Books.

Peterson, C., & McCabe, A. (1983/2013). *Developmental psycholinguistics: Three ways of looking at a child's narrative*. New York: Plenum Press/Springer Science.

Reese, E. (1996). Conceptions of self in mother-child birth stories. *Journal of Narrative and Life History*, 6:23–38.

Reese, E. (1999). What children say when they talk about the past. *Narrative Inquiry*, 9:215–242.

Reese, E. (2013a). *Tell me a story: Sharing stories to enrich your child's world.* New York: Oxford University Press.

Reese, E. (2013b). Culture, imagination, and narrative. In M. Taylor (Ed.), *The Oxford handbook of the development of imagination* (pp. 196–211). New York: Oxford University Press.

Reese, E., Bird, A., & Tripp, G. (2007). Children's self-esteem and moral self: Links to parent-child conversations about emotion . *Social Development,* 16:460–478.

Reese, E., & Brown, N. (2000). Reminiscing and recounting in the preschool years. *Applied Cognitive Psychology,* 14:1–17.

Reese, E., Gunn, A., Bateman, A., & Carr, M. (2019). Telling stories about learning stories. Manuscript under Review.

Reese, E., Hayne, H., & MacDonald, S. (2008). Looking back to the future: Māori and Pakeha mother-child birth stories. *Child Development,* 79:114–125.

Reese, E., Jack, F., & White, N. (2010). Origins of adolescents' autobiographical memories. *Cognitive Development,* 25:352–367.

Reese, E., & Neha, T. (2015). Let's kōrero (talk): The practice and functions of reminiscing among mothers and children in Māori families. *Memory,* 23:99–110.

Reese, E., Sparks, A., & Suggate, S. (2012). Assessing children's narratives. In E. Hoff (Ed.), *Research methods in child language: A practical guide.* Oxford: Blackwell Publishing Ltd.

Reese, E., Taumoepeau, M., & Neha, T. (2014). Remember drawing on the cupboard? New Zealand Māori, European, and Pasifika parents' conversations about children's transgressions. In H. Recchia & C. Wainryb (Eds.), *Talking about right and wrong: Parent-child conversations as contexts for moral development* (pp. 44–70). Cambridge: Cambridge University Press.

Rewi, P. (2010). *Whaikōrero: The world of Māori oratory.* Auckland, NZ: Auckland University Press.

Ritchie, J., & Rau, C. (2010). Poipoia te tamaiti kia tū tangata: Identity, belonging and transition. *New Zealand Journal of Infant and Toddler Education,* 12:16–22.

Sachs, J. (1983). Talking about the there and then: The emergence of displaced reference in parent-child discourse. In K. E. Nelson (Ed.), *Children's language* (Vol. 4, pp. 1–28). New York: Psychology Press/Taylor & Francis.

Salmon, K., & Reese, E. (2016). The benefits of reminiscing with young children. *Current Directions in Psychological Science,* 25(4):233–238.

Sirotkin, Y. S., Denham, S. A., Bassett, H. H., & Zinsser, K. M. (2013). Keep calm and carry on: The importance of children's emotional positivity and regulation for success in Head Start. *NHSA Dialog,* 16(2):113–119.

Snow, C. E. (1990). Building memories: The ontogeny of autobiography. In D. Cicchetti & M. Beeghly (Eds.), *The self in transition: Infancy to childhood* (pp. 213–242). Chicago, IL: University of Chicago Press.

Tangaere-Royal, A. (1997). Māori human development learning theory. In P. Te Whaiti, M. McCarthy, & A. Durie (Eds.), *Mai i Rangiatea: Māori wellbeing and development* (pp. 46–59). Auckland, NZ: Auckland University Press.

van Bergen, P., Salmon, K., Dadds, M. R., & Allen, J. (2009). The effects of mother training in emotion-rich, elaborative reminiscing on children's shared recall and emotion knowledge. *Journal of Cognition and Development,* 10:162–187.

Wang, Q. (2013). *The autobiographical self in time and culture.* New York: Oxford University Press.

Wang, Q., Doan, S. N., & Song, Q. (2010). Talking about internal states in mother–child reminiscing influences children's self-representations: A cross-cultural study. *Cognitive Development,* 25:380–393.

PART V

Specialized needs for play

11

TRAUMA AND IDENTITY

Marilyn Charles

Identity develops within the context of relationships. We are shaped by how we are treated, first through the nonverbal channels of touch, sound, and sensation and then through the words that increasingly organize those sensations. Identity can be seen as an evolving life narrative that is learned in interaction with others, shaped by the categories imposed by cultural narratives. As a psychoanalyst, I recognize that, underneath the labels imposed by medical science, most people seek treatment because they have come to a stopping point in their lives, unable to successfully accomplish the developmental tasks of work and love. In our work at the Austen Riggs Center, we recognize that human experience is only comprehensible in context, and so we try to understand where development has gone awry over the generations, the types of trauma trails that Judy Atkinson (2002) describes. More and more, I see my job as helping young people to develop a narrative in which being stuck makes sense, so that they can address whatever has been left unaddressed, and begin to move forward in their lives from a starting place where their own feelings and experience are at the heart of the story.

Teachers of young children have the opportunity to assist students in self-development at an earlier phase in their journey, supported by the resilience and adaptability of early childhood. My own observation is that what is most necessary for psychic survival is love; love that is directed in a particular kind of way, that seeks children out and finds them where they are; love that tends to *their* needs above one's own. Children look for the reassurance in the human face that marks their valued place in the world. When they find it, then they are free to do the important business of playing towards growth. In this effort, seemingly small rituals can make a big difference as, for example, in the preschool where each child is greeted at the door with a smiling face and an outstretched hand. That good morning hand-shaking ritual is a deliberate invitation to be present in the classroom and participate actively in the learning.

Children whose parents are insufficiently available, in spite of their good intentions, find it difficult to make a place for themselves in the world. In my own childhood, I was not the apple of my mother's eye but rather the child who was born too soon and threw the family into chaos and dysregulation. That disruption came on top of a heritage of an intergenerational transmission of trauma and unresolved mourning that made my parents at times too preoccupied to recognize my needs with anything other than irritation. A left-handed child in a right-handed world, I was never in the place they hoped to find me. Perhaps that out-of-placedness is what brought me to psychoanalysis, which gave me a way of understanding myself in context and of being respectful of the very difficulties that had marked me as a problem.

Psychoanalytic perspectives on child development help us to recognize disruptive behavior or withdrawal as signs of distress. Deprived and traumatized children pose particular challenges for the teacher, whose job it is to teach a child who may be preoccupied by experience she has no way of managing or communicating directly. Play is both the language and the work of the child. Trauma and neglect interfere with the child's ability to make use of their own creative capacities to playfully make meaning from experience and, in that process, to develop a coherent sense of self in relation to the life narrative as it evolves. The attentive adult can see children developing awareness through their play, as they work at establishing meanings such as yes and no, and learning object constancy through early games like peek-a-boo. Such games also establish a mode of communication: Do you miss me when I am gone? Will you respond to my renewed presence with a smile?

These early relational games are augmented by the verbal interchanges between children and caregivers through which the life story evolves. In addition to these evolving conversations, self-identity is further developed through the narratives that accompany games like dress-up or playing at activities like school, cooking, shopping, or working at various professions. The inability to play with meanings complicates this process of narrativization and integration. For such children, art and other creative activities can help them to discover themselves and to develop a language for their feelings so that they can begin to build a map of the social world that includes their experience of it. That grounding also helps the child to find ways to more effectively engage with others. The teacher can aid this process by providing tentative narratives for the child who cannot yet quite provide his own, being very interested in signs that the narrative offered is or is not in line with the child's experience.

Having in mind ways in which trauma reveals itself through the child's demeanor and play can help the attentive teacher to have a better sense of how to help the child towards greater playfulness and, with that, towards more adaptive learning. As noted in Chapter 4, recognizing the general attachment style of a child can help the teacher to imagine how best to approach that child in difficult moments. The securely attached child can be resettled relatively easily, but insecurely attached children respond best when approached mindful of their individual needs and feelings. Particular challenges are posed by children who exhibit hallmarks of the disorganized attachment style, as described by Main and Hesse (1990), such as excessive compliance or disfluent or chaotic speech, movements, or play. The teacher who is able to track the sequence and offer a path back towards activity or other engagement can help to soften and ease the child's distress.

For example, Lucie presents as shy, with large, anxious eyes that avoid contact. Easily startled, she initially paints in total silence, using her brush systematically. Her hypervigilance and the obsessive and deliberate care she takes in her play mark an inhibition common in traumatized attachment. With Lucie, it will be important to be vigilant, as well, but not in a frightened way, rather in a way that marks care, concern, and faith, as the teacher encourages Lucie to move slowly beyond the very tight limits in which she holds herself. With such a child, parallel play, as in painting alongside or tentative, nonintrusive commentary on the child's play, can be ways of marking one's interest in engaging further while leaving the child in charge.

When working with traumatized children who do not engage easily, it is important for the teacher to be able to meet the child where she is. With a child such as Lucie, that may mean being very quiet and initially showing rather than telling, so that teacher and child can begin to work together – likely in parallel – at something, before insisting that words be exchanged. The teacher's tentative naming and willingness to recognize and work with the child's reaction can be essential towards building a more interactive communication between them. With fearful or traumatized children, the risk of compliance rather than engagement is always high, making it important for the teacher to watch for signs of compliance and to encourage individuality and playfulness when they emerge, even when the behavior may be startling. For example, as Lucie began to gain more vitality, she began to intentionally startle the teacher, surprising her by saying 'boo!' as a way of playing with and mastering territory that had been frightening. At that point, Lucie was better able to do her work in more focused fashion, less disturbed by noises that had previously disrupted her. Within such a facilitative classroom environment, she was increasingly able to be playful, even to enjoy making messes, to find words for her experiences, and to begin to engage in interactive verbal communication.

Many children who are living under stressful conditions also experience socio-cultural strains in addition to whatever is occurring within the family itself. Groups in which individuals feel marginalized – whether because of ethnic differences, social class, or economic hardship – can find it difficult to pass along the positive cultural narratives so important to healthy identity development. Such disruptions further complicate the process of identity development that depends on our ability to make sense of our own life story. The lack of continuity across the generations disrupts the process of *embodied simulation* through which we take in information directly from experiences of being-with our elders about how the world works, which also tells us how to see *ourselves* in the larger cultural narrative (Gallese, 2009; Gallese, Eagle, & Migone, 2007).

The concept of embodied simulation helps us to recognize that it is not just the surface behavior that children are imitating but rather a complex mix of verbal and nonverbal meanings (Knox, 2009). Young children, in particular, may be more responsive to nonverbal than verbal communications. Recognizing the power of nonverbal communication helps us to think about how to give more consistent and supportive messages to children. Children take in complex sequences of behavior, including the emotional and other nonverbal meanings that underlie those behaviors. As we know, tone can carry more meaning than the words being said. It is important for teachers to be sufficiently self-aware to recognize when their emotions may be telling a different story than their words, so that they can help the child to make sense of mixed communications. Noticing when we are coming from a stressed position, and giving ourselves a moment to take a breath and downshift, offers the child an experience-near sequencing of those very activities in ways that can be directly taken in and emulated. Using words to name the tension helps the child to develop a language for acknowledging and working with distress.

The child who falls behind is prone to shame, and environmental strains exacerbate this problem. It is important for teachers to be able to recognize signs of shame and to be mindful regarding how to support the internalization of positive identifications in children under their care. This is especially true in areas in which particular groups have been marginalized or where problems attendant to poverty invite shame. Shame tends to be experienced so directly and strongly that it is very difficult to repair, creating a particular challenge for the classroom teacher. The child whose needs are not met tends to feel ashamed, incompetent, or even 'bad.' Shame invites a negative identity and a fear of being seen, which makes it difficult to think, much less play, and also to look other people in the eye and perhaps discover that they do not see us as we see ourselves.

Internalized shame can color the child's idea of what she will see in any human face, making it important for the child to encounter the teacher's smiling face on meeting, and an empathic, caring face during times of trouble in order to attenuate the shame and work towards greater engagement. Being able to recognize the ways in which shame may be impeding positive identity development can help the teacher to build another story alongside, one that marks respect for the child and his cultural heritage and, in this way, to also mark one's respect for the parents and larger community in which the child is embedded. Marking small steps can help to invite greater pride and a sense of mastery and competence in the child.

For the teacher of young children, being empathically present and trying to see the world through the child's eyes can be painful at times. And yet, as the teacher recognizes the distress but also manages to keep her role as a teacher, she is providing an important developmental function. Winnicott (1971) wrote that one of the preconditions for becoming a separate self was to be able to *use* another person. What he meant by this is that there needs to be enough connection *and* enough distance from others that we feel ourselves to be a separate person, capable of standing on our own. Recognizing when a child is flailing, and acknowledging the distress while also insisting on and trying to help the child to meet acceptable standards of behavior, helps the child learn to negotiate this important developmental challenge. In this process, we are also encouraging a positive iden-tification. When we listen attentively and respectfully, we are teaching the child to be respectful not only to others but also to herself. In this way, the *process* of learning can be much more important than the actual content. Through all of our actions, we want to give children the idea that their thoughts, experiences, and feelings *matter*, and that difference can invite interest rather than distance or disdain.

Making use of the possibilities of play

Research tells us that relationships form the core of human developmental pro-cesses. An attuned, attentive relationship provides the safe space necessary for building the capacity to play (Winnicott, 1971). Play is the work of the child. It is through play that he or she tries the world on for size, and figures out how the pieces fit together and how relationships work. Through play, the child is an active participant in these efforts. He is rightfully at the center of the drama, building an idea of *the way things work* in his world. Adversity brings survival needs to the forefront, disrupting the ability to play. The child living under difficult circum-stances may need teachers to actively invite him to express himself as a legitimate and meaningful activity. The teacher's willingness to be curious, playful, and to make false starts, tells the child that it is all right to try and fail, that mistakes are a part of learning. That openness helps the child to begin to make her own meanings in relation to someone who believes that she can find answers within herself. In this way, the attentive teacher can help to open up a process in which the child can learn to make use of her own internal signs and signals, to recognize patterns, to locate desires, and to make choices.

Teachers working in areas where children's development has been disrupted can benefit from learning about the types of attuned attention described in literature directed at therapists. That literature invites us to direct our attention to the various types of nonverbal messages that might be present and available through the child's play, however constricted, and not through their words per se. Such directed attention helps to invite the child to show aspects of their experience that may otherwise either be kept hidden or else erupt in symptoms, such as aggression, crying, or even silence. Providing opportunities for pretend play offers a venue for such communications to emerge. Part of the teacher's job is to *allow* them to emerge, to make tentative attempts at understanding, and to be willing to be cor-rected and shown the way.

On one occasion, for example, a young boy is pretending to fish and pretends to drop a fish into the water. When asked what happened, the child replies, "He died!" The child then turns away and goes back to the paint table. If we take ser-iously concepts like embodied simulation, we can recognize that, as the teacher is taking in, reflecting on and integrating this information, the child is reciprocally invited to recognize layers of meaning, himself. The teacher, for example, may be realizing that the issue of death comes up repeatedly with this child. She can then, rather than trying to suppress or manage such troubling thoughts, encourage the child to play out whatever is troubling him. Perhaps she can find ways to participate in the play, as makes sense to her, to be concerned about the dead fish or the child whose fish has died, trying to remain open to how the child responds to her empathic efforts and to work with what he is able to show in return. Keeping the interaction at the level of play keeps the transaction within the work of the classroom. The teacher does not expect to solve the problem but rather to encourage the child to play with it, recognizing that play is the child's way of making sense of and coming to terms with experience.

Staying within role is very important, helping to keep boundaries clear, safe, and secure. The teacher's empathy communicates itself because it is there, whether or not the child can take it in. If the child seems to be suffering in ongoing ways that do not soften or ease over time, the teacher can bring *that* problem to the attention of the relevant adults who would be in charge of seeking further assistance. In some ways, the teacher is in a difficult position in terms of her role of marking acceptable versus unacceptable behavior, but also recognizing the need for children to be able to make messes and draw outside the lines. As she attends to these at-times disparate aims, she invites the child to be expressive in ways that do not close down the play. Children need to know where those lines are, and those who are not sure about where the edges are will test them. Recognizing such challenges as a need for a clear, coherent, and reliable order can guide the teacher in helping the child to conform sufficiently to be able to also be playful. Chaos and play are not compatible.

The child's internal chaos can manifest in various ways that tend to be disruptive in the classroom. The child who cannot seem to control himself, whose messes impinge on others, tends to invite irritation and efforts to control the behaviors. Rather than just assisting the child in 'doing a better job,' however, it can be more productive for the teacher to try to figure out what he's trying to say. The child's mess may be seen as a sign of the internal turbulence that he cannot contain. From a psychoanalytic perspective, we might be thinking about the meaning of the excess. Through that type of lens, the teacher might wonder about the child's own experience of excess and lack of containment. In this way, the focus turns from irritation over the mess to empathic engagement with the child for whom life so easily becomes a mess. Helping the child to work with and manage messes, then, provides both empathic acknowledgment and a means towards greater mastery, which is so crucial in building self-esteem. Children's behavior always communicates something about their experience. The teacher who is able to be interested in what the child says through their behavior provides containment even in being interested rather than irritated, communicating a 'we're in it together' attitude.

Take, for example, a child who uses paint excessively, filling the palette to overflowing. Such behavior easily invites limit-setting but is also an opportunity for the teacher to empathically engage with the plight of the child, to think through the potential meanings of the behavior and figure out what the child might be trying to communicate that cannot yet be put into words. Much as is described in Chapter 13, the reflective teacher might recognize that a concrete enactment is being played out that communicates, at the level of metaphor, something about being overwhelmed. In an art therapy intervention in New South Wales, for example, one of the supervisors encouraged a reflective stance to such messes, saying, "It's about being overwhelmed by what's coming in . . . It's not about paint. You can talk to him about that. What people want him to do . . . anything he doesn't understand. His little container overflows. Rather than him feeling filled up to the brim . . . he's trying to show you how it feels when he gets filled up and wants to pour it all out. He wants you to know how it feels" (Charles, 2015, p. 687).

Through this type of sensitive encouragement to think about what is happening in the session rather than trying to control it, we can see the parallel process as the supervisor tries to encourage the development of the *therapist's* reflective capacities. From this perspective, the challenge for the teacher is to try to make use of the data as it reveals itself in the moment, and to consider more deeply one's own perceptions and reactions. As the teacher looks for the metaphor, layers of meaning emerge. This type of work requires a willingness on the part of the teacher to be more reflective about her own internal workings, to be willing to recognize when *she* is feeling too much internal turbulence and might need to manage that before she tries to work with the child's mess. Failing to take into account our own contributions makes some puzzles virtually unsolvable, whereas noticing our own reactivity can help us to make sense of interactions that otherwise might seem to be purely driven by the child. Facing our own culpability, even small failures of care or attention, helps the child to more actively recognize and work with her own.

In a stressful moment, we want to be able to downshift, take a deep breath, engage in some introspection and consider various possibilities before acting. That effort communicates itself to the child as a positive value we hold regarding the importance of managing one's behavior rather than impulsively acting on distress. Even when we do not have time to reflect, we can do the best we can in the moment but then later come back to the situation when we have time to consider, "What do I actually think about the interchange?" or, "What might I have said or done that might have been more constructive?" Coming back to discuss an event that was not well resolved at the time marks for the child the need to contend with consequences. Such conversations help to give names to feelings and to organize such disruptions into a coherent narrative that can more easily be thought about and discussed.

As we help the child to recognize and name feelings, we are also helping to build the foundation for a stronger self, a self that will be more resilient in the face of life's challenges (Fonagy, Gergely, Jurist, & Target, 2002). For children, that means building the capacity to be actively playful. Winnicott (1971) usefully distinguishes between play that is ruminative and obsessive, versus play that is creative and fruitful. Play becomes valuable when it has layers "of meaning related to past, present, and future, and to inner and outer, and always fundamentally about [one] self" (p. 35). This is the type of play that we want to encourage, play that helps the child to recognize her own internal experience in context, so that she can begin to build a story that makes sense of that experience in meaningful ways. As described previously, the teacher can aid this process through her willingness to accept the story as it is being told, and try to make sense of it and, in this way, to become a reflective mirror in which the child can respectfully find herself. Part of the process of becoming a separate self is to bump into others and reject what is offered as a way of developing one's ability to choose. For the teacher of young children, it is important to be able to recognize that a child's aggression may be in the service of self-development. Such awareness can help the teacher to support the child's developmental strivings while also shaping behavior.

As we work with children who are too traumatized or inhibited to play freely, we try to be interested in their productions in ways that might open up possibilities. Through our interest and curiosity, the child's playfulness or other feelings might, perhaps, peek through. This is what we found in our art therapy project in New South Wales: that even the most traumatized children were able to make use of the play space in ways that helped to put their development back on track (Tracey, 2014). Art and other opportunities for creative expression can provide fundamental first steps by affording the conditions through which other learning might then be able to proceed.

I was invited in as a consultant to support the young people providing an art therapy intervention at two preschools in areas with high rates of trauma and violence (Charles, 2014a; 2014b). Working from the premise that trauma interferes with mentalization, impeding learning and imagination, this project used art therapy as a means for building self-expression, communication, and personal growth. The art therapists were encouraged to think through the possible meanings of actions rather than trying to control behavior. Rather than just assisting the child in 'doing a better job,' they were encouraged to try to figure out what the child was trying to say. This encouragement to enter more deeply into the process enabled the children to assert aspects of their own identity with pride and to build that pride into their own self-narrative. One severely traumatized and inhibited 4-year-old, for example, was able to explore and assert positive aspects of her heritage, boldly asserting to her white therapist: "I'm Aboriginal, I do dots. You can't, you're not Aboriginal" (Charles, 2014b).

With this child, themes of identity and Aboriginality came forward from the very beginning, as she explicitly defined lines between self and other, the Aboriginal child who 'makes dots' and the white therapist who does not. Another theme that was prevalent in her work was the issue of leaving one's imprint. She played with leaving imprints of her hands in paint on the paper, on the walls, and even on the therapist's hands. Pushing the edges and leaving her mark seemed to be this child's way of making room for herself and inviting recognition. Much like Winnicott's (1971) descriptions of the *use of an object*, we could see the child playing with being able to join in and also to reject, to be able to say goodbye in order to also say hello, which required the art therapist to be able to tolerate both mess and rejection without withdrawal or anger.

This child's preoccupation with limits and time come forward in her repetitive question, "Can we go now?" while not wanting to leave. In this question, we can see her anxiety over intimacy and relying on another and also, perhaps, over transgression. What does it mean to move beyond the inhibitions that had left her so terribly constrained? Notably, for this child, as for the others in the project, the ten-week program substantially affected, not only the capacity to play but also the ongoing ability to be present and to learn within the school setting. We can see in the success of this brief intervention the tremendous resilience of children, if we can leave some space for them to play their way through the challenges they face.

This absorption in play can occur in many ways in the classroom, affording moments in which the teacher who can both feel deeply and also recover from those feelings helps to set in play the same capacities in the other person, through the process of social identification or embodied simulation (Gallese, 2009). This empathic engagement can be both traumatizing and healing for teachers working in stressful environments, who will vicariously experience the pain and the pleasure of the children. As we listen to stories of trauma or watch them unfold through the child's play or artistic creations, we enter into that world at a deep and fundamental level, which affords the potential for *post-traumatic growth* (Tedeschi & Calhoun, 2004). Experiences of mastery help to build resilience, affording greater room for creativity and playfulness for teachers *and* children. Sharing from that creative space helps us to pass along what is best in each of us to future generations.

Conclusion

Increasingly, we think of mentalization and reflective function in relation to the process of becoming a self. Neglected and traumatized children may have the *appearance* of proper selves but, underneath, there may be no real ground on which to stand. In working with such children, we cannot always encounter them directly but rather must be able to play with them, accepting their limits and remaining present as best we might. Much as I was not the child my parents hoped to see, children in devalued positions in the culture tend to feel that they are not the person who can be valued. As Winnicott (1971) taught us, the child must be able to look into the mirror of the human face and find himself reflected there with respect, interest, dignity, and with love. We know that trauma and unresolved mourning impede the development of a coherent identity in the child because the parent's attentive face cannot regularly be found. That deficit leaves a fault line in development in which the child turns to a hypervigilant focus on the other's well-being rather than learning to pay attention to internal signals in order to attend to his own well-being. That reversal makes it impossible to develop reflective function – in the sense of being able to make sense of one's own thoughts and feelings in relation to others' – much less build a solid or secure identity. Such efforts, then, throw identity further off-center, continuing the cycle of trauma we are hoping to relieve.

Play can only be free and creative to the extent that one can rely that there is an environment sufficiently safe on which to land. Part of our job then, is to help children to build a story in which the fragments of their experience can come together into a coherent whole. Research shows that being able to tell one's story is a critical developmental task, one that we can support by encouraging the telling, over time, of the story in which the young person is the star, at the heart of their family, friends, and community. As Winnicott (1971) reminds us, the space of creativity is a potential space, requiring our active efforts as we learn to play in it with one another.

Identity development is negotiated in relation to others who may be like and unlike us but who, importantly, sufficiently recognize us as an individual in order that we might locate ourselves in the engagement. In families that have carried the burden of too much trauma to integrate and absorb into the family narrative, the child is left with the impossible task of carrying that knowledge as a stain, as a point of darkness they are haunted by but cannot make sense of. Such knowledge tends to emerge in the form of a symptom that marks those impossible meanings. The teacher of young children stands at an important juncture between family and community, potentially affording a bridge by which the child can find himself reflected in the eyes of someone who both sees him as an individual and also expects him to meet certain standards of community behavior. Helping a lost child to find himself within the classroom often entails helping the child to play his way into more actively and fully *being*. So, then, the teacher who can meet the child where he is, accepting his experience as valid and meaningful, helps provide the foundation he needs in order to better know himself and thereby to more effectively meet life's challenges.

If we can be open to them, children teach us about the importance of being open to one another so that we can figure out how to be ourselves and also be in relation to others in ways that are mutually enriching. The child who could not find sufficient light in the parents' eyes comes to us in dire need of repair through respectful engagements that nurture identity development. The classroom teacher can play a crucial role in this process by remembering that a positive sense of identity is built in all of the little moments in which we look into another human face and find attentive eyes engaged with our own, open to an encounter. Whatever other challenges the child faces, finding one's teacher there each day, open and receptive to what one might bring to the moment, helps to keep open possibilities for the type of engagement through which the very important work of play and self-development might be accomplished.

References

Atkinson, J. (2002). *Trauma trails: Recreating song lines: The transgenerational effects of trauma in indigenous Australia*. North Melbourne: Spinifex Press.

Charles, M. (2014a). Trauma, childhood, and emotional resilience. In N. Tracey (Ed.), *Transgenerational trauma and the aboriginal preschool child: Healing through intervention* (pp. 109–131). Lanham, MD: Rowman & Littlefield.

Charles, M. (2014b). The intergenerational transmission of trauma: Effects on identity development. In N. Tracey (Ed.), *Transgenerational trauma and the aboriginal preschool child: Healing through intervention* (pp. 133–152). Lanham, MD: Rowman & Littlefield.

Charles, M. (2015). Caring for the caregivers: Consulting with therapists in the trenches. Special Issue: M. Akhtar, Guest Editor, *Psychoanalytic Inquiry*, 35:682–695.

Fonagy, P., Gergely, G., Jurist, E. L., & Target, M. (2002). *Affect regulation, mentalization, and the development of the self.* New York: Other Press.

Gallese, V. (2009). Mirror neurons, embodied simulation, and the neural basis of social identification. *Psychoanalytic Dialogues*, 19(5):519–536.

Gallese, V., Eagle, M. N., & Migone, P. (2007). Intentional attunement: Mirror neurons and the neural underpinnings of interpersonal relations. *Journal of the American Psychoanalytic Association*, 55:131–175.

Knox, J. (2009). Mirror neurons and embodied stimulation in the development of archetypes and self-agency. *Journal of Analytical Psychology*, 54:307–323.

Main, M., & Hesse, E. (1990). Parent's unresolved traumatic experiences are related to infant disorganized/disoriented attachment status: Is frightened and/or frightening parental behavior the linking mechanism? In M. Greenberg, D. Cicchetti & E. M. Cummings (Eds.), *Attachment in the preschool years: Theory, research, and intervention* (pp. 161–182). Chicago: University of Chicago Press.

Tedeschi, R. G., & Calhoun, L. G. (2004). Posttraumatic growth: Conceptual foundations and empirical evidence. *Psychological Inquiry*, 15:1–18.

Tracey, N. (2014). *Transgenerational trauma and the aboriginal preschool child: Healing through intervention.* New York: Rowman & Littlefield.

Winnicott, D. W. (1971). *Playing and reality.* New York: Basic Books.

12

WORKING WITH DIFFICULT CHILDREN IN SCHOOLS

Ionas Sapountzis

Every professional who works with children is likely to have a very clear notion of what a difficult child is, regardless of the child's primary diagnosis. Typically, children who are emotionally volatile and prone to tantrums and aggressive acts are seen as difficult, as are children who are restless and impulsive and children who display self-injurious behaviors. Most of these children are very disruptive in class and meet criteria for more than one diagnosis. But more concerning than the disruption they cause and the learning difficulties they experience is the fact that many of them tend to act in a manner that leaves teachers feeling ineffective and not valued. These are children who do not respond to teachers' efforts and are very difficult to engage with in class.

Added to the multiple challenges teachers face in reducing the level of disruption in the classroom are the expectations of supervisors and parents to address the inappropriate behaviors as quickly as possible. The pressure to achieve tangible results is reflected in the literature. The vast majority of publications on the subject focus primarily on strategies and interventions that specifically target excessive and inappropriate behaviors, while only a handful are devoted to understanding the inner world of such children and how they experience themselves and others. As a result, the functional behavior analysis (FBA) model, which postulates that interventions need to address the underlying functions that contribute to the symptomatic behavior, has come to be seen as the treatment of choice in school.

Despite the widespread application of FBA-based interventions in schools, their effectiveness is not as high as one might expect. In fact, when one looks at the functional behavior plans that are implemented in public schools, one is likely to find that their effectiveness is quite low (Fabiano, 2014; Sapountzis, 2012). The four underlying functions—attention, stimulation, tangible and escape-/avoidance-seeking—are so broad that they fail to capture the complexity of a child's behavior and the emotional turmoil he or she experiences. They fail to capture the "grammar" (Alvarez, 2012, p. 81) of these acts and what these acts signify and reveal about the children. A child who is silly or provocative in class may indeed be motivated to get attention, but the issue is often much more complex than that. As important as the underlying motive and the particular skill deficit is, so is the underlying impulse—the urgency a child feels to gain attention and feel accepted and liked. It is a desire that is rarely satisfied by the responses a child gets for a silly remark. Looking at an impulsive statement only as a manifestation of attention-seeking behavior misses something essential about the child. It misses his subjectivity and his deeper yearning and fails to take into consideration the way the child seeks to satisfy his needs and the experiences he generates for himself.

Many years ago, I found myself missing something essential about a child in my need to develop a functional behavior plan for a 7-year-old boy, Robert, who used to scream loudly many times in class. Robert's screams were initially seen as attention-seeking, as they caused a reaction in class which he seemed to enjoy. They were also seen as stimulation-seeking since he sometimes screamed when he seemed bored. Some of his screams could also be ascribed to the desire to escape, as he was also likely to do it when he was presented with a task that was demanding and required concentration and effort. The behavior intervention plan was textbook-like. Since the average number of screaming incidents was 35 per day, Robert was to get a point if he managed to scream less than 35 times on the first day, another point if he managed to scream less than 34 times the next day and 33 the day after. Meeting his daily goal for four days in a row earned Robert a walk with me the next day to a pizza store two blocks away. Every day, a piece of paper was taped on his desk filled with lines that represented the amount of screaming he could do without losing a point, and every time he screamed he was directed to cross one line out. As long as the total incidents did not cross the red line that marked the goal for the particular day, the objective for that day was met.

Robert's screaming incidents decreased steadily every week, and so every Friday we would go out for pizza. I was satisfied with his progress, and I was amused by the many questions he asked as we walked to the pizza store and back. He would ask me questions about anything that drew his attention, from the types of cars on the street to the different types of grass on the lawns. These questions seemed random until I realized that what he was seeking was not so much information about specific cars or lawns as an opportunity to spend time with an adult who was available and willing to engage with him. One can of course argue that this is proof that the main underlying motive was attention and that the treatment was effective because that need was met, but that remark misses an important point. Robert was not just looking for any attention but for the experience of being attended and listened to. He was, as I learned in my weekly walks with him, a boy who had no contact with his father; a boy who lived with his mother who worked two jobs, several cousins, and numerous other relatives. He was a boy who felt alone despite all the commotion and clatter at home. The trips to the pizza place ended two months later, and the tape was removed from his desk. There was no need for a textbook-like intervention and for weekly slices of pizza. Instead, there was the understanding that Robert would come to my office any time he wanted and got permission—to have a snack, chat about anything that had happened that day, or just have his need to have access to and be welcomed by someone he liked reaffirmed whenever he felt the need for it.

The case of Robert is not unlike cases with many children of all ages when the focus rests exclusively on the symptoms they display and not on their emotional state and the way they experience themselves and the world. It is typical of treatments that focus on the frequency of the screams and not on the fact that a child feels the urge to scream. But as the case suggests, and as most professionals know from experience, children who fail in school, struggle with their peers, and behave inappropriately are not simply motivated by the desires to avoid school work and to gain attention. More important is their internal world and how they experience themselves. These are children whose internal world has been marked by repeated failures and disappointments, by experiences that have left them filled with emotions that overwhelm them and make them feel ineffective. Most of these children have developed very negative views of themselves (Migden, 2002; Salomonsson 2011) and deep down feel that they do not measure up. They are prone to experience even minor failures as deeply painful (Leuzinger-Bohleber et al., 2011) and are quick to react to the threat academic tasks pose by becoming emotional and refusing to do them.

Their impulse to escape demands reflects a wish to avoid what feels difficult and frustrating to them. But it is a wish that is rooted in a deeper fear, the fear of having to face, yet again, how deficient they are and how unlikely they are to be able to perform well. It is an attitude that was present in most kindergarten-to-fifth-grade children my students and I assessed in an inner-city school in New York, where we had to determine whether, despite the considerable services the school offered, the children's puzzling behavior and their failure to progress academically were due to underlying learning difficulties. Indeed, the majority of the children we assessed had underlying learning disabilities that interfered with their learning and affected their adjustment and well-being. More importantly, all children who were struggling with learning displayed clear signs of frustration and agitation. The younger children expressed their frustration by refusing to go on, becoming restless, and complaining of fatigue, while the older children defended themselves by not investing any effort in the task in front of them, acting as if the test and its results did not matter whatsoever.

Partly because that was an excellent school and partly because the children were still relatively young, we did not find any overtly oppositional reactions to our testing. This pattern, however, tends to change for the worse as children get older and become more likely to openly express their opposition to school tasks. As Willock (1987) observed, for many of these children it is preferable to be angry at their teacher and act in ways that elicit the teacher's criticisms than to face the prospect of trying harder only to have their fear of not being able to perform like others be confirmed again. It is preferable, in other words, to induce the teacher's negative reactions and comments and then blame the teacher for being mean and not caring than to face the fact that they tried but could still not perform at a satisfactory level. Calling their refusal to try and their tendency to not respond to their teachers' directions oppositionalism or avoidance misses something essential about these children. It misses their anger and resignation and also the profound hopelessness they feel. Equally important, it fails to recognize the need of these children to protect themselves from the nagging feeling that they are not good enough and that for many of them, being angry at others helps deflect the shame they feel for what they cannot do.

One can argue that the emotional struggles of many of these children and the negative views they develop about themselves may be linked, and in fact may be exacerbated, by organic deficits that have not been effectively addressed or recognized. This has been the case with the children my students and I have assessed over the past years and it is something I have repeatedly witnessed with the children I see in my practice. A child with underlying dyslexia that has not been treated may have many reasons to be resistant, avoidant and even angry over time, just as a child with an ADHD diagnosis may be more likely to seek attention by acting inappropriately. For many others, the suffering they experience and the level of disorganization they display in class may be closely linked with the level of disorganization and conflict that has characterized their families and may be the result of years of neglect and even physical or emotional abuse. Although there are many children from troubled backgrounds for whom school can be a refuge, a place where they can excel and receive recognition, for those who cannot summon the appropriate coping skills and/or are too scarred by past experiences, school is likely to be a place in which their failures and difficulties confirm their negative views of themselves and increase their agitation and sense of marginalization. Regardless of the particular history and underlying reasons that have marked their development, these children are all likely to be vulnerable to interactions and experiences that tap, however fleetingly, into their negative views of themselves. According to Salomonsson (2011), when that happens, the child's ability to understand the other's perception and to communicate with others disappears, and instead the child reacts in a manner that primarily serves to terminate all interaction and to project to others the upsetting emotions he feels inside.

The task of tolerating and addressing inappropriate or explosive behaviors in class becomes considerably harder when the child's internal state remains largely unknown and instead the emphasis lies exclusively on the particular behavior a child displays. The primary emphasis on the symptom, though understandable, risks leaving teachers and psychologists without a broader understanding of the child's make-up, and is likely to result in interventions and responses that are reactive, like the case of a 5-year-old girl with tics and a "mouthing" problem who was placed at a seat that was separated from her peers. The little girl's tendency to put her fingers in her mouth triggered her classmates' reaction and a plan was developed whereby the girl was asked to sit at a desk at the end of the room until the end of the period, anytime she displayed the behavior. Missing from the plan the school psychologist and the teacher agreed on was any recognition of how anxious and different the girl felt and how prone she was to react in a self-stimulatory manner anytime she felt unsure. The practice of placing her away from her peers not only increased her anxiety but must have also confirmed her perception that she was unlikable (Willock, 1987), that others did not want to do much with her.

Understanding the emotional state of children and making sense of bizarre, inappropriate, and off-putting acts helps children feel accepted and recognized. A teacher's understanding can take several forms: it can take the form of a supportive statement, and it can take the form of creating a structure in the classroom that recognizes a child's weaknesses and helps him or her feel supported. It can take the form of sensing the 5-year-old girl's internal state underneath her self-stimulatory act and making sure to not shame her in class—but to instead address the particular incident at another time and to help prevent other incidents from happening by engaging with her and becoming interested in her potential. Or it can take the form of the care with which two teachers from a school for children with emotional difficulties treated a boy who lived in a house with a mentally unstable mother and would often come to school unkempt and hungry. Every day they made sure to have breakfast available for him and every day they made sure to have clean clothes for him to wear. And, every week they took turns taking his dirty clothes home to wash.

This last example may seem a bit unusual, and many educational supervisors may discourage teachers from undertaking that responsibility. But the point is that whatever form a teacher's or therapist's response to a child's act takes, it can only be experienced as supportive by the child when it is based on an understanding of his needs. This is especially important with children who hold very negative views of themselves and are caught in patterns of engagement that leave them feeling cut off and angry. The capacity of adults to entertain possibilities and reflect on causes signals to children, as Bleiberg (2001) remarked, that thinking is safe and that making sense of reactions and fears is possible. It also signals to them that adults are willing to look into what happened, to locate not just what troubles them and what caused them to act the way they did but also what they hope for and what they wish that others would see in them.

The benefits of reaching a different level of understanding was evident in the case of an adorable 5-year-old boy on the autistic spectrum who was regarded as a challenge by many professionals who had worked with him. The little boy would typically barrel into the therapy room, pause for a second or two to gather himself, and then lunge forward toward the shelves with the toys. He would usually reach for one container and yank it open with one decisive move and snatch a plastic teapot out with such a force that it often resulted in the container tipping over and all the other items spilling on the floor. He would then proceed to walk around in circles with the teapot in his hand for a minute or two until something else would catch his attention. He would then leave the teapot on the table or just drop it on the floor and with the same intensity he would reach for another item, which often meant that the contents of that container would fall on the floor as well. He would hold that item for a while as if he wanted to do something with it, only to drop it again and look for something else a minute or two later. He would often walk around the room looking at the shadow he was making with his movements on the floor and would become exited by the changing shapes. One can see many signs of typical autism in these acts, but that kind of knowledge, however accurate, says little about the child and the experiences he created for himself. He seemed absorbed in his sensory world—a boy who would just roam around, darting from one place to another to pick up random objects that caught his attention for a moment and causing considerable disarray as he did it, leaving clear signs of his recent passage behind. He was engaged in ceaseless movement in search of stimulation, but despite his high level of energy and his incessant search for something, he would typically find little satisfaction in what he did.

This little boy was at risk of being seen only in terms of his repetitive behaviors and the disruption he caused. He was at risk of remaining a child who was overwhelming to others, lost in a purposeless state and engaging in acts that left him more cut off and agitated. Over time, it became clear that the boy's anxiety was heightened by the therapist's confusion and uncertainty. In fact, as the therapist noticed, the boy's restlessness and ritualistic behaviors would intensify as the therapist found himself feeling confused and discouraged and wondering what was the purpose of the sessions. As the therapist began to understand this pattern, he began to contemplate how thrown-off he felt by the boy's seeming purposelessness and, in turn, how his own failure to be more active left the boy all alone to contain the anxiety in the room. The boy's continuous movement and the forceful way he reached for items could be seen as clues that communicated how restless he felt because of the lack of purpose in the room and how agitated he became at the therapist's inability to create something for him and, in doing that, to contain his anxiety.

This understanding enabled the therapist to look at the boy's seemingly trivial acts as the beginning of something, something that he could not fully execute and needed the therapist's help to make meaningful. He came to see the boy's restlessness and his reaching for different objects as a communication of what he could not convey with words. He began to feel that what the child needed the most was a sense of purpose and structure, and that included the therapist's capacity to find meaning in the boy's acts and present that information to him. Becoming mindful of the boy's needs enabled the therapist to begin each session with a sense of anticipation, quite a change from his earlier feelings of dread and foreboding. He was now ready to guide him, to help structure his routine, and to facilitate his play. He would point to the teapot as the boy paused after he entered the room and say, "That's what you usually like to start with," and then, as the boy lurched forward, he would be there next to him to lift the lid with him so that the boy could take the teapot out without finding himself becoming the cause of another accident in the room. He would be very attentive for signs that the child's interest in the teapot was waning, and would follow his eyes as he looked around to narrate his next move: "I think you are looking for what to do next." At times, he would have to kneel next to him to point to the items the boy's gaze fell on and would help him reach for the item the boy's gaze seemed to settle on. He also structured the room differently so that the items the boy tended to use—the teapot, the plastic spoons, the clay packets, the balloons, and the finger paints—could be immediately located if he looked for them. He would also insist on a routine, by asking him to place the teapot on the table or the shelf before he picked another item, to put the clay in the container before he picked up the paints or, to put the soiled papers in the garbage basket once he was done. These were all small acts that did not change the fact that the boy needed a solid educational program to grow and learn. But they reflected the therapist's understanding of the child's rhythm (Tustin, 1986) and the sense of purpose he found in realizing how much the little boy needed him to be mindful of him and to know what he was looking for.

Looking at the boy's fleeting and seemingly random acts more carefully and treating them not as meaningless activities but as signs of the child's interests and preoccupation offered the therapist an understanding that the child could not communicate with words. It offered him a sense of perspective and helped him feel more grounded in his responses to him. It is an understanding that is reached when one looks not only at the antecedents and consequences of behavior incidents or at the developmental delays in a child's profile—that is, from a lens that assesses primarily the child's skills and weaknesses—but also at the child's experiences of himself, what the child creates for himself and what he finds and takes in as a result of his acts. It is a lens that seeks to capture the child's subjectivity and to reach the child at that level.

The therapist's role, as Altman et al. (2002) remind us, is to own what the child disowns, to look for the child's experiences underneath his or her acts, however incomplete, off-putting, or bizarre the latter may seem to be. This is a way of looking at a child that is seldom practiced in schools and as a result, the levels of loneliness and disconnectedness that exists underneath offensive and intrusive acts are rarely factored in the intervention plans that are developed. How often do teachers go to a symptomatic child? How often do they seek the unappealing symptomatic child for the purpose of creating something with him or her, a different experience that is sorely needed but which the particular child either cannot secure for himself or herself or has become conditioned to not expect? In a school system that is characterized by the race-to-the-top philosophy and special education policies that are compartmentalized, few teachers can find the time and support to do so.

Two concepts that can be very useful in generating insight into the experiences troubled children create for themselves in the classroom and the reactions they evoke in their teachers are the concepts of transference and countertransference. Transference refers to a person's tendency to transfer in his interactions with others expectations and patterns of relating that have characterized his relationship with significant people in his life, while countertransference refers to the emotions a person evokes in the therapist with his acts. According to the transference concept, children who are angry will bring their volatility and distrust into the classroom. They will bring in their disappointments and conflicted emotions and also their confusion and tendency to cease trying when faced with challenging tasks. They will bring in their defensive mode, their readiness to disengage from others, and to protest and reject. This is nothing new. And yet, when this happens, when problematic children keep acting out despite the teachers' efforts, their acts tend to generate intense counter-reactions in their teachers. In fact, the tendency of teachers and school officials to respond to disruptive acts by distancing themselves from the child who displays them and focusing on rules and conditions rather than on contemplating what the child experiences and how lost he feels may well be an example of destructive countertransference. It could be an example of the anger and impatience a disruptive and hard to manage child can generate in school and the urge teachers and school officials have to not tolerate such acts.

These emotions, when one is able to pause and reflect on them, can give one a sense of how the child's behavior affects him and shapes his reactions. But what is very valuable in understanding the concept of countertransference is that the emotions teachers or school psychologists feel can provide them with a clue to the child's underlying emotions that contribute to the particular behavior. For instance, the teacher of a first grader with attention deficit and language delay expressed how confused she felt when listening to the boy and how hard it was to understand what he was saying. The teacher also said that the boy often gave responses in class that suggested that he understood very little of what was being discussed. She attributed her confusion to the language difficulties the boy had and his impulsive manner of speaking. But her confusion captured more than the effect the boy's language delays had on her. It captured the boy's confusion and anxiety when he sought to express himself and, with that, the ineffectiveness and loneliness he experienced when he felt that others made little sense of what he was saying. Recognizing the confusion, the child must have felt when he sought to express himself helped to shift the angle of the teacher's understanding from the exclusively neuropsychological to the personal and experiential.

The capacity to look at the frustration, irritation, or indifference one feels toward a child and wonder whether these emotions are likely to resonate with emotions that are similar in the child—and therefore whether they communicate something about the child's experience—can often lead to realizations that can change one's perspective. The capacity of teachers to do that in class—to wonder about the extent to which their emotions and reactions capture something essential about the child—can change their perception of the child and how they experience him or her. Admittedly, this is not easy to do. It is very hard to pause and look at one's reactions in order to gauge the effect a child has on oneself and what that says about the child when one feels frustrated or annoyed. In those moments, the child is often experienced as a burden, and his behavior may be so offensive or intrusive that a teacher cannot but feel disrespected or rejected. These emotions, unless understood and processed, are likely to color the teachers' reactions and in turn are likely to be felt by the child. But, to repeat, without seeking to understand these dynamics and the reactions these children evoke, children and teachers are likely to get caught in exchanges that are cyclical, where their negative acts elicit negative reactions that in turn confirm and intensify negative attitudes that add to the confusion and annoyance each participant experiences.

The reciprocity of these emotions and the reactions they trigger in the child and the teacher can explain several puzzling incidents I experienced when I worked at a school for children with emotional difficulties which, at the time, I could not understand. Prior to the start of the school year, the teachers and I would devote considerable time to reviewing the files of the most difficult children to prepare ourselves for their transition back to school. Everything went smoothly initially, but invariably after the first few days the incidents started and the children's emotions erupted in full force. In fact, their emotional reaction was often very intense and rather disproportionate to what had transpired in the classroom. This was very difficult to understand given how caring and attentive the teachers had been. From a behavioral perspective, the students' explosive reactions made little sense. It was only when I contemplated the role of transference and countertransference, what the children expected and feared underneath their genuine desire to do well, and what the teachers (and I) feared and expected underneath their efforts to reach the children, that what happened began to make sense. For these children who had been failed many times in their lives and who had many experiences of failing, any new incident of failure, whether triggered by their difficulty with an academic task or by a conflict with a classmate, confirmed their expectations and triggered catastrophic reactions. Already at the age of 7 or 8, they were very sensitive to interpersonal slights and to experiences of feeling unable to learn, and they reacted intensely to these emotions. In retrospect, the teachers' interest and kindness may have intensified their frustration. Failing to perform well in a class that was led by a nice and supportive teacher may have confirmed their fear of how bad they were and may have fanned their anxiety and anger. It may also have intensified their sense of betrayal and abandonment when they had to face the consequences of their acts. What happened next depended on whether the children's meltdowns and tantrums left teachers feeling rejected and angry or whether the teachers were able to treat the children's tantrums as part of their ongoing struggles with themselves and as a reminder of their fragility. The children who were in classes run by teachers who took their outbursts less personally and saw them in the context of what the children were struggling with did better and seemed to develop a more trusting relationship with their teachers. They were still prone to tantrums when they felt threatened or overwhelmed, but they gradually developed the sense that their teachers were not put off by the reactions they could not control, that teachers did not end up seeing them as less than who they wanted to be. As I witnessed many times, their growing faith in their teachers enabled them to regulate their reactions more effectively in many cases and to pull themselves back from the brink of another explosive reaction.

The previous description points to another important factor in understanding transference and countertransference dynamics and being able to derive information from a child's act. It points to the fact that a teacher, who understands what a child struggles with, can tolerate his inappropriate acts better than one who does not. This dynamic can explain why some teachers can be very reactive toward a particular child while others may be less affected by the very same act and more willing to contemplate what might have caused the child to act in a particular way. It can also account for the reasons why some teachers persist with a particular child and seem less persistent or more impatient with another. Looking at transference and countertransference dynamics can enable teachers and therapists to make better sense of their reactions toward a child, and that is not a small feat. Many difficult children can elicit such intensely negative reactions in the classroom that without being able to put them in context and understand the impact they have, teachers and psychologists may find themselves reacting in a manner that repeats the experience that has characterized the children's relationships with adults.

Reflecting on a child's mental state and the emotions and perceptions that constitute his or her reality enables teachers to have a better grasp of what is happening in the classroom and the experiences the child generates with his or her acts. More importantly, the willingness to look at the predictable cycles of actions and consequences from the perspective of the child helps to convey the teacher's faith in the child. It also helps to offset the child's experience of adults as not making sense of and not seeking to know him or her. Common in almost all children who struggle in school is their tendency to avoid reflecting on experiences and to treat the consequences they elicit as not related to what they did. It is an attitude that helps many children avoid facing what feels very upsetting to them, including some troubling possibilities about themselves. The lack of self-reflection, however, leaves them in a state where emotions and consequences are experienced as events that just happen to them and are not related to their acts and what happened before (Bleiberg, 2001).

What do students who fail and feel unliked or marginalized expect in schools? What does a child with severe learning disabilities expect from school, and what does the school do with these expectations? Failure to acknowledge and explore these issues and to recognize how children's expectations shape their outlook toward learning is likely to contribute to practices that miss the depth of their agony. As Salomonsson (2011) pointed out, when the children's experiences are colored by images and expectations of themselves and others that feel bad and overwhelming, the children's capacity to process and contain them disappears. What was characteristic in all the protocols of the young children from the inner-city school my students and I assessed over the past years was their resignation from any positive expectations and their tendency to not respond much to their teachers' efforts. They were all prone to leave themselves out of the pictures they drew and the stories they told as if they felt not worth enough to include themselves in them. Understanding the difficulties of these children to learn and adjust in schools requires more than just the capacity to identify academic and executive deficits and generate a list of reinforcement preferences. It requires the capacity to contain their projections, such as their outbursts or impulsive acts, as well as in many cases the absence of projections (Alvarez, 1992), like their seeming indifference to anything in class.

Perhaps most importantly, such understanding requires being able to hold for them the idea of a potential they have often resigned themselves from and to persist with them. Yet, as Fonagy and Target (1996) have argued, the experience of others' being mindful of their difficulties and seeking to make sense of what they experience enables children to develop the capacity to reflect on their emotional state and to recognize the emotional states of others. It enables them to become more aware of themselves and others and to make connections between emotions and acts and also between acts and consequences. Unfortunately, it is an approach that schools nowadays seem less more inclined to focus on. Instead, the focus is on treatments that have immediately measurable goals and offer the reassurance that concrete steps are being adopted. But without taking in the totality of the child and what his or her behavior difficulties point to, one runs the risk of finding oneself looking at behavior charts and realizing, as I did 20 years ago, that although the graphs are pointing in the desired direction the child remains unknown, and is seen only through the prism of his or her deficits.

Present in every act, present in most children's disruptive or inappropriate behaviors, is not just confusion, anger, or a sense of ineffectiveness but also the wish, however faint or disowned, for what is missing and what needs to be found. Present also is their wish for the steady and encouraging gaze of grown-ups who can make them feel seen and appreciated and can acknowledge their potential. It is a gaze that is more likely to be found in teachers and therapists who are attuned to the emotional turmoil these children experience and to their wish to feel effective and to be liked.

References

Altman, N., Briggs, R., Frankel, J., Gensler, D., & Pantone, P. (2002). *Relational child psychotherapy*. New York: Other Press.

Alvarez, A. (1992). *Live company: Psychoanalytic psychotherapy with autistic, borderline, deprived and abused children*. London: Routledge.

Alvarez, A. (2012). *The thinking heart: Three levels of psychoanalytic therapy with disturbed children*. London: Routledge.

Bleiberg, E. (2001). *Treating personality disorders in children and adolescents: A relational approach*. New York: Guilford Press.

Fabiano, G. A. (2014). Interventions for high school students with Attention-Deficit/Hyperactivity Disorder: Considerations for future directions. *School Psychology Review*, 34(2):203–209.

Fonagy, P., & Target, M. (1996). Playing with reality: I. Theory of mind and the normal development of psychic reality. *International Journal of Psycho-Analysis*, 77:217–233.

Leuzinger-Bohleber, M., Laezer, K.L., Pfennig-Meerkoetter, N., Fischmann, T., Wolff, A., & Green, J. (2011). Psychoanalytic treatment of ADHD children in the frame of two extraclinical studies: The Frankfurt Prevention Study and the EVA Study. *Journal of Infant, Child and Adolescent Psychotherapy*, 10:32–50.

Migden, S. (2002). Self-esteem and depression in adolescents with specific learning disability. *Journal of Infant, Child and Adolescent Psychotherapy*, 2(1):145–160.

Salomonsson, B. (2011). Psychoanalytic conceptualizations of the internal object in an ADHD child. *Journal of Infant, Child and Adolescent Psychotherapy*, 10(1):87–102.

Sapountzis, I. (2012). Creating continuities and reversing perspectives: Psychodynamic contributions in school psychology. *Journal of Infant, Child and Adolescent Psychotherapy*, 11(2):1–14.

Tustin, F. (1986). *Autistic barriers in neurotic patients*. New Haven, CT: Yale University Press.

Willock, B. (1987). The devalued, (unloved, repugnant) self: A second facet of narcissistic vulnerability in the aggressive, conduct-disordered child. *Psychoanalytic Psychology*, 4(3):219–240.

PART VI

Culture and play

13

CREATING REFLECTIVE SPACE IN THE CLASSROOM

Ana Archangelo and Fabio Camargo Bandeira Villela

Teachers recognize the importance of respect for difference and yet, our conversations about teaching about tolerance, sociability (getting along with others), and respect for diversity can include more rationalization than reason. Such conversations often include moralizations offered as if it were truly possible to directly affect the hearts and minds of the students in ways that would promote more welcoming reactions to difference that are less hostile to diversity. And yet we know that, particularly for young children, experience is much more profound and compelling than verbal instructions.

Conversations about pedagogy are often used to justify methodologies based on information, clarifications, and explanations about whatever is seen as different. In practice, however, these well-intentioned efforts tend to fail because they overlook very real tensions that underlie all too human fears of the unknown – and of the known. Even people living in the same country can be part of subgroups with different ideas and values. When differences in perspective that affect who is "I" and who is "other" are ignored, we can fail to come to grips with even very basic notions of how "sameness," "strangeness," and "difference" are constituted for one person versus another. This failure leads to the type of *uncanny* sense Freud (1919/1964a) discusses regarding Jentsch's link between feelings of uncanniness and intellectual uncertainty. Jentsch concludes that: "The better orientated in his environment a person is, the less readily will he get the impression of something uncanny in regard to the objects and events in it" (Freud, 1919/1964a, p. 220). This position leads to the conclusion that whatever is "uncanny," "strange" is frightening *because it is unknown* and, if one becomes familiar with the unknown, the "uncanniness" or the "strangeness" is reduced. In contrast, according to Freud, whatever we experience as uncanny is of a different order. For Freud, the uncanny remains frightening precisely because it relates to what is known, old and long familiar, and not something that is unknown. Therefore, information and explanation do little to overcome the uncanniness.

Using Freud's idea for the "uncanny," we can consider that conversations in schools about *getting along together* have been naïve because they are based on presumptions of unfamiliarity, as though, if we just had the correct information, we would solve the problem. When we speak about accepting, tolerating and welcoming diversity, we are necessarily talking about human difficulties in dealing with something that feels strange or different. However, if the tension has less to do with the unknown and more to do with what is familiarly disconcerting in ourselves, then the relation between *sameness* and *difference* becomes much more complex and profound with both rational and irrational aspects.

From that framework, in order to have constructive conversations about diversity, we need to recognize that we all find diversity disconcerting and uncanny in the Freudian sense of the term. Thus, adopting the expression presented by Archangelo, Oyama, and Pompeu (2012), we should, rather, think of diversity as "the point of inflection which leads to conflict and coincides with it" (p. 306). In other words, we need to recognize that the experience of the uncanny tends to come, not from real differences in the other, but rather from what we cannot tolerate in ourselves that we displace and locate in the other. From that perspective, we can see how our attempts to overcome the uncanny feelings will fail unless we can encounter the human presence that *seems* external and strange.

To overcome this dilemma and achieve real engagement between people, we need enough trust to experience some degree of contact with what is uncanny, what is strange within ourselves. For that contact to occur, the external world must be stable enough that contact with the uncanny within ourselves can be recognized, contained, and welcomed. When we are working with children living in unstable environments, this challenge is even more difficult and yet crucial to their well-being and development.

From this perspective, we can recognize the potential importance of the classroom – and the classroom teach – in providing protective containment for the developing child. When all is going well, social conventions and language itself – all the ways in which members of a human group relate with each other, or in which its members demand their rights to live and be – constitute a protective container. We can envision that social container as a membrane that protects the individual enough to dare to learn more about one's internal world including the at-times difficult, confusing, or unacceptable feelings that can otherwise seem uncanny.

You can see how education about diversity would not easily break through this type of resistance, which would make immediate acceptance of diversity impossible. However, it may be possible (at least conceptually) to think about it over time (in contrast to immediately). In this chapter, we argue that one promising vehicle that aids us in being able to grapple with diversity and difference is aesthetic experiences, in terms of "the qualities of feeling" (Freud, 1919/1964a, p. 219), if we can play with them rather than resisting or being overwhelmed by them. We contend that, in contrast to what is strictly rational, the acceptance of diversity becomes possible if there is a certain differentiation between one's own body and those of others, a private space in which to reflect on and regulate one's feelings. In creating a boundary in which one might have aesthetic – feelingful – experiences, one also creates a space in which the psyche – internal reflective space – can develop.

Today, this question of internal space, within which the self can develop, overlaps another of equal complexity. With increasing migration, traditional boundaries of self-other relations are changing, making it more difficult to locate oneself in space or identify one's "territory." Originally, the concept of territory described the set of space and people in a given State in which fundamental agreements, without conflict and tension, are assumed (Valverde, 2004). The key idea was that of territorial unity, which guaranteed a certain constancy for the notion of "same" and "other." However, increasing geopolitical disputes and migration have brought about the need for new ways of conceiving of territory, including the power relations involved in decisions about the physical and symbolic control of space (Valverde, 2004).

Looking at the process of the acceptance of diversity in relation to the idea of territoriality and of bodies that move in space, it is possible to think of the child's need to be present in their body as a way of developing a "territory for lodging." That challenge is heightened by the fluidity of territory these days in relation to changing networks of social relations and disputes for power between various groups (Valverde, 2004). Negotiation of limits or boundaries between "us" (the same, insiders) and the "others" (strangers, outsiders) becomes increasingly complex. These boundaries can be fenced off or transparent but generally they are mobile, appearing and disappearing, expanding and retracting, as a function of the claims of different movements and forces over time.

Encountering the uncanny in the classroom

For the early childhood teacher, these evolving relationships become a challenge in helping children to locate themselves in space and time, and to build a solid identity that does not close off otherness, but rather can tolerate and be enriched by it. When territoriality is constantly changing, modifying what is identified as the "same" and the "other," how can one think about identification and differentiation when the groups with which one identifies (and in which one must trust) form and reform; and when barriers are permanently erected between "allies" and "enemies," between "us" and the "others," but then razed, especially when these definitions are often invisible and mutant? Reliance on the external world, on the cultural soup that encompasses us and sustains our adventure in search of contact with what is internal, has become far more difficult nowadays.

Concern about the fluidity of territoriality seems to have arrived in the school. Among the several questions that might be asked about the effects of territorial fluidity[1], one is of special interest in this chapter: How can a school affected by territorial fluidity in present-day experiences deal with the uncanny, which, according to Freud, prevents us from recognizing the familiar, yet strange, in ourselves, thus pushing us towards intolerance in relation to diversity and to the other?

We believe that if the school is capable of using this fluid territory as a space for experimentation and investigation so that the child is able to explore in the company of an adult, it will favor contact with the internal world and with what is different, promoting emotional and mental development. However, if the fluidity represents a space of instability and lack of support, it will tend to intensify defenses and hinder the development of the child, especially for those who arrive at school with a history of abandonment or traumatic experiences.

We are living at a time in which intolerance is widespread, and it would be worthwhile to reflect on any element that may suggest new ways of understanding this intolerance and, possibly, action to be taken. One of the areas in which intolerance has flourished is that of gender. The episodes that will be presented here can help us think about the impact of fluidity, the meanings attributed to it by the child, and the consequent demands on adults and the school.

The vignette to be presented is taken from research conducted as part of a project for the program of teacher training in Brazil[2], coordinated by one of the authors. In general, during moments of play and while listening to stories, children repeatedly raise questions about a world in which "being a boy" or "being a girl" are muddled or nonexistent.

Vignette

After reading the book *Menina bonita do laço de fita* (Machado, 1986)[3] and talking about the story, the children were asked to draw a picture of "Who I am" and "Who I would like to be." Caique [fictitious name] drew what follows (see Figure 13.1).

> Who I am: At the beginning of the activity, Caique draws himself without feet, with something in his mouth and apparently falling. Careful observation reveals that the following phrase had been written and then erased: "I don't know". The student apparently did not feel comfortable representing how he was, despite the fact that earlier that day, he had said he was the little girl on the board. This suggests a certain internal conflict. On the other hand, he felt comfortable drawing an imaginary scene that included a fairy on the part of the page set aside for drawing what he would like to be.
>
> (Mendonça, 2018, p. 72)

The next week, the story "The Lake of the Monsters" (Tiberius, 2018) was presented and the children discussed it. They were then asked to draw monsters (see Figure 13.2). The teacher of Playtime reported the situation in this way:

> Caique, who was quite creative, drew his fears in the same way as his beloved fairies. Some of his fears were Frankenstein, vampires, zombies, wolves, Iara and the Mummy. All of his pictures were drawn as if they were little girls
>
> (Mendonça, 2018, p. 76).

FIGURE 13.1 How you are and how you would like to be
(Report of research carried out by Archangelo, cited in Mendonça, 2018, p. 72)

The treatment given by the research worker provides a clue as to how to understand this in the face of the concerns revealed by the children and how the school can serve as a protective membrane favoring the development and integration of the child in an environment of fluid territoriality. This environment is one in which reflective space can be developed.

Reflective space: Five levels of the presence of an adult in the classroom and three fundamental feelings about school

In another work (Villela & Archangelo, 2014, pp. 40–41), the concept of *meaningful school* was formulated. This refers to the type of classroom environment that can serve as a field favorable to the development of significant experiences along

FIGURE 13.2 The monsters
(Report of research carried out by Archangelo, cited in Mendonça, 2018, p. 77)

with evolving ideas about the meanings of those experiences for each child, encouraging the development of mentalization as described in Chapters 4 and 11. We developed the idea that for the school to be considered as significant for the child, it must be able to promote three basic feelings: welcome, recognition, and belonging (Villela & Archangelo, 2014, pp. 41–47). These feelings, however, are not necessarily uniformly present, neither for all students nor for all school situations. It is thus necessary for the feelings of welcome, recognition, and belonging to be set as goals for the school, as well as serving as pivotal points for reflection about singular experiences. These goals should orient not only the decisions and general actions of the institution but also decisions and actions involving specific children in specific situations in relation to a specific adult in a given time and space.

By suggesting five levels for the presence of an adult in the promotion of the experience of *being*, we intend to extend the discussion to include information about how these basic feelings can be promoted. The purpose is to delineate paths by which territorial fluidity can be created as a space for experimentation and growth, rather than a space of instability and lack of support, as discussed previously. Whether fluid territoriality compromises or favors development and psychic integration will depend on the approach of the adult in relation to this fluidity.

For each of the five levels described, the participation of the teacher is considered in relation to specific situations or activities that are complex, tense, and in some way involve conflict for a given child. We trust that the adult participation in each of the levels can be generalized beyond the specific example, in relation to the emotional development of the child, to intervention in the process of integration, self-expansion, and the resolution of conflicts of individuals or even groups.

The five levels cited will be illustrated with the vignette and the drawings presented previously. An attempt will also be made to relate the five levels to the three basic feelings of a child in relation to the school.

Level 1: Regularly offer "significant emptiness" – space just to be in the company of an adult inside the classroom.

The presence of an adult at this level is involved in the organization and offering of a space in which fluidity can be an antidote to the rigidity of stereotypes and prejudice. This space is constituted in various physical, material and mental dimensions, depending on the activity to be developed, and without stereotypes or prejudice being the original reason for the activity.

The offer of space indicates that the adult plans and accompanies the activities, which are destined for each and every one of the students. Even without a focus on a certain student, each child tends to feel the presence of the teacher and become involved in the activities as if they were specially designed for him/her. This involvement makes the experience significant and makes it possible for the student to perceive that they can count on the help of the teacher, if necessary.

Taking the example of Caique described previously, one can say that the invitation to draw and the offering of paper are examples of this level. But we can also go beyond the example. The significant emptiness would also be the offering of sheets of colored paper for the pictures, rather than white ones, thus giving the children the chance to choose a color considered to be "for boys" or "for girls," without any mention of this stereotype being made.

Level 2: Actively offer a psychic presence, even though silently.

We could say in Winnicottian terms that the adult needs to mirror who the child is (Winnicott, 1971). When recognizing the hesitation of a child in the face of the desire to choose a material usually considered inappropriate, or to express an idea often seen as inadequate, or even to exhibit a not harmful but socially unacceptable behavior, the adult should be ready to approach the child and, without saying anything, encourage them to continue. Such encouragement comes from facial expressions, a look of approval, or a gesture that shows physical and psychic proximity. This attitude not only authorizes the child to experiment with different ways of acting, thinking, and feeling but also makes them legitimate beyond the usual expectations and conventional ways of being.

Even if involved in a certain conflict, the presence of the adult encourages the child to overcome their uncertainties and to creatively and freely experience "being in the fluid territory" or "being in the world" thus approaching greater integration.

Returning to the situation described in the vignette, in the case of the recognition of the hesitation of the child in the face of a choice of colors traditionally related to being a "boy" or a "girl," one can say that the adult approaches the child, without saying anything, but with an encouraging expression that endorses their right to make their own choice, in this way providing a receptive mirror of the child's individuality.

For the first two levels ("Regularly offer 'significant emptiness'" and "Actively offer a psychic presence, even though silently"), the presence of an adult/teacher strongly favors the feeling of welcome for the student in the classroom. And it is via the feeling of welcome that the student feels at home in the classroom and with the teacher. The student also perceives that he/she is receiving special attention, personal, and unique. They feel physically and psychologically safe, developing an intimate certainty that they can turn to the teacher when faced with difficulties or anxiety be it with internal conflicts, identity formation, and interpersonal relations with colleagues and teacher or even with their own family (Villela & Archangelo, 2014, p. 42).

Although the feeling of welcoming can be linked to these two levels (and serves as a background for the next three), it is on the second level that it is most profound. By actively offering a psychic presence, the teacher is not referring directly to aspects of the activity, but to psychological aspects of the student, tacitly encouraging them and facilitating the adequate resolution of tensions as well as integration and the expansion of the self. After this second level, the intervention of the adult is focused on the mental attitude of the student in the face of the activity, no longer on the activity itself in the strictest sense.

The next two levels of the presence of an adult in the promotion of the experience of being ("Offer a mind capable of containing and processing the conflict without rationalizing it and moralizing the atmosphere" and "Offer the option of *parroting*") also promote the feeling of welcome, but in a more specific way, the feeling of *recognition*, which is more complex and results from an adequate welcome. Recognition in its *external* meaning refers to the valuation of the activity of the student by the teacher. Its more specific and *internal* meaning – which is what interests us here – refers to the feeling of finding oneself in the other and in contact with another who is the same – the teacher – and with whom he can talk and be recognized as an equal (Villela & Archangelo, 2014, pp. 42–44).

Level 3: Offer a mind capable of containing and processing the conflict without rationalizing it or moralizing the atmosphere.

On this level, the presence of the adult is necessary not only for supplying an open environment and encouraging the child who is hesitant in relation to her desires. It is also necessary to manage processes of splitting that become explicit in moralistic attitudes, stigma, and prejudice, and which tend to trigger a hostile environment.

The presence of the teacher in level 3 releases and provides support for whatever, in the words of Bion, is "true," in contrast to what is "right or wrong" (Bion, 1965). When one speaks of "right or wrong," one sees an object as good or bad, sacrificing the complexity of experience in the attempt to calm the anxiety that it mobilizes in us (Klein, 1997). By electing a victim and condemning someone as guilty, our psyche avoids attributing, in fantasy, a form and destiny for numerous other aspects of the experience.

In general, when faced with situations of tension or conflict between children, the teacher tends to take the position of mediator between them. However, if she appears to act as mediator, often implicitly or even unconsciously, she ends up also acting as judge, counting on rationality and authority to mediate the conflict for an ending in which the supposed aggressor understands how wrongly he has acted and asks for forgiveness from the supposed victim.

Because of this hazard, in level 3, it is fundamental that the teacher abstain from such a position and avoid rationalization that will end up as moralization. As Bion (1965) suggests, the adult must be able to tolerate the conflict that each participant is involved in and implicated in. By avoiding rationalization, it is possible to recognize common aggressive, prejudiced, and polemic attitudes that, to a certain extent, are held by each and every one, although they may be voiced by only one student. The teacher, in level 3 of presence, will face the difficult task of processing the uncanny that is circulating and thus of freeing the class from the environmental tensions. When the uncanny is processed by the teacher, it becomes tolerable and can be processed by the mind of each of the students, thus becoming less threatening.

The processing of anxiety by an adult makes it less threatening, and thus easier to integrate the experience. This processing makes taking responsibility for the uncanny as experimented within the classroom more possible rather than expelling it and blaming it on another student or on another school situation. In general, the teacher who acts on level 3 does not explicitly call attention to the processes of splitting that take place during the experience. He only deals personally with these processes, integrating them into his own experience, but these can then be shared with the children. In this way, he loans his capacity of mental processing to them. As Bion (1962) says, the child can thus introject not only the experience that has been processed but also aspects of this mind that was capable of processing it.

In the case of the child who rejects a colleague for choosing the "wrong" color and the "wrong" sheet of paper, the adult brings the open space back but without emphasizing the splitting going on. One example of what could be said in such a situation would be, "Do you know that my best friend has blue hair?" That type of remark maintains the "true" in the situation, but without any mention or judgment in relation to the attitude of the students. And what is true? The answer would be: "The choice of a color is (or should be) only a question of taste." But such an affirmation has symbolic implications that are available for other experiences without mentioning them. It condenses, in a processed form, the conflicts arising from prohibitions and judgments related to gender identity. It brings such conflicts into an area in which they can be played with, demystifying them and thus making it possible to gain space and representation in the mind of the child.

Children are affected by such observations because they overthrow moral meaning, expanding the field to thought and feeling, repositioning that area outside the condition of judging or being judged. And if the child does not feel judged, they can integrate parts of themselves rather than using mechanisms to banish the unwanted parts.

Something quite close to the previous example was experienced during our project, something that convinces us of the strategic potential of this approach. One boy, who initially complained about his schoolmate's choice of a "girl" color, reacted to the management of the teacher and returned the white paper he had chosen, saying, "Give me the purple one."

Level 4: Offer the option of parroting.

The level 4 of the presence of the teacher in the classroom initially appears the same as the level above, since it also "offers the students the containing mind that some of them are lacking" (Archangelo, 2007, p. 343). But there are important differences that justify the description as a new category. In level 3, the tensions and conflicts result predominantly from the confrontation of inclination and desire of the children, and the external and internal prohibitions that define parameters of being and also the criteria for moral judgement. In level 3, the teacher should maintain the fluidity of the space, avoiding a conspiracy between forces that replace experimentation in the different ways of feeling, behaving, and thinking with ingenuous submission to moralizing narratives.

Although in level 4, the objective of the teacher has still been to make "tolerable and more integrated what has been expelled," what is at stake is "[t]he promotion of a certain recognition of what has gone in pieces" (Archangelo, 2007, p. 344).

On this level, there are many examples of children who live territorial fluidity as instability that compromises development. The presence described in level 4 is necessary because the systematic absence of a containing mind provokes deep internal suffering or even a certain disintegration of mental space. When working with traumatized children, teachers must be aware of this possibility. School activities often lack meaning in situations such as this one, which requires a profound investment by the teacher in the restoration of the capacity to unite the parts that have been expelled and disintegrated of the child's self, leading to what Archangelo (2007) has called *parroting*. As the author points out, it

. . . would enable the child to delimit and organize his own internal space, so that he can reintroject those parts and, hopefully, the parts he needs in order to learn. What I am suggesting – which I will call the process of *parroting* – is a means of being a good container without being intrusive to the child: a way to help the child listen to what goes on within himself. [. . .] The parroting approach could metaphorically be expressed as follows: The child would say: "Listen to what I'm saying, that's me, these are fragments of myself. I cannot bear and contain what I am." And by parroting, the adult would reply: "Listen to what you've said. There is a unity if we bind the parts. And this unity may not be unbearable at all, though you feel differently."

(Archangelo, 2007, pp. 343, 344)

In the activity of "who I am; who I would like to be," the different drawings and the poorly erased register of what had been ("I don't know") provide evidence of how conflicting child experience can be in many aspects. In the case of Caique, the sequence of offerings by teachers seems to have been sufficient for a certain integration between the doubts and future possibilities he could have in mind. One can say that the activities constituted a good enough container for less integrated elements to find space for processing, integration, and development, as we can see in the progressive richness of elements and colors in the pictures.

However, it is not always the activity itself that is a sufficiently integrating container. Through time, the teacher may perceive that the child persists in the same conflict, often withdrawing and rejecting learning at school, or revealing extreme difficulty in organizing time and space. It is possible to say that, symbolically, the poorly erased "I don´t know" in the picture infiltrates various dimensions in the experience of the child, forcing processes of turning off and disintegration.

In these instances, it is up to the teacher to intervene more directly, such as is proposed in the concept of *parroting*. To offer another example from the previous vignette, if Caique had persevered in the conflict, it would have been the role of the teacher, in level 4, to verbalize the observation about how many possibilities of expressing oneself there are, despite the suffering revealed in the badly erased "I don't know."

In levels 3 and 4, as pointed out previously, the feeling of recognition is present and predominates. By offering the child a containing mind, the adult demonstrates recognition of the anxiety and affliction of the child but, above all, makes it possible for the child to recognize the teacher as similar, in realizing that we all share the human task of mentally processing our emotional experiences.

The final level of the presence of an adult in the promotion of the experience of *being* ("Offer one's own capacity to create worlds") is especially important in the development of the third feeling pointed out previously, that of *belonging* (Villela & Archangelo, 2014, p. 44). An unnamed experience or conflict is named and expressed through the mind of the teacher, gradually being incorporated by the student and achieving meaning. Therefore, the student radically experiments with the symbolic space of the school, the classroom and the word, imparted by the teacher, who intentionally attempts to tune in to the internal and experiential world of the student. In this way, the teacher attempts to respectfully mirror what is of singular and unique importance to that child.

Level 5: Offer one's own capacity to create worlds.

The presence of the teacher in level 5 requires a profound capacity for observation and for listening for what is missing (Bion, 1965). It is the observation of the non-word, the non-memory, the non-story; recognizing the lack of internal resonance about what takes place in the environment. It is not an absence that can mobilize or move the subject but rather an absence that obstructs the construction of meanings for experience and, therefore, growth. In Bionian terms, this no-thing can be seen as the bad object that promotes destructive attacks on the mind, the force within us that can turn towards evasion rather than growth (Bion, 1984). To be present at this level, the teacher must be disposed to face adversity; she must be constantly alert to timing so that a specific intervention can echo the ideas of or make sense to the child.

At this level, the adult should be an observer who can focus on the inert body of the child, notice the manipulation of a toy that hides the absence of true spontaneous play, the sounds that pass for words, or any automatic reactions of whatever type. These behaviors must be recognized as *imitations* of play that mimic playful behavior patterns in the child who cannot play, whose internal dialogue and confrontations with the internal world are too impaired to integrate and make use of experience. The very lack of feelingful-ness in these behaviors can be seen as a cry for help from such children.

With traumatized or neglected children, the teacher must listen to the unsaid and be able to recognize what we call here "empty (non-significant) emptiness." If such a sterile environment is present and predominates, it is the mind of the adult that produces possible meanings for that body, for that game, for those words. He should invent possible scripts for various games, demonstrate enthusiasm in the face of vague and empty words, create stories for the unrecognizable lines left on paper, decipher mathematical sentences, and intuit family stories. In this way, the teacher provides the narrative function so essential to meaning-making and identity development, as described in Chapters 10 and 11.

Moreover, in this case, the symbolic intervention of the teacher is similar to the interpretative procedure of clinical psychoanalysis, described by Freud (1937/1964b) as "construction in analysis." The presence of the teacher in level 5 is aimed at integration of the ego and the expansion of the self, as is the intervention in a present-day psychoanalytic clinic. Despite this similarity, however, the investigation of the unconscious, which marks Freud's clinic, is not the goal, as the context of the classroom is of a different nature. The goal here is learning, which, for the young child, rests on the ability to play.

For children who need the presence of an adult in level 5, territorial fluidity is a synonym for instability and, frequently, for devastation. For such children fluidity makes unfeasible the constant, stable contact that the child needs; it interrupts the fragile attainment of meanings produced by the creative mind of the teacher.

The teacher must guarantee the maximum of stability possible, loaning her own mind so that a few visible threads of the experience of the child can be intertwined with the experiences of the group. In this way, a personal narrative can be developed over time by the child.

The presence of the teacher at this level is solitary; it requires that he sustain frustration and create something that often dissipates in the air in the face of an apparently indifferent or apathetic child. It is a gift. Adelia Prado, a Brazilian poet, says in her poem "Leitura" (Reading): "I always dream that something generates, is not dead. That which seems not to be alive, fertilizes. That which seems to be static, waits."[4] It is a wager like that of Adelia Prado that sustains the work of the teacher in level 5. His gestures will make it possible for the child to find some insertion in time and space, with the objective of fertilizing a mind that is waiting, yet to be born.

Final considerations

To maintain the spatial metaphor suggested by the use of the term of territory, one can say that the child lives territoriality as the presence or absence of feeling welcome, the presence or absence of significant others to help maintain contact with the uncanny circulating in the classroom, which makes it possible to elaborate and develop meaning and understanding. In dealing with otherness and finding oneself face to face with one's internal world, the child can deal with different forms of changing territorialization and deterritorialization – to locate him or herself as a separate, unique, and feelingful person – as long as he or she feels welcome. Otherwise, the possibilities for the development of tolerance and respect of difference will have been lost.

In our contemporary turmoil, everyone is required to deal with liquidity of experience (Bauman, 2001); the child looks for a receptive, containing mind that furnishes experiences of "feeling oneself felt." Stability would thus be in the adult way of doing what Ogden (1994) calls "interpretation in action," an interpretative action that, since it has direct significance for the subject, is not felt to be intrusive and uncanny but is rather capable of helping them deal with the strange-familiar. To a certain extent, this hospitality prepares the child to take up residence in his own body and, with this assured, to have significant experiences with the "other," with less fear of what might arise from such experiences. Safe and convivial residence is not as demanding as "Heimlich," in the sense in which it is, "Concealed, kept from sight, so that others do not get to know of or about it, withheld from others" (Freud, 1919/1964a, p. 222). Therefore, the strange – familiar is less uncanny, like something "Heimlich, belonging to the house, not strange, familiar, tame, intimate, friendly, etc." (Freud, 1919/1964a, p. 221) – and can thus be recognized in oneself and in the other. In this way, the creation of reflective space within the classroom makes possible a true respect for diversity – within ourselves and with one another.

Notes

1 For instance: Do the tensions in the schools today already point to a territorial dispute taking place between the children and the space of teaching and learning (or between adults and children)? Do the discourse and pedagogical practice in defense of tolerance and respect for diversity account for the psychic effects of this scenario marked by territoriality?
2 Sponsored by the Interinstitutional Program of Scholarships for Introduction to Teaching (PIBID) of the Coordination for the Improvement of Higher Level Personnel (Capes), a foundation of the Ministry of Education (MEC).
3 Translated into English in 1996, published by Kane/Miller Book Publishers, under the title *Nina Bonita* – A white rabbit begs a black girl to tell her the secret in order for him to match her beautiful color.
4 Original in Portuguese: "Eu sempre sonho que uma coisa gera, nunca está morto. O que não parece vivo, aduba. O que parece estático, espera" (Prado, 1979).

References

Archangelo, A. (2007). A psychoanalytic approach to education: "Problem" children and Bick's idea of skin formation. *Psychoanalysis, Culture & Society*, 12(4):332–348.
Archangelo, A., Oyama, D. K., & Pompeu, M. (2012). O Conflito da Diferença na Escola: Uma Visão Psicanalítica. *ETD – Educação Temática Digital*, 14(1):299–313.
Bauman, Z. (2001). *Modernidade Líquida*. Rio de Janeiro: Zahar.
Bion, W. (1962). *Learning from experience*. London: William Heinemann.
Bion, W. (1965). *Transformations: Change from learning to growth*. London: William Heinmann Medical Books.
Bion, W. (1984). *Second thoughts: Selected papers on psychoanalysis*. London: Maresfield Library.
Freud, S. (1964a). The "uncanny". In J. Strachey (Ed. & Trans.), *The standard edition of the complete psychological works of Sigmund Freud* (Vol. 17, 1917–1919, An infantile neurosis and other works, pp. 217–256). London: Hogarth Press; Institute of Psycho-analysis. (Original work published 1919)
Freud, S. (1964b). Constructions in analysis. In J. Strachey (Ed. & Trans.), *The standard edition of the complete psychological works of Sigmund Freud* (Vol. 23, 1937–1939, Moses and monotheism, An outline of psycho-analysis and other works, pp. 255–270). London: Hogarth Press; Institute of Psycho-analysis. (Original work published 1937)
Klein, M. (1997). *Envy and gratitude and other works*. London: Vintage.
Machado, A. M. (1986). *Menina bonita do laço de fita*. São Paulo: Ática.
Mendonça, L. C. (2018). *Análise de Questões de Genêro: Observações do Subprojeto Pibid/Pedagogia* (Master Dissertation). Campinas: Faculdade de Educação – Unicamp.
Ogden, T. (1994). *Subjects of analysis*. London: Karnac.
Prado, A. (1979). *Bagagem* (2nd ed.). Rio de Janeiro: Nova Fronteira.
Tiberius, J. (4 de 11 de 2018). *MOLWICK*. Fonte: Jose Tiberius. www.molwick.com/pt/contos/520-contos-criancas.html
Valverde, R. R. (2004). Transformações no Conceito de Território: Competição e Mobilidade na Cidade. *GEOUSP – Espaço e Tempo*, 15:119–126.
Villela, F., & Archangelo, A. (2014). *Fundamentos da escola significativa* (4 ed.). São Paulo, SP, Brasil: Loyola.
Winnicott, D. W. (1971). Mirror-role of mother and family in child development. In D. W. Winnicott, *Playing and reality* (pp. 111–118). London: Tavistock.

14

CULTURAL ISSUES IN RELATION TO PLAY FOR TEACHERS

Athena A. Drewes

As families migrate within their country or immigrate to other countries for safety, work, and educational benefits, the number of children and families from culturally diverse backgrounds is rapidly increasing across the globe. It is essential for teachers to become more aware of this global shift and its impact on the populations served (Drewes, 2009). It is becoming more essential that we be sensitive to the cultural differences among the children we work with and help the children embrace these differences as well as help the children build upon the unique qualities of their cultural identities.

The implication for educators is that not all children play alike or that play is valued in all families. How children play with peers or interact in a group setting and even how they learn best may depend on their cultural upbringing.

The importance of play and its relationship to culture

Play is a crucial activity throughout all cultures (Drewes, 2009). It is not only a natural and pleasurable experience for children but it contains therapeutic and healing components (Schaefer & Drewes, 2013). Further, play is extremely vital for early learning; the way children learn language and literacy skills, critical thinking, problem-solving and self-confidence, along with healthy brain development, creativity and physical skills. It is through play that children also form friendships, develop social competence and emotional maturity, among other skills (Schaefer & Drewes, 2013; Drewes, 2009; Vandermaas-Peeler, 2002). Play is so important for normal child development that the United Nations High Commission for Human Rights, UN Convention on the Rights of the Child (www.unicef.org/crc) has recognized play as a *right* of every child in *every* country.

By playing, children are able to successfully understand and master their culture, which in turn, allows for the successful integration into social structures resulting in cultural survival as well (Monroe, 1995; Drewes, 2009). Further through play, children are able to learn about their society's rules and what is acceptable behavior (Monroe, 1995; Drewes, 2009). Children can then learn to sort out not only their similarities but also what is different about themselves and others (Levin, 2000; Drewes, 2009). Immigrant children and those living within a multicultural society need to become not only competent in their own culture, but also competent with the dominant culture that they interact with (Fleer, 1999; Drewes, 2009). Play helps them to do that.

Play is so important for a child, that the converse, play deprivation, has serious consequences across all cultures as well. Children who are unable to play are ostracized from group activities which results in the lack of learning how to get along with others within the culture through the social characteristics of play, a key element (Frost and Jacobs, 1996; Drewes, 2009). Cultural norms and attitudes toward play, along with opportunities for play, determine how different types of play are stimulated and whether the adult, especially the teacher, sees play as a good thing or a waste of children's time (Edwards, 2000; Drewes, 2009). Differences in play and play behaviors across cultures can also be seen in the degree to which play is viewed as a survival mechanism and to what extent children are permitted or encouraged, by not only their parents, but also teachers, to take risks, and how play fighting may be viewed, and what the responsibilities are of the children to each other as well as to adults (Johns, 1999; Drewes, 2009). How much freedom the child has to explore and practice adult roles through play, as well as whether the environment provides easy access to materials for creative and constructive play are also important cultural considerations (Edwards, 2000; Drewes 2009). The teacher is a critical person for helping to facilitate play and having the necessary materials and encouragement. For children to acquire cultural competence, teachers and parents need to understand that it is a slow and gradual process that is achieved through many observations, experiences and interactions in the classroom, on the playground and with parents and peers.

Play also becomes a powerful way for children to learn about the world in a safe place, school. They can learn new concepts, transform their experiences into unique personal creations, build meaningful connections between their home life experiences and those at school and in the community. They can also learn about each other's families and diverse backgrounds.

Children's development of cultural awareness

It is important to understand how children develop their cultural identity and attitudes, in order for the teacher to help foster its development. Children learn cultural awareness through experiences with their bodies, social environments, and their cognitive developmental stages (Derman-Sparks & ABC Task Force, 1989). By age 9, racial attitudes tend to stay the same unless the child has a life-changing experience (Aboud, 1988). Before age 9, teachers and families can have a good chance in helping children develop positive feelings about their racial and cultural identity (Biles, 2014).

Preschoolers (ages 3–4) begin to notice differences among people. They are learning to classify and sort based on color and size. They begin to comment on hair texture, eye shape, and other physical characteristics, asking to know how people got their color, hair texture, and eye shape. Seeing that their own bodies are changing and growing, it is not unusual for them to wonder why skin color and other physical traits don't change. Black children may voice dislike for their skin color, hair texture, or another physical trait (Biles, 2014; Clark, 1963). By age 4, children will begin to prefer one race. Their thinking is limited, distorted and inconsistent, making it easy for them to believe stereotypes and form pre-prejudices (Biles, 2014).

In Kindergarten (ages 5–6) children continue to ask questions about physical differences, and start to understand explanations given for these differences. They are developing social skills and becoming more group-oriented. By age 6, most children will understand the concept of fair and unfair, and will use these concepts as they try to deal with issues (Biles, 2014).

In Primary Years (7–8), children acquire racial constancy. They now have the understanding that a person's skin color will not wash off or change but remains the same as that person grows up. Children at this age also consider multiple attributes at one time, understanding how one person can be a member of several different groups (i.e., part of a family, a classroom, a culture, and a race). They can also understand feelings of shame and pride, aware of racism against their own group. They are able to empathize and show interest in learning about the world. At this stage, it is crucial for teachers to encourage children to accept and celebrate their differences, helping them to develop a positive self-concept, feeling positive about racial and cultural identities that reflect diversity in their environment (Biles, 2014).

> Simeon, an African-American girl, age 4, went over to where the dolls were during free play. At first, she picked up an African-American doll and briefly held it. She soon put it down, preferring the doll with fair skin, blonde hair and blue eyes. Holding and caressing it, she showed it to her friend, who was Caucasian, and said, "This is me. See how pretty she is?"

Sampling of various cultures and play

Play differs across cultures and socioeconomic status (Roopnarine & Johnson, 1994). It is important to understand how a child's play may be impacted by their cultural norms around playing. Immigrant children may have difficulty creating friendships during play time because of the differences in the way they learned to play, based on parental and cultural views, and may find difficulty with the competitiveness that they may encounter in their new country. Inadvertently, teachers may be encouraging group play or competitive games, only to find the immigrant child refusing to join in or standing outside of the group activity.

This following section outlines various ethnic cultures and how children's play is viewed. Teachers may find that immigrant children and families in their classroom have difficulty playing with peers. Understanding the underlying cultural views that the children may have been exposed to or the parents actively support, can help to lessen any misunderstandings or conflict between the child and their new cultural orientation in the school.

For example, Euro-American culture tends to stress the cognitive benefits of a child's play or the acquisition of individual independent social skills through play. Families with strong African-American, Asian-American, or Hispanic-American backgrounds tend to be somewhat more group-oriented in understanding of social relationships compared to families from Euro-American cultures. Euro-American families have more eye contact, offer and receive toys, share, lend, take turns, and even have organized cooperative play (Roopnarine & Johnson, 1994). In contrast Korean-American families strongly believe that academic activities are more highly valued than play but may see that the academic activity itself can be enjoyed as a kind of play (Hyun, 1998).

Indigenous peoples

Hamilton's (1981) observations of child rearing practices in Arnhem Land, Australia, found that non-Aboriginal mothers of European heritage used everyday household objects from the environment to distract, pacify and amuse their child as well as to allow the child to explore, whereas Aboriginal mothers seldom did this. The means toward emotional contentment was through the social interaction with the mother, through an oral experience (Fleer, 1999; Drewes, 2009). Hamilton (1981) found Australian Aboriginal children did not engage in the fantasy games of similarly aged non-Aboriginal Australian boys. Their play consisted of exploring their environment, risk-taking, and developing physical skills (Fleer, 1999; Drewes, 2009).

United States – Native Americans

Indigenous cultures within the United States span over 500 recognized tribes with diversity within and across them. There is the pervasive belief in the sacredness of life, where religious experience is constant and surrounds the individual at all times (Drewes, 2009). There is a belief in the cyclical or circular pattern of life, with traditional homes, dances, communication, and play all having a circular arrangement and movement occurring in a clockwise fashion (Farrer, 1990; Drewes, 2009). The spoken word is considered important with thinking before speaking expected. Consequently Anglo-Europeans may misread the thoughtful pause and silence as withdrawal or as a stereotypical characteristic of a stoic and silent people. Sacred knowledge is passed down in oral forms with elders as the repositories of the knowledge (McDonald & McAvoy, 1997; Drewes, 2009). Native Americans concentrate more on playing a game well rather than putting down an opponent or being competitive. Competition is seen as a motivating, stimulating force that spurs the group and individual toward greatness (Drewes, 2009). Everyone tries to do their best but not at the others' expense, and winning and losing is not seen as relevant.

Native American children often play in a group with relatives and family members, and this is preferred over solitary play or joining activities with non-Native American children. Activities and physical games are conducted in a circular arrangement. Physical proximity is also a normal way of communicating for indigenous American children and adults, standing close to the side of the other person with whom you are talking. Keeping eyes straight ahead or cast down with the body not moving until the interaction is terminated (Farrer, 1990; Drewes, 2009). Adults and children can become offended if the other person (e.g. teacher) moves away from their body contact.

> White Feather, 4 years old, would often come up to her teacher to show her what she drew. She would place her shoulder touching her teacher's arm and would be physically in contact with her teacher whenever she wanted to say something. With eyes downcast, White Feather, would pause, taking time to say what she wanted. Her teacher, limited for time to interact, and uncomfortable with the close proximity of White Feather, along with her slowness to express herself, began to find herself feeling irritated. During outdoor play time, White Feather, preferred to play exclusively with her cousin, and would use the "jungle gym," an intricate working of steel that they would climb. But instead of climbing straight up, the children preferred to go in circles, spiral-like, slowly getting up to the top.

Mexico

Mayan children's play from rural Yucatan, Mexico had play themes that were exclusively about what they saw the adults doing in daily life, along with little elaboration or complexity throughout the play. Roles and play scripts were almost always ritualized with children not changing from being human and only utilizing actual objects (Fleer, 1999; Drewes, 2009). There were no imaginary objects or people in the children's play. In turn, adults did not join in the play nor did they seem particularly entertained by watching the play and did not reward the play by attention or praise (Fleer, 1999). Play was not valued in its own right with adults preferring the children to observe and learn through watching and engaging in a productive activity or that the play should contain work elements (Drewes, 2009).

Africa

Children in Liberia have over 90 forms of play from make-believe, games, use of toys, storytelling, dancing, musical instruments, and adult play. Natural materials and objects are turned into toys. Storytelling is prominent with children from age 9 upwards telling stories that contain animals talking to each other and to people, humans, and having access to magical powers and spirits in human form (e.g. witches). Hunting games were common in many parts of Africa serving as imitative play as a prerequisite for actual adult work (Drewes, 2009).

China

In China parents use playtime as a teaching time, demanding mature behavior, expecting the child to listen attentively to their elders and behave accordingly. Pretend play is used to teach proper conduct and Confucian thought emphasized with role-playing social rules and adult customs (Chow, 1994; Drewes, 2009).

India

Western Indian parents take three distinct roles in their children's play: instructive – telling the children what to do; restrictive – cautioning and protecting them from something harmful; or participative – playing with the children (Oke, Khattar, Pant, & Saraswathi, 1999; Drewes, 2009). Some universal games, such as tag, hide-and-seek, and ball-and-stick games were played but often the children converted almost anything they could find into play materials. Pretend play included being film stars and using dialogues from films as well as use of festival rituals being played out and sung. Almost three-quarters of the play observed involved physical movement: chasing, jumping over obstacles, racing, and dancing despite limited play spaces (Oke, et.al, 1999; Drewes, 2009).

Korea

Korean mothers frequently used food as a way to comfort their young children, offering continuous and immediate gratification. Mothers had a high expectation for their child's success. Toys were utilized to improve creativity, develop positive feelings, and promote and enhance physical and psychological development (Hupp, Lam, & Jaeger, 1992; Drewes, 2009).

Muslim culture

Immigrant children from Muslim communities come from a variety of ethnic and cultural backgrounds, and speak many different languages with their religious beliefs, values, and practices creating issues and challenges for teachers. In 2010, approximately 12.9 percent of the United States population consisted of immigrants (U.S. Census Bureau, 2011). Of this, about 0.6 percent (9 million) were Muslim immigrants (Pew Research Center, 2011). Immigrant children from Muslim backgrounds in the United States come from 57 nations and speak 60 different languages (Center of Immigration Studies, 2012). Arabic is the most commonly spoken language followed by Begali and Punjabi (Al-Romi, 2006; Md-Yunus, 2015).

Important cultural aspects to remember when teaching Muslim children include that the family is an important social unit as well as the valuing of the extended family. Family interests outweigh personal interest with parents demanding complete obedience and devotion to the family and community. Children are best educated by memorization and repetition rather than concepts of reflective questioning. This may be the opposite of how a teacher generally teaches. Use of visuals, concrete examples or manipulatives, demonstrating, using gestures, repeating instructions, allowing the child to write in their native language or illustrate their answers, or use audio recordings of English books and computerized lessons have proved to help the children understand better (Md-Yunus, 2015; Adams & Kirova, 2006). It is important for teachers to be aware that Muslim parents are not in favor of children's pursuits in extracurricular activities in school.

Young children, however, are free to choose whom they play with and the play area, but free mixing among young men and young women is prohibited after puberty. Male teachers should generally avoid eye contact with Muslim mothers and female teachers should avoid eye contact with Muslim fathers. Clothing is expected to be loose for both men and women (Md-Yunus, 2015). There are culture-specific beliefs regarding watching television, listening to music, and pursuing secular activities that do not in some way enhance spirituality and these may impact classroom teaching styles and events. Teachers should be aware that some Muslims may have reservations regarding music. Some types of music might not be acceptable to Muslim parents. Islamic teaching prohibits loud, violent, or depressing music. More orthodox Muslims might request musical activities be conducted with unaccompanied voices. In addition, art projects involving human forms might be a concern for some Muslims (Ismail, Yunus, Ali, Hamzah, Abu, & Nawawai, 2009) whose belief in one God has led them to question the use of photos or pictures of human beings, animals, or even statues that might be considered idols. Although, Muslims do allow such depictions when made by children or when created as toys for children (Ismail et al., 2009). But some parents may be offended by school personnel requests to have children bring stuffed animals to school for show and tell activities (Borhan, 2004). Muslim parents consider stuffed animals in the same way as they do art projects, which involve human forms. Teachers will need to be sensitive to this potential concern and also be prepared that some parents may request that the children be excused when class photos are taken or not permit their child to be photographed in the classroom. Muslims are not allowed to keep dogs and puppies as pets or to touch these animals (Borhan, 2004), which could create conflict if a teacher or child brings in such a pet into the classroom. In addition, parents may feel offended by books, stories, or movies that glorify these animals, requiring the teacher to be sensitive in picking out books for story time or the viewing of Disney movies in class.

Culture and learning

Vygotsky (1978) formulated a sociocultural theory of learning that stresses that children "construct knowledge within a cultural context through social interactions with adults and peers" (Reynolds, 1998). Particular skills and learning that is valued by a culture, including symbols and spoken language, become the tools that help to convey meaning and in turn influence the surrounding environment (Berk & Winsler, 1995). Vygotsky stressed that imaginary play becomes the child's growing edge and is the most effective means for stimulating a young child's cognitive development because of the use of symbols to communicate meaning to other players (Berk & Winsler, 1995). It is in the play that the child then recreates experience by using symbols that reflect the cultural milieu. Therefore, play becomes socially constructed and dynamic.

Cultures vary in how information is obtained, such as through the internet, through elders, nature, spirits, or symbols, or even through oral tradition. Cultures also solve problems in their own unique ways based on their distinctive values, philosophy, and beliefs. There are also different ways of communicating non-verbally, which is critical for teachers to understand and watch for in their class-rooms. Some children will not make direct eye contact when talking to a teacher, as it shows lack of respect in their culture; some may smile because they are embarrassed or do not understand and are afraid to raise their hand to ask a ques-tion, rather than the smile indicating feeling happy; others may not smile (such as in the Korean culture) because it signals shallowness and thoughtlessness (Dresser, 1996).

Different cultures also learn in different ways. In the United States, students often will work in groups and work collaboratively whereby they learn from one another. Teachers would then be a facilitator while the activities would be student-centered. However, in other cultures the teacher is always the center of class activities, the sole authority figure, with students not daring to ask questions, as it would be seen as a challenge to the teacher's authority; and as such there are no collaborative activities but rather memorization of information would be required (Pratt-Johnson, 2006).

Some cultures view conflict as a positive thing, while other cultures see conflict as something to be avoided. In the United States, conflict is not usually desirable, but the culture encourages individuals to deal directly with conflicts when they arise. While Asian countries see open conflict as embarrassing or demeaning with differences best worked out quietly and written exchanges would be preferred over face-to-face encounters (Dupraw & Axner, 1997).

It becomes a challenge for the teacher to replicate culture authentically in every part of the curriculum. But of most importance is being sure that the curriculum, room arrangement, guidance, and transitions are authentic and meaningful, hon-oring the cultures of the children being taught.

Blending play and culture in the classroom

Rather than reducing time to play in order to meet the demands of state mandates and standards, teachers may have to advocate for playtime or find ways to blend or fit it into the curriculum. Content-rich curriculums can allow children to have opportunities for continual and in-depth learning including play. Teachers can support children's play by providing a variety of things to do while observing what unfolds and supporting the child's actions through assistance and by acknowledging their words and actions (Jones, 2011). It is important that teachers support critical thinking and curiosity through play with materials and relationships (Jones, 2011). Through the observation of play, the teacher can learn about the cultural environment of the child and what materials might need to be added to the play area.

Teachers of young children should explore and be comfortable with the materials offered the children (such as blocks, books, and paint), along with the ideas and feelings that emerge from the children. By exploring "what else can you do with these items" and thinking about "what could children do," the teacher can help to foster the process rather than the product. Comments such as "tell me about your building" or "what is happening here (in the play)?" helps to foster and encourage oral language and can allow for explanations of what the children are building, how they built it, and encourages engagement in practicing storytelling and making stories up on the spot. All of which are essential in helping children with literacy development (Jones, 2011).

Effective teaching, especially for children from different cultural backgrounds, builds the curriculum upon what the children already know. You can extend and enhance learning, facilitate social interactions as well as assist children in joining play. By providing scaffolding to support children's learning and development, you help to expand the child's play experience regardless of their cultural background. For example, "Why do you think the doctor can help the baby?" or "Why does the baby need to go to the doctor?" (Rice, 2014)

Play and learning can be integrated throughout the day (Eklind, 2004; Rice, 2014). Children need opportunities to work out feelings, emotions, and fears that they are unable to address or even acknowledge overtly (Schaefer & Drewes, 2013; Rice, 2014). Teachers can facilitate this integration by embracing and using play as a valuable tool for children's learning through facilitation, engagement, and appropriately individualizing play opportunities for each child's developmental level. But the teacher may need to plan for play and it may even need to be intentional. Having opportunities for play may need to be created within the classroom curriculum in order to allow for higher-level thinking with the teacher conscientiously thinking about how to incorporate play time, the space for play, and the materials for play (Rice, 2014).

Teachers may find that they have to advocate for play with administrators and families in order to help foster play for every child's development and by securing a prominent place for play in their curriculum planning. Teachers are in the perfect position of being able to help educate parents (and administrators) on the value of play and, in turn, garnering parental support for including play in the curriculum (Rice, 2014).

Following are some suggestions for ways that teachers can help to foster developmentally appropriate play for the multicultural children in their classrooms.

- Build relationships with your multicultural students and their parents. Learn everything you can about the children's home cultures, but be sensitive to the things community members or parents are or are not willing to share with an outsider. If and when possible, visit your student's home and neighborhoods. Invite caregivers, parents, and grandparents to share something of their lives in their native culture with all the children in the classroom.
- Listen empathically – and listen actively and carefully, putting yourself in their places and learning to read between cultural lines.
- Look for cultural interpreters – in the school or community who can assist you in order to add to your cultural fund of knowledge and to assist you in interpreting cultural questions and sharing cultural concerns.
- Take advantage of available resources such as books, articles, films, music, and audio recordings; go to local cultural fairs and community festivals; read about your students' culture, listen to music, and visit their grocery stores to learn about customs and foods (Pratt-Johnson, 2006). Try to learn phrases from their language.
- Observe multicultural play and see what themes emerge and that can be used to help build the curriculum as well as help to develop an appreciation for the similarities and differences between home and school.

Creating a multicultural classroom play environment

(Suggestions from: Cronin & Jones, 2014; Drewes, 2004; Drewes, 2009; Hyun, 1998.)

- Where possible, encourage administration to hire staff from the children's cultural/language backgrounds.
- When possible, make sure there is ample time for sustained, unstructured, child-initiated play to occur.
- If there are frequent interruptions or brief opportunities for play, it will diminish the value of play in the children's eyes and discourage them from being able to develop sustained play and get the most from it.
- Learn everything you can about the children's home cultures. Ask questions!
- Provide representation from children's home cultures as regular aspects of the play environment and group times. Books about the cultures, toys, and games from the culture (or having the children teach their peers a game from their homeland) can help to enrich the curriculum as well as help in integrating the child into the classroom and peer relationships. Remove materials and visuals that might promote stereotypes. Display photos and collages from magazines of all the multicultural children and families in your classroom, in the community, or society. Make your classroom environment inviting with tapestries, fabrics, music, pictures, art work, etc. that is culturally relevant to your students and families.
- Avoid isolation of a child from peers. Understand that culturally the child may not be comfortable in competitive games, or joining in with a group but

would readily join in dyadic play or with another child with similar cultural backgrounds.

- Have stories that represent the different cultural groups in the community. Help parents to create "home books" by taping them in both a home language and English, which would allow children to begin to experience and learn another language.
- Have parents share photographs and stories with their children. Encourage parents to spend time in the classroom to focus on sharing about their home lives: who lives there, what the family members' job roles are, what languages are spoken, and where did their families come from. Use a world map to put little pin flags on to show locations of where the families or ancestors lived or a world globe to show locations of countries and the distance to their current land and the diversity of cultures in your classroom.
- Include familiar props and multicultural looking dolls and families. Make available paints, markers, crayons, and paper that reflect a variety of skin tones (Crayola's multicultural division sells these items). Art and craft supplies, games, play foods, multicultural dolls, and books are all now available online and through catalogs representing many different cultures. For example, the nonverbal communication of emotionally-laden material may be typical of many Asian cultures so that items such as origami paper for folding, rice paper for painting, and red clay should be available (Drewes, 2004) for children to express themselves. Pencils, markers, crayons, and paints with multicultural skin tones allow children to draw and paint pictures more representative of their self-image and physical characteristics (Drewes, 2009).
- Foster creative play, such as creating a restaurant with play dishes and play food, menus (from area restaurants or creating their own; written in both languages used), utensils, and other materials from the different cultural groups in the classroom. Include dress-up clothes that may also be like those worn by the men, women, and children in their culture and toy tools that match those used in the child's community.
- Display items in an accessible and reachable way (Bodrova & Leong, 2007).
- Invite parents/caregivers to come into the classroom to talk about where their families came from, trips they have taken to see family, as well as share the language they spoke or speak, and foods they enjoy and cook (even bringing food in to taste and share).
- Share your own cultural background.
- Have props available for dramatic, open-ended play that allows for creativity and opportunities to think, plan, and carry out the play. For example, in one classroom within the Tungasuvvingat Inuit Head Start Program in Ottawa, Canada, the teacher included not only the usual preschool items (blocks, Legos, puzzles, supplies for writing and drawing, computer), but also books that were in Inuktitut (native language) and stuffed animals commonly found in the Arctic. Dulled ulus (women's knives) at the playdoh table, miniature rubber seals, dolphin, whale, a kamutiik (arctic sled), child-size amauti

(traditional baby-carrying parka), and caribou skins were available for the children to use in their play. Inuit drums and music were available; a water table contained sea green water, a large rock and pebbles, a sea turtle and dolphins and several big clam shells reflecting the native waters and sea animals; and the children's cubbies had their names in both Inuktitut and English (Reynolds, 1998).

- Encourage multicultural parents/caregivers to lend recordings of music that their family enjoys. Teach your classroom children songs and dances from different nations of the world. The children will begin to see how people are similar in liking to sing and dance but different in the way they express it. Talk about how different music sounds: loud, soft, fast, slow, and with different instruments. Have parents/caregivers bring in some of the musical instruments from their countries for the children to hear and experience.

Necessary props to include

- In order to help honor and support multiculturalism in your classroom, try to supply materials that represent the diverse experiences of the children you teach. Include multicultural dolls, family figures, and animals native to their cultural lands. Have materials and props that will allow children to create their roles around themes that interest them, such as travel. Include such props as suitcases, postcards, unused airline tickets (Hyun, 1998).
- Avoid materials that are highly structured, stereotypical, or might promote competitive behaviors. It is best to include open-ended materials and toys such as blocks, play dough, cardboard boxes, and dress-up items.

Games and activities to help children build cultural understanding

Hello in Different Languages – The group tries to come up with the word(s) for "hello" in as many different languages as possible (Biles, 2014).

The Story of My Name – Explore where each child's name came from and what the name means in order to help build intercultural respect and understanding (Biles, 2014).

Match-Ups Skin-Color – Put out a number of nylon, knee-high stockings in various shades (tan, black, white, pink, yellow, red) and encourage children to try them on their hands and arms or legs and feet to help increase their awareness of skin color. Ask, "Can you find a stocking that is the same color as your skin?" and, "Is it lighter or darker than your own skin?" Emphasize that skin-color differences are interesting and desirable (Biles, 2014).

Alike and Different – Using 3x5 index cards, black ink pad, pen and magnifying glass, have the children make prints of their thumbs by pressing them on the ink pad and then putting their thumb on the cards. Label each print with the child's name. Let them use the magnifying glass to see how the prints are alike and different. Point out how each person has patterns on the skin of their fingers and each person's fingerprints are different from anyone else's (Biles, 2014).

Proverbs and Traditions – Ask the children's families to supply sayings that are common in their culture or cultural traditions that they have in their families. Choose a broad topic, such as love, birthdays, holidays, etc. Chart the responses to see how different cultures express similar ideas (Biles, 2014). Have the children compare the different names they use for their grandparents.

Summary

It is crucial that teachers realize the importance of play in the social, emotional, and cultural growth of their classroom students and become advocates promoting opportunities and time for unstructured play to occur. By setting up a culturally rich and inviting classroom, children can explore their own culture and those of their peers, thereby lessening the likelihood of bullying or isolation and increasing tolerance and acceptance.

References

Aboud, F. (1988). *Children and prejudice*. New York: Basil Blackwill.

Adams, L.D., & Kirova, A. (2006). *Global migration and education*. Mahwah, NJ: Lawrence Erlbaum.

Al-Romi, N.H. (2006). Muslim as a minority in the United States. *International Journal of Educational Research*, 33(6):631–638.

Berk, L., & Winsler, A. (1995). *Scaffolding children's learning: Vygotsky and early childhood education*. Washington, DC: National Association for the Education of Young Children.

Biles, B. (2014). Activities that promote racial and cultural awareness. Retrieved 11/1/16, www.pbs.org/kcts/preciouschildren/diversity/read-activities.html.

Bodrova, E., & Leong, D. (2007). *Tools of the mind: The Vygotskian approach to early childhood Education* (2nd ed.). Upper Saddle River, NJ: Merrill/Prentice Hall.

Borhan, L. (2004). Teaching Islam: A look inside an Islamic preschool in Malaysia. *Contemporary Issues in Early Childhood Education*, 5(3):378–390.

Center of Immigration Studies. (2012). *Muslim immigrants in the United States*. www.cis.org/a rticles/2002/back802.html.

Chow, R. (1994). Beyond parental control and authoritarian parenting style: Understanding Chinese parenting through the cultural notion of training. *Child Development*, 65:1111–1119.

Clark, K. (1963). *Prejudice and your child*. Boston, MA: Beacon.

Cronin, S., & Jones, E. (2014). Play and cultural differences. www.childcareexchange.com.

Derman-Sparks, L., & the ABC Task Force. (1989). *Anti-bias curriculum: Tools for empowering young children*. Washington, DC: National Association for Education of Young Children.

Dresser, N. (1996). *Multicultural matters*. New York: Wiley & Sons.

Drewes, A.A. (2004). Multicultural play therapy resources. In E. Gil & A.A. Drewes (Eds.), *Cultural issues in play therapy* (pp. 195–207). New York: Guilford Press.

Drewes, A.A. (2009). Cultural considerations. In K. Stagnitti & R. Cooper (Eds.), *Play as therapy: Assessment and therapeutic interventions* (pp. 159–175). London: Jessica Kingsley Publishers.

Dupraw, M., & Axner, M. (1997). Working on common cross-cultural communication challenges. www.wwcd.org/action/ampu/crosscult.html.

Edwards, C.P. (2000). Children's play in cross-cultural perspective: A new look at the Six Cultures Study. *Cross-Cultural Research*, 34(4):318–338

Farrer, C.R. (1990). *Play and inter-ethic communication: A practical ethnography of the Mescalero Apaches*. New York: Garland Press.

Fleer, M. (1999). Universal fantasy: The domination of Western theories of play. In E. Dau (Ed.), *Child's play: Revisiting play in early childhood setting* (pp. 67–80). London: Paul Brookes Publishing.

Frost, J., & Jacobs, P. (1996). Play deprivation and juvenile violence. *Play Rights*, 18(4):6–9.

Hamilton, A. (1981). *Nature and nurture: Aboriginal child rearing in North-Central Arnhem land*. Canberra: Australian Institute of Aboriginal Studies.

Hupp, S.C., Lam, S.F., & Jaeger, J. (1992). Differences in exploration of toys by one-year-old-children: A Korean and American comparison. *Behavior Science Research*, 26:1–4.

Hyun, E. (1998). *Making sense of developmentally and culturally appropriate practice (DCAP) in early childhood education*. New York: Peter Lang.

Ismail, H., Yunus, A., Ali, W.W.Z., Hamzah, R., Abu, R., & Nawawai, H. (2009). Belief in God based on the national philosophy of education amongst Malaysian secondary school teachers. *European Journal of Social Sciences*, 8(1):160–170.

Johns, V. (1999). Embarking on a journey: Aboriginal children and play. In E. Dau (Ed.), *Child's play: Revisiting play in early childhood setting* (pp. 60–66). London: Paul Brookes Publishing.

Jones, E. (2011). The play's the thing: Styles of playfulness. www.childcareexchange.com.

Levin, D.E. (2000). Learning about the world through play. *Early Child Today*, 15(3):56–64.

McDonald, D, & McAvoy, L. (1997). Native Americans and leisure: State of the research and future directions. *Journal of Leisure Research*, 29(2):145–167.

Md-Yunus, S. (2015). Muslim immigrant children in the United States: Practical suggestions for teachers. Retrieved 10/15/16, www.childresearch.net/papers/multi/2015_01.html.

Monroe, J.E. (1995). Developing cultural awareness through play. *Journal of Physical Education, Recreation and Dance*, 66(8):24–30.

Oke, M., Khattar, A., Pant, P., & Saraswathi, T.S. (1999). A profile of children's play in urban India. *Childhood*, 6(2):207–219.

Pew Research Center. (2011). Religion and public life project. www.pewforum.org/2011/01/27/the-future-of-the-global-muslim-population.

Pratt-Johnson, Y. (2006). Communicating cross-culturally: What teachers should know. *The Internet TESL Journal*, 12(2). http://iteslj.org/Articles/Pratt-Johnson-CrossCultural.html.

Reynolds, G. (1998). Welcoming place: An urban community of Inuit families. *Canadian Children: Journal of the Canadian Association for Young Children*, 23(1):5–11.

Rice, M. (2014). What is the teacher's role in supporting play in early childhood classrooms? Retrieved 10/15/16, www.ttacnews.vcu.edu/2014/what-is-the-teachers-role-in-supporting-play-in-early-childhood-classrooms/.

Roopnarine, J., & Johnson, J. (1994). A need to look at play in diverse cultural settings. In J. Roopnarine, J. Johnson, & F. Hooper (Eds.), *Children's play in diverse cultures* (pp. 1–8). Albany: State University of New York Press.

Schaefer, C.E., & Drewes, A.A. (2013). *Therapeutic powers of play: 20 core agents of change*. New York: Wiley & Sons.

United Nations High Commission for Human Rights. Retrieved 11/3/16, www.unicef.org/crc.

U.S. Census Bureau. (2011). Population distribution and change. www.census.gov.s

Vandermaas-Peeler, M. (2002). Cultural variations in parental support of children's play. In W.J. Lonner, D.L. Dinnel, S.A. Hayes, & D.N. Sattler (Eds.), *Online readings in psychology and culture* (Unit 11, Chapter 3, pp. 1–9). Bellingham, WA: Center for Cross-Cultural Research, Western Washington University. Retrieved9/19/2016, https://www.researchga te.net/publication/228997834_cultural_variations_in_parental _support_of_children's_play.

Vygotsky, L.S. (1978). *Mind in society: The development of higher psychological processes*. Cambridge, MA: Harvard University Press.

15

CULTURE AND PLAY AS KEY ELEMENTS OF IDENTITY FORMATION AND ACADEMIC PERFORMANCE FOR CHILDREN OF COLOR IN PRIMARY EDUCATION

Kirkland C. Vaughans and Renee Vaughans

As we discuss the significance of culture and play as vital constructs facilitating early childhood education and a positive sense of racial and cultural identity, we will primarily be doing so from the vantage point of African American and Hispanic children. We believe these comments will have serious implications for other children of Color who also experience themselves as "Othered," a term signifying their exclusionary status within American society. We also believe that the concerns raised here have functional value to children across the globe who bear the status of recent immigrant or refugee. We will therefore be examining the role of culture primarily as a facilitative agent in establishing an attachment to school or, alternatively, the consequences of a failed attachment to school.

Culture is most often understood to constitute a set of conscious beliefs, attitudes, and practices that are inherited from one's ethnic, racial, or religious origin. While such an understanding has much merit, this chapter will be addressing culture as both a force external to the person and as a powerful internal psychic structure that is a determinant of identity. As a major building block that provides a sense of cohesion to one's sense of self, ethnic, or racial heritage, as well as to one's school and community, one's culture can be considered a psychological nutriment.

Developmental research studies indicate the impact of culture as an internal dynamic even prior to birth. For example, Music (2011) cites research that shows that the cries of newborns are impacted by their culture, such that French babies at birth cry "with rising melody contours" while the cries of German babies have falling contours (p. 72). According to Music (2011), a British child psychologist, we should not view culture as a distinct topic but more as "another lens for examining the whole range of questions concerning children's psychological and emotional development" (p. 810). To not consider cultural influences on early child development leaves us in the quandary of subscribing to the dubious notion of the "universal child," which in all likelihood would be patterned after a Eurocentric model of childhood. Pedagogically engaging a child from such a posture would minimally result in cultural mis-attunement, or worse, a devaluing of one's cultural heritage, rendering mute the potency of culture as an effective instrument for engaging the learning process. As Shore (1996) illustrates, such a belief system originates from a false presumption in which, "Culture is conceived as one of the contents of mind rather than as a defining attribute of mind" (p. 22).

Before proceeding, we wish to issue four caveats regarding the idea of cultivating culture in early education, after which we will also address some parallel impediments to play that arise in the field of education. On the face of it, cultivating culture in early education certainly sounds like a nice idea, as well as a worthwhile pursuit, however, such programs may also induce some negative feelings in teachers and teacher assistants. Such negative feelings are most likely to occur in those who are not familiar with their own cultural leanings and biases toward others, particularly when such an approach lacks administrative support. Should such negative feelings emerge, they do not necessarily portend failure of this venture. Instead, if processed with another colleague, they may in fact become an avenue to a deeper understanding of one's own unrecognized cultural issues, as well as a new potential source of genuine engagement with cultural others. According to Music (2011), negatively viewing other cultures that differ from our own in significant ways is practically a universal phenomenon, in part rooted in our strong beliefs that our practices are the right way of behaving. Particularly when there is not adequate administrative support, it is especially important that teams of teachers from different classrooms collaborate in this effort and develop a thinking space among them in experiential trials to heighten cultural awareness. Such teacher pairing allows for mutual support and immediately expands the learning base, preparing the ground for the school to expand its cultural horizon.

A second reason has to do with the very divided and angry mood in many nations today. In the United States, for example, this divisiveness is particularly salient regarding immigration and immigrants. Under the threat of deportation, many of the Hispanic children that we work with have become very constricted in their willingness to share information or feelings regarding family matters. As a result, these children are unfortunately characterized by school officials as resistant, unappreciative, or uncaring.

Our third concern has to do with the assumption that not developing such programs is the equivalence of neutrality: It is not. The absence of cultural education conveys a powerful message to both students of Color and to White students that cultural issues are not of valid interest and that there is nothing productive to be gained from their inclusion. Failing to address cultural issues, for all students, would probably constitute more of the same, leaving the problems further entrenched. This situation was noted by Walter Dean Myers (2014), a children's book writer who commented on the depressing fact that in 2013, while 50 percent of the children in the United States claimed ethnic or racial heritage other than White, less than 10 percent of the books published that year pertained to children of a minority status. This lack of diversity in children's books, he believed, left their cultural stories off the bookshelf.

Teachers need also be alerted to the fact that they may encounter a strong resistance from students of Color. Given the present political climate, many children of minority ethnic or religious status are quite apprehensive about their own welfare and the welfare of their families. There is a strong sense of dis-ease within these communities. Children may feel a sense of reluctance about having their cultural, religious, or racial differences highlighted in any way, fearing that it could lead to governmental reprisals. Despite these challenges, early childhood educators hold an extremely important position, because of their ethical and pedagogical authority, that they can use to help those in their care to expand upon opportunities for understanding themselves more as well as understanding others better.

Our final programmatic concern has to do with having immigrant students and students of Color explore their culture, race, and ethnic heritage, while omitting White students from this same exploration. Failure to include white students in the exploration of their culture conveys very detrimental messages to the entire student body. First, it says that White students are simply the norm and are not raced like the other students. Second, it creates a rather voyeuristic perspective towards the cultural attributes of the Students of Color. In the United States, this situation is in part enacted on a national basis during the month of February, which is celebrated as Black History Month, and again in September, with Hispanic Heritage Month. What goes undeclared is White culture and ethnicity. White children, I believe, can greatly benefit from an acknowledgement and national celebration of their ethnic roots and cultural heritage. Such programming conveys a sense of cultural diversity as a basis for mutual understanding and of collective cohesion. Likely similar situations exist for those of you teaching in other countries where there are racial or cultural divides.

Social and developmental considerations

Presently, cultural and racial diversity in the United States is reflected by the presence of 100 different linguistic and ethnic groups who, by the year 2030, are expected to constitute more than 50 percent of children under the age of 5 (Shonkoff & Phillips, 2000). It appears that all cultures share in common strong beliefs about how children should be raised. Kenneth Clark, the Black psychologist of the famous doll studies that demonstrated the harmful psychological impact of school segregation on young Black children, strongly impacted the 1954 Supreme Court decision ruling outlawing racial school segregation. Clark (1955) noted:

> One of the most characteristic and impressive things about the American people are their dedication to their children . . . Almost no sacrifice is too great for parents to make if it will benefit their children. Parents will work, scheme, attend church, buy life and endowment insurance, move from country to city, from city to Suburbs, from one neighborhood to another, from south to north, from east to west—All for the welfare of their children.
>
> *(p. 3)*

While we certainly believe that Dr. Clark's claims are legitimate, we also claim that they are true as well for the vast majority of mothers across the world. To the Western eye, however, other groups' motivations may at times be hard to decipher. For example, Music (2011) describes Fulani mothers who cover their infants in cow dung in order to trick the evil spirits into believing that their children are unworthy of being taken. Closer to the United States are the mothers who prepare their youngsters to cross borders on their own in the hope of a better life in America, not knowing if the children will survive the journey or if the mothers will ever see them again.

While acknowledging the importance of culture, Tronick (2007), a developmental child psychologist, satirically notes that, "Culture is often referred to, even deferred to, but only superficially and rarely well" (p. 6). If we take Tronick's comment to heart, it suggests that the focus of this chapter has to be about how teachers can teach themselves to learn about a multicultural perspective, rather than learning it in a book. So, before discussing play that is based in cultural meaning and learning, we want to make a few suggestions that may assist us in developing an orientation to cultural learning and understanding.

Work with these young children requires not only an openness to them but, perhaps more importantly, an openness to oneself. Notably, an awareness of one's own cultural attitudes and biases should become more pronounced as you gain more experience and exposure. In their promotion of and support for cultural diversity in Australia, The Australian Early Childhood Mental Health Initiative found that many parents were ambivalent about the program due to worries regarding the loss of cultural identity among their own children. They were able to productively remedy these concerns by involving the parents more and developing personal relationships with them. This example stands out, not because of its success, but as a lesson to focus on the meaning of one's intervention to the other, despite one's best intention, and also, importantly, brings us back to our focus on play as an essential tool that underpins learning for us all.

Wood (2013) emphasizes that an essential benefit of play is the creation of "relational interactive spaces" (p. 12) that facilitate the development and expression of cultural identities for children. Wood also acknowledges that some children may be culturally inhibited or unaware of adults as copartners in play. She further warns that a significant number of children from impoverished African and Asian nations have experienced poverty as the most significant pattern to their way of life. As a result, these children did not involve themselves so much in imaginative play or play prior to the completion of chores. Their play largely served as rehearsals to meet the challenges of the hard life that awaited them. These findings support the necessity for educators to first observe, listen, and talk to their students in order to adequately assess which play exercises might be beneficial to the child, through a shared understanding. What is most essential in the efforts of educators is to understand that when their pedagogical programs entail play that is mediated through a multicultural approach, such efforts convey to these children an abiding respect and sense of care. Mindful inclusion of culture as a fundamental determinant of identity helps to ensure that the children's cultural identity will serve as a protective shield against psychosocial stressors in their communities.

Cultural influences on play

While all of the leading experts in the field of child development agree on the developmental importance of play, what is often overlooked is what constitutes play for a minority or culturally "Othered" group of children, whose play may easily be interpreted as a violation of the social code of the dominant group. Let us offer a few examples. The rough and tumble play of Black and Hispanic boys, especially from impoverished circumstances, are often viewed by educators as a prelude to more aggressive behavior or an actual fight that must be circumvented. The culture of gender probably plays a significant role in how this type of play is perceived. Rough and tumble play is largely engaged in by boys, and not by girls, while the majority of early childhood educators are women. Hughes (2010) distinguishes rough and tumble play from other forms of aggressive activity; the former is characterized by play fighting that involves hitting, wrestling, and chasing with multiple children participating simultaneously. There are other notable distinctions: Rough and tumble play constitutes mock aggression and actually pulls children together. It is inherently social in nature, unlike aggressive fighting that drives children apart. For instance, with Hispanic boys, soccer and tag football are popular games that are inherently rule-bound and enhance cooperative play, role taking, and social cooperation. For many of these children who are not faring well academically, such engagement becomes the choice opportunity for them to feel good about themselves. Observing their zestfulness, their immersion in these games, and the high premium on winning leaves one with a sense that, for many of them, these games are the equivalent of the actual Olympics.

Youngsters play soccer at school the same way they see their older brothers, cousins, and fathers playing, in a rough and tumble fashion that requires the skilled use of their bodies. When a White child complains to teachers that he has been hit, the result can be a punitive response of, "No more playing that game. You play too rough." Teachers appear to be more comfortable presenting these boys with Lego, iPad, and video games, none of which aid in the development of gross motor skills or the release of gross motor energy—sorely needed for children cooped up in classrooms where they feel "Othered."

In addition, some educators are surprised by the fact that many impoverished children have no toys, and mistakenly equate this circumstance with a lack of interest in play. They do not understand that play is a universal and necessary development task of childhood that can take many forms, depending on the context. Aggressive or rough and tumble play is often incorrectly perceived as synonymous with hostility or actual fighting. Little recognition is given to its requirements of role-taking, phantasy formation, and rule guidance.

A second frequent source of cultural conflict occurs when Black boys play basketball. Their cultural attitudes are reflected in the street or public park tournaments that they witness and that their older brothers, cousins, and other role models are involved in. There is an emphasis on ball control, maintenance, and accuracy. Teaching staff often suggest a shared time with the ball as well as provisions for all players to have a chance at shooting the ball. Such attitudes are directly contradictory to these boys' training and background and would never be tolerated on their home court. In both examples, when the boys do not comply with the new suggestions or when another student complains of feeling left out, the teacher's response is frequently to stop the games altogether, until the "Other" boys play as the White children require.

Conclusion

Play is necessary for optimum development in early childhood, for all children. But children play differently in different cultures. It is vital that early childhood educators recognize cultural influences in the play of their charges and in their own conscious and unconscious experience, in order for them to be responsive and inclusive of all children. Ignoring cultural influences is not neutral—it results in children feeling excluded and forbidden to discuss their differences. Teachers should examine themselves and their own backgrounds and cultural assumptions and then bring that sensitivity to their classrooms.

References

Clark, K. (1955). *Prejudice and your child*. Boston, MA: Beacon Press.

Hughes, F. (2010). *Children, play, and development*. Los Angeles: SAGE.

Myers, W.D. (2014). Where are the people of color in children's books? *New York Times*, March 15, 2014.

Music, G. (2011). *Nurturing natures*. Hove, UK: Psychology Press.

Shonkoff, J., & Phillips, D. (Eds.). (2000). *From neurons to neighborhoods: The science of early childhood development*. Washington, DC: National Academy Press.

Shore, B. (1996). *Culture in mind: Cognition, culture, and the problem of meaning*. New York: Oxford University Press.

Tronick, E. (2007). *The neurobehavorial and social-emotional development of infants and children*. New York: Norton.

Wood, E. (2013). Developing integrated pedagogical approaches to play and learning. In P. Broadhead, J. Howard, & E. Wood. (Eds.), *Play and learning in the early years* (pp. 9–26). Los Angeles: SAGE.

PART VII

Teachers and play

16

ENGAGING CHILDREN IN HEALING WORK

Michael O'Loughlin

The power of story

I find it disturbing that we can so easily forget the basics of human connection. As training for child professionals has become more technical, it has become more distanced from the lives of children. We see this in psychotherapy, where manualized therapies—in which therapists literally follow a script from a therapy manual—are increasingly in vogue. We also see it in early childhood education in, for example, the decline of play in preschool and kindergarten environments and a concomitant increase in the use of worksheets and prescribed academic curriculum. What happened to cultivating curiosity and wonder in children? What happened to cultivating an interest in how a child's feeling state can affect her capacity to learn, to know, and to imagine?[1] In her book *A Child's Work: The Importance of Fantasy Play*, Vivian Paley (2004) reports an interview with a preschool director who stated:

> I'm not inclined to encourage fantasy play any more if my teachers can't handle it . . . If the teachers are worried about what's coming out, especially with the fours and fives, everyone is better off if we stick to lesson plans and projects.
> "Has the play changed that much?" I asked.
> The teachers think so. Maybe it's the increased tension since 9/11. Children do seem less prepared, more at risk. We're on safer ground with a somewhat academic curriculum. It's more dependable.
>
> *(p. 7)*

Donald Woods Winnicott (1896–1971), a British pediatrician and psychoanalyst radically changed our understanding of work with children. Both from his work

with mothers and infants and from his role as a consultant during the mass eva-
cuation of children from London during World War II, Winnicott developed an
exceptional sensitivity to the needs of suffering children. As Adam Phillips (2007)
noted in his biography, Winnicott placed a premium on the child's *feelings*. Contrary to other notable British analysts of that period (e.g., Anna Freud and Melanie
Klein), Winnicott was not interested in making pronouncements *about* children:
He believed that rather than coming with knowledge to help a child, his job was
to allow the child to teach *him* what he needed to know to understand that child.
Thus, Winnicott believed that, a child's symptoms, "such as shyness, enuresis, fid-
getiness, eczema were no longer a physiological malfunction but an intelligent and
therefore intelligible solution to emotional conflict" (Phillips, 2007, p. 49). The
child had a story to tell, and Winnicott's job was to get the story. That story might
emerge through drawing, through play, through conversation, or through somatic
symptoms such as fidgeting, nail-biting, stomachaches etc., any of which might
earmark an underlying concern. The therapist's job was to engage sympathetically
with the child so that the underlying difficulty would be revealed.

Nowhere is this more evident than in Winnicott's (1971) elegant squiggle game,
a game in which therapist and child spontaneously complete each other's drawings.
The fundamental purpose of working with a child, for Winnicott, was *making
contact with that child*. Sadly, with the busyness of school curriculum and the pressure
to *do* things, the possibility for existential moments of healing is disappearing
rapidly from our schools. Winnicott assumed that every child "longs for someone
to bring understanding" (quoted in Phillips, 2007, p. 51). This suggest that a primary function for anybody working with children is to respond to this longing by
cultivating a stance of *receptivity* to a child's emotions and *sensitivity* to the deeper
meaning underlying symptoms such as anger, anxiety, 'laziness,' oppositionality,
etc. This, as Winnicott (1965) noted, requires a *facilitating environment* that allows
the child space to tell her story knowing that she will be heard: Knowing, as Max
van Manen (1986) noted, that she will not only be seen by the receiving adult but
that she will also *experience being seen*.

To become a healing space, therefore, a space where the kind of existential *I—
Thou* encounter discussed in the work of theologian Marin Buber (2010) is possible, a classroom ought to be a place where stories can be exchanged and a place
where new storying and re-storying possibilities can emerge. This imagining of
school as a place that privileges story requires an acknowledgment that *both* teachers
and children come to school with stories. It is in the meeting of these stories that
interesting pedagogical moments are created and healing journeys can begin.

Teacher stories: Reasons for teaching

In what follows I will begin with some autobiographical work that lays bare my
interest in the terrible effects of trauma on children, in the possibilities of working
through traumatic feelings, and in the consequences of silence and the problems
that are created if a school environment creates a demand for children to keep

secret any shameful or traumatic events. I will then sketch the outlines of a way of working with traumatized children that honors their stories and their need to be heard. This work is not for the faint of heart. It requires teachers to be prepared to receive children's pain and anguish, and this in turn demands of teachers that they be emotionally ready for such work. In her book *Trauma trails*, Australian Aboriginal author and trauma specialist Judy Atkinson (2002) reminds us that encounters with children's trauma can stir up unexpected emotional reactions:

> Facilitators of healing must therefore know themselves, as Mary discovered. "My expectations were to just get some tools to help our mob. I wasn't counting on all that stuff coming up for me and having to work through it. I don't think it really occurred to me that I would have to work on myself first before I could help my mob."
>
> *(p. 210)*

My own emotional reactions to schooling and to children run very deep. As I have recounted elsewhere (O'Loughlin, 2009; 2013; 2017a; 2017b) I went to school already a very traumatized child. I had a persistent stomach disorder as an infant that caused me to go into arrested development, and that led my parents to insist on moving me to another hospital in our local small town in rural Ireland after the physician in the first hospital had advised them to prepare for my funeral. That decision saved my life. By all accounts I made a remarkable recovery, but the lengthy absences from a relationship with my mother caused by my hospitalizations, as well as my persistent gastric problems, and some life-long residual motor delays, caused me to grow up feeling delicate, fragile, and very anxious. I was unable to participate in the robust games my male peers enjoyed, and this, coupled with a somewhat cerebral disposition, left me often feeling isolated and taking flight into the comfort of books. Refrain from my childhood: "Look at Michael, he has his head always stuck in a book."

School was inhospitable to my presence. My interest in reading and ideas was of no value because the school focused on very simplistic rote learning primers, and no additional conversation or discussion occurred. We were not expected to have opinions or ideas nor were we expected to develop our own points of view on anything. Rather than build on local knowledge, the curriculum was generic and rote-learning oriented. In particular, there was no space for the voices of marginal families such as mine. My family had been imposed on the local farming community when the county authorities purchased a scattering of small plots of land and built subsidized houses for poor families. We were viewed as outsiders. A local farmer drove his children to school, every day, for example, and when it rained—which was often—he allowed other neighborhood children in the van. However, if my siblings and I—or any of our outcast compatriots from other homes earmarked for the poor—tried to clamber aboard, we were excluded. The school itself reinforced this same sense of exclusion, rendering it impossible for economically marginal and socially excluded children such as myself to find ourselves reflected in the curriculum or even to gain basic respect or to earn love because of our human presence.

I suffered persistent anxiety, evidenced for example by nail-biting and frequent gastric disorders, made worse by the regimen in my elementary school. My school was no safe haven. None of the three teachers in my rural school ever acknowledged my medical history or the emotional vulnerability that I experienced because of my childhood hospitalizations. Most likely, it never occurred to them to inquire into my circumstances or learn my story. I never experienced warmth, sympathy, or even the kind of recognition that Max van Manen (1986) described, when he noted that every child needs to *be seen* and to *experience being seen*. To the contrary, a climate of fear and brutality prevailed, one that mirrored that described so poignantly by Patrick Chamoiseau (1997) in *School Days*, his account of schooling in colonial Martinique. Contrary to needing to be seen, we *feared* being noticed, because there was an ever-present risk of punishment for any student who caught the teacher's eye. We were beaten regularly and we were ridiculed publicly for even the slightest infraction of rules, or for any errors in our academic work. Worse, just as happened to *Pink,* the hapless boy in Pink Floyd's rock opera, *The Wall* (Parker, 2005), ridicule and humiliation from teachers abetted shaming and bullying from fellow students—many of whom were apparently willing to laugh with trepidation at the travails of a fellow student, knowing that the presence of a peer in the hot seat meant that they had earned a temporary reprieve from humiliation.

My advocacy for children, therefore, is rooted in loneliness, gnawing anxiety, and a tentativeness about my place in the world, which, while it did not absolutely prevent me from taking leaps of imagination, made the psychic cost of such leaps very high. How, I wonder, can we sensitize adults to creating emotionally facilitative spaces in which children can feel free from anxiety and feel uninhibited in the use of their imaginations? How can we sensitize adults to the deep concerns that may preoccupy children's minds? At its most basic, how can we persuade child professionals to recognize that every child has a story and a longing to be understood? I cannot forget the little girl that Alex Moore (2013) brings to us in his recent essay:

> Yeah. [And] you can't concentrate, because there's something in your head and it stays there . . . It's a bit like when my dad died and I came back to school. It was really difficult . . . I kept on thinking what my mum was doing, because I stayed with my mum for a week at home.
>
> *(p. 291)*

As teachers, therefore, we bring many emotional predispositions to our work with children. Contrast my anguished advocacy, for example, with the more typical *reasons for teaching* that many young women bring to the profession. In Joanna Lipper's (1996) documentary, *Inside Out: Portraits of Children*, 6-year-old Georgia is filmed on a gazebo in her backyard. She is standing in front of an easel, holding a pointer, and ranged in front of her is an impressive array of stuffed animals all of which, with the exception of one errant creature, appear to be paying rapt attention. "Pay attention class," she says in stentorian tones as she begins to teach a lesson on the characteristics of owls. When my daughter was young she enacted a very similar didactic scene, in her case using rolls of paper towels as a stand-in for students! Many of the female student teachers I work with tell me similar stories of an enduring and almost embodied affection for teaching, often expressed through the kind of didactic enactment just discussed. This early emotional attachment for girls to the idea of teaching—tied as it is to traditional feminine conceptions of nurturance, as well, perhaps, as to fantasies of authority and control—offers a powerful motivation for teaching. Although the subject is insufficiently studied, I suspect it explains the pull of teaching for many young women. Perhaps to avoid what Madeleine Grumet (1988) refers to as the "bitter milk" of separation from their mothers, young women find continuity and security in the perceived maternal functions of teaching. There is a large net gain for children in having teachers who have a deep emotional attachment to the profession and who are approaching the field with an intrinsic desire to be in a nurturing pedagogical relation with children.

The down side, as Deborah Britzman (1991) revealed in her book, *Practice Makes Practice*, is the risk that because of their nostalgic attachment to the idea of teaching, young female teachers may be vulnerable to reproducing elements of a traditional, teacher-centered didactic pedagogy from their own school years. In the world of schools, where administration is often male-dominated, young women who are eager to teach, eager to please authority, and anxious to reproduce the nostalgic experiences of their own imagined schooling, are vulnerable to being taken advantage of by school administrators who are only interested in compliance with curriculum directives and with generating the highest test scores possible, and who have little interest in the subjective experiences of children or the emotional quality of classroom life. A major contribution of the writings of Britzman (2003; 2006; 2009; 2010) and others[2] is to honor the complexity of the work of teaching and to recognize that *emotional work, imagination, and meaningful engagement* are at the heart of good teaching.

Not all teachers have a nostalgic pull toward teaching. Some teachers enter the field to try to create school experiences that counter their own disappointing experiences in schools. For example, I am an accidental teacher. I only entered the profession because, in the Ireland of my youth, coming from a family that lived close to subsistence, getting a government-subsidized two-year teacher diploma was the only way to get my foot on the first rung of the university education ladder. Like everybody who has ever sat in a traditional classroom and been apprenticed to a regime of enforced deference to authority, and to a curriculum in which knowledge was reduced to rote memorization and test scores, I entered teaching handicapped by having a very traditional, teacher-centered notion of teaching. It was all that I knew. School had not been kind to me, and, perhaps, as a result, I developed a strong wish to teach differently and to create moments of change and possibility for children. I can recall reading Paulo Freire's (1970) newly published *Pedagogy of the Oppressed*, as I paced the school playground on lunchtime patrol during my second year as a teacher. My story, as someone who suffered at the hands of what was often a harsh and dismissive school system, is not so atypical either, though my own experience with student teachers suggests that new teachers who view teaching through a nostalgic filter may be more numerous in the field. In thinking of teaching, then, clearly the *reasons for teaching* matter, and our history in schools shapes what we aspire to achieve as teachers.

To put it more formally, autobiography is key, and teacher educators would be wise to assist beginning teachers in reflecting on their school experiences so that they might exhume, interrogate, and refine their *reasons for teaching*. For those of us interested in the possibilities of schooling as a vehicle for deep emotional work, for social justice, and for the development of a critical imagination, such inquiry is essential. Unfortunately, as institutional teacher education has become increasingly co-opted by the necessity of preparing teachers for "evidence-based practice," high-stakes testing etc., the space for this kind of deep preparation has evaporated, to the extent that it ever existed (see Biesta, 2009; O'Loughlin, 2016a). I believe, however, that it is possible for teachers who are committed to social justice, opportunity, and the nurturance of imagination, to create spaces where children can do this work. A teacher's chances of being creative and emotionally sustaining are greatly improved if she finds ways of working at understanding her own auto-biography and refining her reasons for teaching.

The nature of the wound: Absence of story-making

Trauma, as Marilyn Charles (2003) noted, can be described as individual, familial, or cultural. A child can be the victim of individual trauma (e.g., being a victim of bullying or assault; suffering effects of serious illness or bereavement); a victim of familial trauma (i.e., where the family dynamics are severely disrupted and neglect, incest, violence, or other family trauma threatens a child's life chances); or a victim of collective or cultural trauma (i.e., where a child is part of a whole group which has suffered catastrophic losses, through, for example, war, genocide, or displace-ment as a result of a natural disaster). Some children—such as traumatized refugee families—may actually suffer from individual, familial, and cultural trauma at the same time. Norma Tracey's (2013) work with vulnerable aboriginal Australian families also illustrates the consequences for children of multiple, overlapping traumas. There is agreement among trauma experts that trauma that cannot be spoken about, travels across generations. Selma Fraiberg et al. (1975) used the term *ghosts in the nursery* to describe the many traumatic events that can haunt the lives of even the youngest children. If children are not given opportunities to tell their stories, and if they are not given opportunities to voice their suffering, their hopes, their desires, and their aspirations, the probability of that suffering passing on to the next generation is great. Selma Fraiberg et al. (1975) captured the transmission of trauma and sadness this way: "The sad and distant face of the mother was mirrored in the sad and distant face of the baby. The room was crowded with ghosts" (p. 181).

Thus, for any professional who works with children, the stakes are extremely high: At its simplest, the challenge for all of us who work with children is to cultivate spaces of receptivity and possibility so that children may tell their stories and thereby face their ghosts, master their suffering, and develop a capacity to imagine and live their lives otherwise.[3]

Australian aboriginal writer Judy Atkinson (2002) introduced a concept that is key for teachers, caregivers, and therapists of young children, namely the concept of *lore*. Lore refers to traditions and customs based on the wisdom that comes from experience and that is transmitted in practical teachings from parent to child across generations. In communities that have suffered catastrophic events, lore collapses. For instance, after Hurricane Katrina in New Orleans, over a million people were displaced, and many of those never managed to return to their old communities, thus losing family ties and generational links. Atkinson (2002) says that the rupture of family and community bonds disrupts the flow of information and lore from one generation to another and produces *lorelessness* (p. 45). This is a condition where people feel disconnected from ancestral wisdom and family, and lose the sense that they are part of what Rosenman and Handelsman (1990) call *group story*. "Cultural genocide," Atkinson reminds us, is "when people come to believe that they themselves are of no value, that their cultural practices and traditions are inferior, and hence so are they, that they are nonpersons with no value" (2002, p. 72).[4] Traumatized communities are surrounded by ghosts, and children who have been wounded by war, dislocation, refugee status, natural disasters, or generations of deprivation carry a huge ghostly inheritance from the long litany of suffering their families and communities have endured.

In *No Voice is Ever Wholly Lost,* Louise Kaplan (1996) illustrates the effects of this kind of trauma on children. From her study of children of Holocaust survivors, Kaplan explained how a parent's suffering can turn children away from pursuing their own developmental path and redirect them to being caretakers of their parents' suffering. The puzzling question, as Kaplan notes, is how a child, in the presence of a parent who does not speak of a trauma, manages to pick up on that suffering. It seems that the parent's emotional blankness or depression elicits a child's concern. This can be detected, Kaplan notes, in the disproportionate space that the parent occupies in the child's mind. Children who refuse school, for example, often do so because concern for a vulnerable mother looms so large that the child simply cannot dare to leave her side. A caretaking child—often known as a *parentified* child—then, suppresses the possibility of articulating a desire for her own growth and well-being in order to secure the future of the parent. Such reversal of the normal pattern of family relations—in which the child now becomes caretaker to the parent— is caused by the parent's inability to share her or his feelings, and this results in an unhealthy "precocious attunement" (Kaplan, 1996, p. 226) or excessive concern for the parent on the child's part. Kaplan (1996) summarizes the process elegantly: "Because of these abrupt and unexpected derailments in dialogue, the child becomes a witness to what happened to the parent" (p. 227). Kaplan (1996) illustrates the terrifyingly ordinary ways in which children may become preoccupied with their parents' trauma, this way:

> The survivor parents unconsciously focus on the issues that were and still are crucial to their salvation. Though the mother still cannot remember her starvation, she transmits the emotional experience of starvation through her preoccupation with buying, preparing, serving, and eating food. The father transmits the physical degradations he endured by being preoccupied with cleanliness and the elimination of feces . . . When a girl is innocently competing with her mother for her father's attentions, the mother may suddenly decide to snip off her daughter's ponytail and send her to school with a crew cut. Of course, when the mother arrived at the camp at the same age the daughter is now, that is what her captors did to her. To survive the psychological trauma of her mother's hostile gesture, the daughter develops an unconscious fantasy that she has been selected by her mother to perform a special mission. She, and she alone, can repair her mother's trauma by sacrificing her own desires and longings. She becomes obese, thus effectively concealing her beauty under layers of fat. Or she starves herself until her body is transformed into the body of a concentration camp prisoner (Kaplan, 2006, pp. 226–27).

How then can we shift such children from preoccupation with parental suffering toward an interest in their own hopes and dreams? Alice Miller (1996), author of *The Drama of the Gifted Child*, argues that traumatic re-enactment only stops when mourning for the terrible losses of the past is facilitated. This requires that adults who work with children find the courage to engage children in conversation about painful and difficult aspects of their own lives so that the children may then be free to pursue their own interest and desires. It seems to me that this is a key responsibility of teachers of young children.

Restorative pedagogy: Creating safe spaces for deep emotional work

Restorative pedagogy refers to the idea of teachers creating healing spaces in their classrooms—spaces which evoke children's deepest feelings, which draw on the lore that constitutes their very being, and which allow teachers and children to feel recognized at school. This is difficult to accomplish if children's experiences are overwritten by curriculum mandates, high-stakes testing pressures, and harsh or punitive forms of discipline that deny children's feelings, that fail to honor their experiences, and that fail to provide opportunities for children to construct meaning for themselves and imagine their own possibilities. Writing as far back as 1955, psychoanalyst Arthur Jersild (1955) made a plea for teachers to create safe emotional spaces in classrooms. That plea is just as relevant today:

We contribute to the growing child's isolation and loneliness whenever we, in effect, tell him [sic] that we do not wish to know how he feels. Yet there is much in the school life of both boys and girls that would make the sturdiest child express intense emotion if the pressure against it were not so strong. In some schools, it is true, there is much gaiety and laughter, but painful emotions are often squelched. At the elementary school level, for example, millions of children feel the sting of failure, the lash of sarcasm, and the pain of rejection. If all these children, and others who encounter countless hurts, some deliberately and maliciously imposed, some that arise in the natural course of life's struggle— if all these were free to cry, as well they might, there would be a flood of tears at school. But such signs of distress would be unseemly. It is better, for the sake of decency and order, to keep up a pretense that all is well. And by a strange irony, which persists in our culture from a more primitive time, it is more appropriate, if one is deeply moved, to show it through signs of anger (sarcastic laughter, for example) than through grief and affection. An outpouring of feeling would be frightening to teachers who have rigidly schooled themselves never to let the hurts and tender emotions of their own lives show in public.

We ask the child to hold back his tears and swallow the lumps in his throat, swallow his rage and his fear and his pride. We ask compassionate teachers to do the same. To do this is like swallowing a sword. It can be done, but it is not easy; it takes long practice and it leaves scars.

(pp. 68–69)

A core principle of work with all children—and most particularly children who have experienced trauma—is to create classrooms as safe emotional spaces where teachers engage in *deeply meaningful encounters* (see Cyrulnik, 2009) with children. A first step is to acknowledge that children are capable of intense feelings and have a capacity for anguish as deep as that of any adult. Trauma theorists would suggest that the most powerful thing we can do in the presence of trauma is to *bear witness to suffering* (O'Loughlin, 2007). For teachers, this translates into the importance of *deep listening* (see Lewis, 2013 and Tracey, 2013). A capacity for empathy, a sense of attunement to the fluctuations in a child's emotions, and the creation of a nurturing communal space in which worries, anxieties, and personal stories of suffering can be absorbed by a community of peers, offer significant possibilities for healing. This, then, calls on teachers to be emotionally self-aware; to cultivate emotional receptivity to their students' feelings; and to believe in the fundamental power of narrative as a tool for helping children to story and re-story their lives so that they can begin to name their experience and develop the capacity to experience dreaming, imagination, and possibility. Here, then, are a few key principles, that might guide teachers in setting up safe, healing spaces that nurture a kernel of creativity in each child:

1. Learning occurs best in anxiety-free zones. A harsh or punitive approach to discipline; the presence of public shaming or ridicule; or an excessive emphasis on test scores or other indices of achievement, can greatly increase a child's

anxiety and shrink the space for creativity, enjoyment, and learning (see O'Loughlin, 2017a).

2. Each child needs to be seen. In my therapy practice, I greet each child as she or he enters my office, and I insist on a goodbye as they leave. As Max van Manen (1986) has emphasized, every child needs to be seen, and to experience being seen. I recommend greeting each child personally as she or he enters the classroom, and saying a personal goodbye to each child at the end of the day.

3. As Marilyn Watson (2003) noted in *Learning to Trust*, schools are *relational places*. Relationships require time and effort to gestate—and this is especially true for those children whose capacity to build trusting relationships is impaired due to the effects of trauma, separation, or excessive conflict at home.

4. Emotional attunement is critical. If a child seems dejected, withdrawn, or out of sorts, it is important to reach out to that child to inquire about her or his feelings. Children carry many worries, and a teacher who is *interested* can be an invaluable source of support for a child who is burdened by, for example, fear of failure, family worries, anxiety about schooling, immigration status, fear of being bullied etc. Attuned interest leads to the creation of spaces for a child to open up so that what burdens that child can be talked out and worked through.

5. When children express anger, defiance, or withdrawal, or when children refuse to engage with schoolwork, these reactions are best understood as symptoms, not problems. A teacher who views such behaviors as problems, will react and try to eliminate the problem. This may require confronting the child and risks escalating into a battle where the teacher has to resort to an authoritarian stance to keep the child in line. An attuned teacher will understand that anger, defiance, and what is often called "laziness," are symptoms, and will seek to probe *what lies beneath*. Every child has a backstory, and behavioral symptoms merely alert us to that backstory. At such moments, it is best to take a child aside—or speak with a parent or guardian—in order seek to understand what that backstory is, so that resources can be mobilized to alleviate the child's difficulty. As I explained earlier, children long to be understood.

6. Marilyn Watson (2003) has written about how classrooms ought to be places where affiliation and attachment matters. Children feel a need to belong and they will thrive in an environment that meets their needs for security and safety. This calls for the idea of a *classroom as a community*, a place in which children feel they belong; they feel they are known and seen; and an atmosphere is created in which children are expected to take care of each other in a climate of inclusion, respect and nurturance, and in which shaming, ridicule, and bullying are not tolerated. Alfie Kohn (1996) described the choice teachers face as one between enforcing *compliance* and building *community* with children. This stark choice between a pedagogy of compliance and a focus on the creation of a supportive classroom community needs to be weighed carefully by teachers.

7. Ultimately, for each individual child, it is vital that the classroom is an invitational space—a space in which children can be heard and in which the

teacher models a form of receptivity that allows children to share their experiences, their worries, their suffering, their hopes, their aspirations and their trepidations. Surface behaviors are viewed merely as symptoms or information that leads us to seek to understand possible underlying disturbance or tension. If the child longs to be understood, our purpose ought to be to strive to respond to that longing with respectful understanding. Ultimately, attuned work with children is at least as much about the capacity of adults to listen mindfully and restoratively, as it is about children's capacity to speak their truths.

8. Children will transfer both positive and negative feelings from family relationships onto teachers. Positive transference, where, for example, a child begins to view a teacher as a good mommy, is easy to handle and typically evokes a positive response of love from a teacher. A child who has developed a negative, distrustful, or hostile attitude to primary caregivers, may, however, bring a negative transference to school, and express hostility to even the most loving teacher. This, in turn, may evoke a negative harsh or punitive transference response from a teacher who is unable to receive and understand the reasons behind a child's negative emotions, or unable to see the veiled hurt beneath a child's anger or aggression. Psychoanalysis teaches us to suspend judgment and to view any kind of transference response—positive or negative—merely as useful information to help us understand the struggle a particular child has in building relationships or even in just being in the world of school. A teacher should never take a negative transference personally. Rather, the teacher should seek to understand *what lies beneath* the anger, disappointment, hostility, despair, or other negative emotion a child may exhibit.

9. In terms of building a communal, supportive space, regular class meetings provide a space where children can share their stories; where a teacher can allow students to experience participatory decision-making; and where the relational complexity of being a in a group together can be processed.

Curriculum that seeks to address the unconscious

The conception of children that underlies much of educational practice is predetermined and prescriptive. Focusing primarily on prepackaged information, often reduced to fill-in-the-blank worksheets, school curriculum is designed to be generic so that it can be delivered didactically to all kinds of children in all kinds of contexts, in order that outcomes can be measured in standardized and supposedly "evidence-based" ways. Such an approach to education negates the individuality of both teachers and children and creates a curriculum that distances teachers and children from their own deep emotions and from their cultures and contexts. An alternative is to think of teaching as *situational* and *critical* and curriculum as locally constructed *with* students. It is in a context of situated learning, in which children can find themselves in the curriculum, that a pedagogy of storying and re-storying becomes possible.

The call, here, is rather old-fashioned. It entails a recognition that children are active seekers of meaning and that schooling must be a place of dialogue and questions if children are to claim a place in the world. Staking such a claim requires opportunity to engage with children's lived experiences, with their histories, with the lore that comes from their family and community, and with their imaginations. Deep aspects of children's experiences can be accessed, for example, through use of film, poetry, music drama, folklore, fiction, and other media that evoke the unconscious and that allow each child to begin to think of what kind of place they will occupy in the world. I think of a teacher as a person who accompanies children a piece of the way on their life journeys, assisting them in documenting their life stories, in articulating their ambitions, and in pursuing their dreams. American psychiatrist Harry Stack Sullivan (1955) postulated that we are all more simply human than otherwise (p. 32). This is an idea that we forget at our peril. Children need our full presence as human beings, and we have an ethical responsibility to provide them with nothing less than a connection to a vital teacher who will fully engage them as developing human beings.

Because of the enormous pressure to limit and control the work of teachers and children. I recognize that the philosophy of teaching I advocate is pushing against the tide as schools become increasingly programmed and managed environments. Nevertheless, I conclude here with a few pedagogical and curricular recommendations that could enhance the school experience of children, particularly those whose experiences deviate from the idealized, abstract, middle-class norm for which standardized, prepackaged school curriculum is written.[5]

1.   To experience empowerment, children must become active participants in their own learning. Children can only find their voices and write themselves into the curriculum, if regular participation opportunities are made available. Children must speak and write their way into understanding. Prepackaged curriculum and what Paulo Freire (1970) referred to as the banking model of education—in which nuggets of information are deposited in students' minds—negate meaning-making and the development of imagination, and leave children powerless.

2.   Teaching work that invites autobiography creates a space for children to build on their own life stories. Children must create connections between new knowledge and ideas and their existing understanding, and the best entry point for this is through discussion and collaborative learning activities, and through a writing process that allows each child to explore ideas and make meaning for themselves. Autobiographical work also provides teachers with a very powerful way of understanding each child's backstory. A useful way to think about this is that every child comes to school with a backpack filled with genealogy, ancestral memory, values, hopes, dreams, possibilities, and challenges. Inviting these ideas into the classroom conversation offers the possibility of developing a deep curriculum infused with meaning.

3.   It follows from this that at least some aspects of curriculum and the learning process should be organic and should evolve through dialog and the co-construction

of ideas and projects. Children need to reach for meaning, and work though to an understanding of novel and complex ideas. Schooling, too often, is based on the assumption that knowledge is absolute, and there are always right and wrong answers. Teachers who believe that all understanding is partial, and that we have to grope toward meaning, teach very differently from teachers who follow a generic curriculum slavishly.

4.   Ultimately, if we are to invite every child to become a critically engaged citizen, and if we are to relieve the burdens of children who come to school with limited horizons and potentially foreshortened futures due to the adversities they have experienced, we would be wise to rethink the invitation that formal schooling offers our children. Schools provide the main venue for preparing children to become concerned, critically informed citizens, and people who live in the world with confidence and creativity. We need to create spaces where teachers are free to do the work of caring for and engaging with children that has always called our greatest teachers to this vital profession.

Notes

1   For further discussion please see O'Loughlin (2016a; 2017a).
2   For psychoanalytic accounts of working with children, in addition to the cited works by Deborah Britzman, please see Boldt and Salvio (2006); Boler (1999); Field, Cohler, and Wool (1989); Grumet (1988); O'Loughlin (2009; 2013a; 2013b; 2016; 2017a; 2017b); O'Loughlin and Johnson (2010); Taubman (2012).
3   See e.g., O'Loughlin (2010), "Ghostly presences in children's lives."
4   For a discussion of refugee children as "nonpersons," please see O'Loughlin (2016b; 2016c).
5   These ideas are elaborated further in my book, *The Subject of Childhood* (2009).

References

Atkinson, J. (2002). *Trauma trails: Recreating song lines: The transgenerational transmission of trauma in indigenous Australia*. North Melbourne: Spinifex Press.

Biesta, G. (2009). Good education in an age of measurement: On the need to reconnect with the question of purpose in education. *Education, Assessment, Evaluation, and Account-ability*, 21(1):33–46.

Boldt, G., & Salvio, P. (2006). *Love's return: Psychoanalytic essays on childhood, teaching, and learning*. New York & London: Routledge.

Boler, M. (1999). *Feeling power: Emotions and education*. New York: Routledge.

Britzman, D. (1991). *Practice makes practice: A critical study of learning to teach*. Albany, NY: SUNY Press.

Britzman, D. (2003). *After education: Anna Freud, Melanie Klein and psychoanalytic histories of learning*. Albany, NY: SUNY Press.

Britzman, D. (2006). *Novel education: Psychoanalytic studies of learning and not learning*. New York: Peter Lang Publishing.

Britzman, D. (2009). *The very thought of education: Psychoanalysis and the impossible professions*. Albany, NY: SUNY Press.

Britzman, D. (2010). *Freud and education*. New York: Routledge.

Buber, M. (2010). *I and thou*. Eastford, CT: Martino Publishing. (Originally published 1937)

Chamoiseau, P. (1997). *School days*. Lincoln: University of Nebraska Press.

Charles, M. (2003). The intergenerational transmission of unresolved mourning: Personal, familial, and cultural factors. *Samiksa: Journal of the Indian Psychoanalytic Society*, 54:65–80.

Cyrulnik, B. (2009). *The whispering of ghosts*. New York: Other Press.

Field, K., Cohler, B., & Wool, G. (Eds.). (1989). *Learning and education: Psychoanalytic perspectives*. Madison, CT: International Universities Press.

Fraiberg, S., Adelson, E., & Shapiro, V. (1975). Ghosts in the nursery. *Journal of the American Academy of Child Psychiatry*, 14:387–421.

Freire, P. (1970). *Pedagogy of the oppressed*. New York: Continuum.

Grumet, M. (1988). *Bitter milk: Women and teaching*. Amherst: University of Massachusetts Press.

Jersild, A. (1955). *When teachers face themselves*. New York: Teachers College Press.

Kaplan, L. (1996). *No voice is ever wholly lost: An exploration of the everlasting attachment between parent and child*. New York: Simon & Schuster.

Kohn, A. (1996). *Beyond discipline: From compliance to community*. Alexandria, VA: ASCD.

Lewis, P. (2013). The child, childhood, and school. In M. O'Loughlin (Ed.), *Psychodynamic perspectives on working with children, families and schools*. Lanham, MD: Jason Aronson.

Lipper, J. (Director), (1996). *Inside out: Portraits of children*. [DVD]. New York: Films Media Group.

Miller, A. (1996). *The drama of the gifted child*. New York: Basic Books.

Moore, A. (2013). Love and fear in the classroom: How "validating affect" might help us understand young students and improve their experiences of school life and learning. In M. O'Loughlin (Ed.), *The uses of psychoanalysis in working with children's emotional lives* (pp. 285–304). Lanham, MD: Jason Aronson.

O'Loughlin, M. (2007). Bearing witness to troubled memory. *Psychoanalytic Review*, 94(2):191–212.

O'Loughlin, M. (2009). *The subject of childhood*. New York: Peter Lang Publishing.

O'Loughlin, M. (2010). Ghostly presences in children's lives. In M. O'Loughlin & R. Johnson (Eds.), *Imagining children otherwise: Theoretical and critical perspectives on childhood subjectivity* (pp. 49–74). New York: Peter Lang Publishing.

O'Loughlin, M. (Ed.). (2013a). *Psychodynamic perspectives on working with children, families and schools*. Lanham, MD: Jason Aronson.

O'Loughlin, M. (Ed.). (2013b). *The uses of psychoanalysis in working with children's emotional lives*. Lanham, MD: Jason Aronson.

O'Loughlin, M. (2016a). A manifesto for critical narrative research and pedagogy for/with young children: Teacher and child as critical annalist. *Journal of Pedagogy*, 7:11–24.

O'Loughlin, M. (2016b, June). Psychoanalysis, subjectivization, and the limit case of the refugee. Presented at Association for Psychosocial Studies Conference, University of West of England, Bristol, UK.

O'Loughlin, M. (2016c, November). Refugee or shelter? The ethical precarity of what we do to children and families fleeing violence. Paper presented in plenary panel at 24th Reconceptualizing Early Childhood Education Conference, Taupo, New Zealand.

O'Loughlin, M. (2017a). The possibility of nurturing a kernel of creativity in a child. In D. Caracciolo & C. L. Weida (Eds.), *The swing of the pendulum: The urgency of arts education for healing, learning, wholeness*. Rotterdam: Sense Publishers.

O'Loughlin, M. (2017b). The emergence of the speaking subject: Child therapy and the subject of desire. In B. Seitler (Ed.), *From cradle to couch: A remembrance of the work of Sylvia Brody*. New York: International Psychoanalysis Books.

O'Loughlin, M., & Johnson, R. (Eds.). (2010). *Imagining children otherwise: Theoretical and critical perspectives on childhood subjectivity*. New York: Peter Lang Publishing.

Paley, V. (2004). *A child's work: The importance of fantasy play.* Chicago, IL: University of Chicago Press.

Parker, A. (Director). (2005). *Pink Floyd: The wall* (25th Anniversary Deluxe Edition). [DVD]. Sony Legacy.

Phillips, A. (2007). *Winnicott.* London: Penguin Books.

Rosenman, S., & Handelsman, I. (1990). Identity as legacy of the Holocaust: Encountering a survivor's narrative. *The Journal of Psychohistory,* 18(1):35–69.

Sullivan, H.S. (1955). *The interpersonal theory of psychiatry.* London: Tavistock.

Taubman, P. (2012). *Disavowed knowledge: Psychoanalysis, education and teaching.* New York: Routledge.

Tracey, N. (2013). Working at the interface of education and trauma in an indigenous pre-school: The importance of "deep soul listening." In M. O'Loughlin (Ed.), *Psychodynamic perspectives on working with children, families and schools* (pp. 133–152). Lanham, MD: Jason Aronson.

van Manen, M. (1986). *The tone of teaching.* Portsmouth, NH: Heinemann.

Watson, M. (2003). *Learning to trust: Transforming difficult elementary classrooms through developmental discipline.* San Francisco, CA: Jossey Bass.

Winnicott, D.W. (1965). *The maturational process and the facilitating environment.* Madison, CT: International Universities Press.

Winnicott, D.W. (1971). *Therapeutic consultations in child psychiatry.* London: Hogarth.

17

TEACHER STRESS

Impact, challenges, and solutions

Deborah Mugno and Jennifer Reid

Introduction

Preschool teachers face many stressors on a daily and sometimes hourly basis. Long hours, low wages, physical demands, and unpredictable situations top the list. Research confirms teacher reports that there are increasingly more children in preschools who have difficulties associated with poverty, parental violence, substance abuse, and children who are also exhibiting overall developmental challenges (Johnston & Brinamen, 2006). Even the most astute and highly trained teachers are often not equipped to handle some of the situations that are put before them.

According to Zinsser et al. (2013), the stress of the preschool or early school teacher in turn has a direct impact on classroom climate and the behavior of the children in the classroom. Pianta (1999) suggests that teacher-child interactions are one of the most significant and impactful experiences in a child's day, thus the dilemma: stressed teachers bring stress to classrooms and to students. Dworkin (2001) makes the point that teachers naturally try to defend against their own stress, but to do so, they may withdraw from desired and caring relationships with students. Preschool expulsions also increase when teachers are more stressed (Gilliam, 2008).

How might teachers better support the emotional and social development of the children in their classrooms and create a stable, positive emotional climate for their students as well as for themselves?

In this chapter we will examine the common stressors experienced by teachers of young children, explore their impact, and offer viable suggestions for short- as well as long-term solutions. As a result of extensive research in the field and the continuing development of best practices, there are many practical and promising ways to address teacher stress.

Sources of teacher stress

The sources of work stress in early school settings differ from person to person, program to program, and day to day, but there are common themes that umbrella the early childhood teaching profession. An extensive survey of adult full-time employment (Substance Abuse and Mental Health Services Administration, Office of Applied Studies, 2007) revealed that those employed in early childhood education are among workforce groups reporting some of the highest levels of stress and depression. When individuals experience higher degrees of stress, they are more likely to express negative emotions such as anger, depression, and sadness (Feldman et al., 1999; Zinsser, 2013). Stress has a direct impact on the relationships that teachers have with children (Hamre & Pianta, 2001) and the nature of these teacher-child relationships can actually predict academic and behavior problems up until eighth grade (Biglan, Hayes, & Pistorello, 2008).

Faulkner et al. (2014) purport that teacher stress, particularly in preschools, is the result of both the organizational characteristics in a particular workplace and an individual's capacity to deal with challenging situations; that is, the stress a teacher feels is due to both external environmental and regulatory factors, and internal, individual coping capacities.

Organizational Factors

Organizational factors vary from school to school, but the most common include:

Low wages

Low wages adversely affect the likelihood that a teacher will remain in the early childhood education profession. Working with young children requires stamina. Teachers are always "on" and unfortunately, the monetary rewards for such are frequently not commensurate with the physical and emotional demands of the job. Add to the equation personal financial worries, and the stress quotient rises.

Disputed professional status

Early childhood educators are often denied the status of professionals, regardless of the degrees they have earned, amount of training they have received, or their years of experience.

Parent-teacher relationships

Many educators, particularly teachers of young children who work closely with parents, have difficulty establishing relationships with parents and working collaboratively to benefit the child. This lack of support from parents leads to inconsistencies in discipline from home to school and can create boundary issues related to teacher and parental roles. Some parents try to micromanage their child's pre-school experience which can undermine teachers' authority as knowledgeable and competent educators of young children. The research of Faulkner et al. (2014) demonstrated that teachers frequently experienced some of their greatest stress during parent interactions.

Physical demands

Stress related to long hours and physical demands can lead to general health and mental health problems, affecting performance and practice. Sorenson (2007) found that teachers who experience high stress are likely to have more physical difficulties such as headaches, muscle strain, backaches, sleep problems, and blood pressure problems. They are also more likely to express emotions in negative and less healthy ways. This in turn impedes effective classroom interactions and can create staff absentee issues in a profession where bringing in substitutes interrupts the consistency of caregiving, a tenet which is essential in working with young children.

Lack of social support

Relationships with peers and supervisors have a significant impact on the day-to-day atmosphere in any organization, but this is particularly true in the teaching profession and seems to be a consistent factor across all levels of teaching from preschool through high school. When people, and specifically teachers, have more social support, their physical and mental health tends to improve (Betoret, 2006; Perrier et al., 2010). Berkman et al. (2000) define social support as having an individual or group of individuals who provide resources, abstract and/or tangible, to another.

Program/policy conflicts

When a program's philosophy is not in sync with a teacher's ideas about child-rearing and child development, or policy decisions conflict with one's professional beliefs, teachers can lose the motivation and enthusiasm that attracted them to the profession in the first place. Instead of experiencing their job as fulfilling, it becomes a source of frustration and lacks satisfaction (Moriarty, et al., 2001). Low job satisfaction results in teacher turnover and teacher turnover affects the professional quality and stability of an entire school or center. Research conducted by Zinsser & Curby (2014) found that a substantial proportion of teacher behaviors can be attributed to school characteristics including policies that dictate programmatic as well as administrative tenets.

Challenging child behaviors

The vast majority of early childhood educators, including those with early childhood special education training, report that students with behavior problems continue to be the most challenging children to work with, those on the autism spectrum rating as most difficult (Ruble, Usher, & McGrew, 2011). Teacher burnout, stress, and depression rates tend to be higher in schools and in classrooms with higher levels of student disruptions (Dorman, 2003; Hastings & Bahm, 2003; McGrath & Huntington, 2007). Hemmeter, Corso, and Cheatham (2006) report that the highest priority training need cited by early childhood educators was that of working successfully with children with challenging behaviors.

Internal individual factors

Life continues. Teachers may have many roles outside of their professional duties and some have second jobs to compensate for the field's low wages. Family dynamics, social relationships, spiritual beliefs, life events, etc., all contribute to a teacher's capacity to deal with challenges in the workplace. Many of these factors are ones that he/she often has little ability to control. Teachers also respond to challenging issues in different ways based on past experiences, knowledge, and temperament.

Teacher personal history/life experience

Perrier et al. (2010) state that prior attachment orientation continues to play a role in how one handles events and situations. Whether they are consciously aware or not, teachers' own early childhood experiences (i.e., how they were treated and helped by their parents and early caregivers) influence how they perceive and respond to both positive and negative behaviors in the classroom. Some teachers may find that they are unable to deal with certain children or behaviors, while others are unaffected by the same or similar behaviors.

Teacher reflective capacity

Some teachers are better able to recognize and regulate their own negative emotions and frustrations than others. Their personal experiences, knowledge of child development, their own social and emotional competence, and even topics in pop culture might explain the difference in how they perceive behaviors. The behavior whining, for instance, viewed objectively, is an attempt to communicate discomfort but, subjectively, can be seen as attention-seeking, demanding, helpless, lazy, among many other possible interpretations of the behavior. The range of teacher reactions can include:

- From a frustrated or annoyed position: "Please stop whining!"
- From an angry or controlling position: "You will not have my attention when you use that voice," or "I'm not listening when you talk like that."
- From a dismissive position: "You are just fine," or quietly ignoring the behavior.

- From a position of pity or identification with the behavior: "It's okay, sweetie, I will help you."
- From a position of understanding that the behavior has meaning: "It seems like you are trying to let me know that something is really bothering you."

Reflection is essential to professional growth. Not only does it provide an opportunity for teachers to identify and think through the consequences of their responses, it acts to reduce teacher stress by putting teachers in proactive rather than reactive positions, helping to neutralize their own personal experiences that may also trigger stress-evoking responses. Although there are a number of models that have been developed to structure teacher reflection, the basic components include similar questions. A teacher trying to manage a child with challenging behavior might ask herself:

- What is the child's behavior?
- How am I responding?
- How effective is my response?
- Do I have any personal insight on why I might be responding in this way?
- Is there another way to think about and respond to the child's behavior? If so, what can I do differently?
- Take the example of the child who constantly interrupts at circle time and go through the previous exercise. If a teacher constantly responds to the interrupting child from an annoyed or even an angry position and the behavior continues, the teacher's response is obviously ineffective. Perhaps that particular teacher was so annoyed because she/he was brought up in a family or school setting where interrupting was considered very impolite and disrespectful. But, let's think about the child. Is there another way to interpret this child's intent? If he is one of eight children with a single mom and has little opportunity to be heard at home, interrupting may be the only way he can have a voice. Can this teacher take the child's perspective and respond in a different way? Consider the following suggestions:
- "It must be really hard for you to wait your turn when you are so worried that you might not get to tell me about . . . , but Kate is talking. I do want to hear what you have to say and your turn is next."
- "I can tell that you must have something important to say, and I promise that you will have a turn right after your friend Kate, as we go around the circle. I will not forget."

Journaling, videotaping, and peer review are also methods that aid with reflection. In the context of reflection, as teachers examine their own assumptions about children, they will better understand how their responses affect a child's behavior and be able to change responses that are unproductive, that create personal stress, and that may evoke personal anger as opposed to empathy.

For example, if a teacher assumes that all children really want to be good and please adults, she/he may respond very differently when children present challenging behaviors.

In the following list are core assumptions derived from basic principles of children's emotional development. Keeping these in mind is often a helpful tool when teachers are faced with difficult situations and challenging behaviors.

1.   Children have rich inner lives. They attribute meaning to their experiences and have their own perspective on experiences. *Children think about a lot, experience and perceive stress, and have opinions at a very early age.*
2.   Children's behavior always has reasons. *Always!*
3.   All children are doing the best that they can to be successful in their worlds. *Children want to be good; they want to please others.*
4.   A child's emotional growth occurs in the context of deep, sustained relationships. *It's all about relationships!*
5.   Childhood proceeds with regressions and progressions. *Normal development does not follow a straight trajectory. Even adults regress in certain situations.*
6.   Children develop protections against unpleasant emotions. *Children use defense mechanisms in the same way as adults. (We will explore this concept further later in the chapter.)*

Teacher self-efficacy

Questions around the coping capacities of teachers also relate to their feelings of self-efficacy. When teachers feel that they can have control in creating desired outcomes, they tend to be more motivated to persevere. Teachers encounter emotionally-charged situations on a constant basis, many of which provoke strong emotional reactions. If teachers believe they can do little, they may resort to more palliative techniques such as avoidance, denial, or putting a positive spin on events. These types of emotional and avoidance reactions are an effort to reduce personal emotional reactions to stress. They may be helpful in the moment but likely do not recognize or address the source of the stress. Finding ways to manage teachers' own reactions to stress in itself can create more stress (Carson, Templin, & Weiss, 2006; Montgomery & Rupp, 2005). When teachers have confidence in their abilities to affect change and handle difficult classroom situations, they report less stress and tend to be less prone to burnout (Schwarzer & Hallum, 2008; Ware & Kitsantas, 2007).

Both external and internal factors have a significant impact on teacher stress and there is also considerable overlap between the two. How do teachers cope with the demands of their workspace? What ways of coping are effective? Maladaptive? Given the range of stressors and the multitude of variables that are the source of teacher stress, what can be done? How can one effectively move from coping to more proactive resolutions?

Coping and stress reduction

Defense mechanisms

Negative emotions such as shame, guilt, anger, or fear are signals to the mind that something is amiss in one's subjective estimation. Anxiety is a signal that there is some assessed danger. Sometimes a danger is real, such as the edge of a cliff, while other times it is only perceived, and takes the form of an uncomfortable thought or feeling (e.g., anger or rage). Defense mechanisms serve the purpose of protecting against or warding off these perceived dangers. Defenses are unconscious, operating behind the scenes in the mind, often so much so that the original thought or feeling remains hidden from consciousness. *We all use defense mechanisms and when a defense is effective, it does reduce the level of anxiety.* While defenses are brought into action unconsciously, an increased awareness of them and of the purpose they serve is very helpful in guiding the reflective exploration of reactions to stress and anxiety. Common defenses and examples of how a teacher might use them include:

- *Denial,* or looking on the bright side more than the actual evidence supports rather than confronting the problem: "I am *sure* that this child will work out her shyness in time."
- *Regression,* a process of giving in to pressure and using ways of coping that may not directly confront challenges: "I sure need a mental health day. Dealing with those kids five days in a row is just too hard."
- *Acting out,* or unconsciously showing one's feelings through behaviors rather than confronting and expressing them verbally, such as when one is persistently late for work.
- *Externalization,* a process of placing one's own positive or negative feelings or attitudes in others: "The kids in the class are really afraid of that child when he gets angry."
- *Reaction formation,* a process of feeling and therefore acting in the opposite way of how one genuinely feels, such as showering a person with gifts or compliments when one is angry.
- *Dissociation,* or disconnecting from one's self, also referred to as compartmentalization, such as when one zones out to avoid situations that are uncomfortable or overwhelming: "I don't even remember what happened today. I must have just tuned it all out."
- *Repression,* or the blocking of unwanted thoughts or feelings: "I am not stressed; just a little tired today."
- *Displacement,* a process of redirecting negative feelings about one person to another safer target: "My co-teacher is really supportive; it's the parents who are the problem."
- *Rationalization,* or trying to find a reason that may be *part* of the truth to explain an event: "It wasn't my fault he was sent to a different school. They couldn't afford the tuition here anyway."

- *Sublimation,* or the transformation of negative thoughts or feelings into an action that is productive and socially acceptable, such as when one takes on more work in reaction to feeling angry or upset about work.

For teachers, there is typically not an accepted forum nor the time for expressing unpleasant feelings about various aspects of their work. Elfer and Dearnley (2007) state that the repression of emotion is common in settings of "care work" due to worries about being viewed as unprofessional and also due to the fact that there are typically few opportunities for emotions to be considered and discussed in these types of workplaces. Teacher who can openly share and explore their frustrations without judgement or criticism are better able to gauge their own reactions in difficult situations. They can examine what works, what doesn't, where or when they use defenses, and how their reactions influence the responses of others.

Palliative solutions

Solutions that contribute to the reduction of teacher stress typically fall into two categories: palliative strategies and direct actions (Kyriacou, 2001). Palliative solutions are focused on reducing the strength of reactions to stress by minimizing, or providing strategies to better tolerate the effects of stress; they typically do not address the source of the stress. *Palliative solutions can be helpful and, at times, critical* to maintain emotional equilibrium in a difficult situation. Often workshops, self-help publications, blogs, etc. provide tips to help teachers' stress using palliative techniques, many of which are effective in the short term and their impact should absolutely not be undervalued. Palliative techniques or solutions can be mental, physical, or both, and include such activities as:

Relaxation techniques/activities. Some of the more familiar relaxation techniques include controlled deep breathing, progressive muscle relaxation, meditation, nature walks, gardening, journaling, taking quiet breaks, listening to music, use of fidgets or stress balls, etc.

Physical activity

Exercise has long been known as a way to reduces stress. Vigorous exercise produces changes in the brain, releasing endorphins.

Self-talk

Self-talk is the *intentional* process of repeating positive and motivating statements throughout the day and in response to negative thoughts. "I can do this," "I am a good person," and "I won't take this personally," are examples of positive self-talk.

Mindfulness

There is an increasing interest in mindfulness training for people in all walks of life, and new research has demonstrated that the benefits of being more mindful (i.e., focused on and accepting of present moment reactions) can be an effective tool in the professional development and coaching of teachers (Whitaker, et al., 2014). The goal of Mindfulness-Based Stress Reduction (MBSR) training is to help individuals change the way that they think and react to stress. Mindful co-workers create calm workplace environments and mindful teachers create safe emotional environments in their classrooms. Depending on its focus and its use, mindfulness can be considered both a palliative solution and a direct-action activity (Gold et al., 2010).

Most important in this discussion of palliative solutions is the capacity of teachers to identify the palliative strategies they use and to determine whether they are adaptive or maladaptive. Having only palliative tools may not be sufficient, so what are the long-term solutions to address stress reduction? The good news is that researchers and leaders in the field of early childhood have taken this problem of teacher stress very seriously and are examining organizational and system changes that are successfully tackling the issues that contribute to the challenges in the classroom.

Direct action solutions

Researchers have consistently documented dysfunctional and negative organizational characteristics as stress factors. Many of these factors fall under the governance of school directors or other administrators (Barford &Whelton, 2010; Baumgartner et al., 2009). McGinty, Justice, and Rimm-Kaufman (2008) found that when directors were able to facilitate a sense of community for and among teachers, teachers demonstrated much higher levels of commitment and job satisfaction.

Director-initiated activities and teacher participation

According to Zinsser and Curby (2014), teachers' behaviors in classrooms are in large part attributable to factors at the center level. Management practices create the emotional workplace climate. Research by Baumgartner et al. (2009) found that teachers relied heavily on directors for help with problem solving. What can directors do to generate sound social support to teachers and how can teachers be more proactive in the organizational setting?

Directors can clarify roles and expectations.

One of the aspects most frequently related to job strain is the quandary of unclear expectations (Reffett, 2009). Directors should be sure that job descriptions are explicit and reasonable and that clear procedures are in place for performance appraisal. Expectations and policy descriptions for working with parents must be well defined and health/safety requirements sufficiently documented.

Teachers can and should ask for clarification on roles and expectations before accepting a teaching position. Contractual agreements further concretize policy and performance procedures.

Directors can encourage input on decision-making.

Scheduling opportunities for regular staff meetings where staff can openly discuss issues and participate in joint decisions that affect both children and teachers is best practice. Pooling ideas and reflecting on the positive and negative consequences of existing practices opens possibilities for changes that foster staff commitment.

Teachers can actively participate in staff meetings, not only voicing difficulties, but also offering viable suggestions for the resolution of those difficulties when they arise.

Directors should provide consistent meaningful feedback.

Sharing skills and knowledge as well as recognizing efforts and achievements is essential to developing good working relationships between staff and administration, and also among staff themselves.

Teachers can and should ask for more feedback from administrators as well as from peers when they fell it is needed.

Directors can support teacher expression/reflection.

Building in time for staff to express their frustrations and challenges, and reflect on their own feelings and reactions to the situations that they face in their classrooms reaps many benefits. A reflection model similar to the one described earlier in this chapter can be adapted to address a specific problem or to meld with a particular school philosophy. Reflection is *an essential process* for helping staff feel that they are heard and understood, and to develop healthy alternative perspectives for problem solving.

Teachers can make a regular practice of self-reflection and be willing to share their insights for active problem solving and for reframing more specific, meaningful solutions.

Directors should provide and encourage breaks.

Providing a comfortable space away from the noise and bustle of classrooms where staff can create their own emotionally supportive climate demonstrates that the needs of staff are recognized and honored. Just as children need soft cozy spaces, teachers also benefit from spaces where they can relax in comfort and calm. Allowing teachers to have a part in creating that comfortable space is critical for it to be effective and useful.

Teachers should take advantage of breaks as true downtime and, if at all possible, not use break time to catch up on other aspects of work.

Directors should provide resources and professional development.

Downer et al. (2009) state that the teaching profession, must, "move beyond one and done workshops." Teachers need more; they benefit at a much higher level from practice and mentoring that includes opportunities for self-observation with supportive feedback.

Teachers should take advantage of the opportunities presented and offer suggestions for professional development content.

Directors should encourage open and honest communication.

Staff must feel comfortable enough to express opinions openly, not only related to classroom activities but also center policies and procedures. Clear avenues for handling complaints should be established and opportunities for informal staff communication provided. Celebrations, offsite events, team building exercises, and staff retreats are all ways to build support and cohesion as well as positively affect morale.

Teachers should be specific and honest about their needs and share their successes as well!

Directors should support and champion community involvement.

Directors and staff should be encouraged to participate in larger community efforts.

In order to increase awareness of the importance of early education and the value of the early childhood educator, participation in community events that include higher-level funders and policy makers is not only important but critical. Increasing awareness can also take the form of letters to legislators, newsletters, blogs, social media posts, etc.

Teachers can and must be advocates for their profession and participate in such community activities when opportunities arise.

Teacher-initiated activities

Classrooms that are designed to foster independence and meet the social, emotional, and physical needs of the children can aid in reducing stress levels in the children, and in turn, teachers' stress levels. Components of a safe emotional environment for young children include:

Physical environment

- Quiet/cozy spaces for children to independently remove themselves or take breaks

- Access to developmentally appropriate toys and activities, including a wide variety of sensory materials for children to express themselves and to soothe when needed
- Defined boundaries and labeled spaces that children can independently navigate
- Materials that reflect the children's interests

Emotional environment

- Regular parent-teacher communication
- Support of communication between parents and children, including notes in cubbies or lunchboxes, notes to parents (dictated, if necessary) from children, and supervised child accessibility to phone for check-ins with parents if needed
- Ample preparation for changes in the environment (changing center activities, circle time seating) and changes to the daily schedule
- Preparation for and introduction to visitors entering the classroom
- Open access to transitional objects as needed
- Familiarity with all staff in the building and substitute teachers
- Engagement of children on their level, including talking with them on their eye level and sitting with them during mealtimes

Social Support

The elements of building a strong community are embedded in the concept of social support. Social support, as defined earlier in the chapter, is an individual or a group of individuals who provide resources, abstract and/or tangible, to one another. A social support could be a co-worker, a consultant, the center director, one's family, friends, or even a higher being. A programmatic social support that is rapidly becoming a source for early childhood educators is the model of early childhood mental health consultation (ECMHC). The ECMHC model provides consistent social support from a non-judgmental, highly competent colleague. This is an option that more and more administrators, described by Johnston and Brinamen (2006) as the "gatekeepers" for change, have begun to explore. The impact of such a program can be far-reaching, and *significantly* affect the emotional wellbeing of staff, children, and families.

The Early Childhood Mental Health Consultation (ECMHC) programmatic model

The ECMHC programmatic model is a systemic approach, focused on the school program to work through specific issues that affect more than one child, staff member, and/or family (Cohen & Kaufmann, 2005). Programmatic ECMHC is primarily an indirect approach where early childhood mental health consultants build the capacity of staff (and parents) to support healthy child emotional development and manage challenging behaviors, one of teachers' major sources of stress. Consultants coach and mentor directors and teachers using a collaborative approach, providing strategies that recognize their diversity in philosophy and culture, capitalizing on their strengths, and offering pragmatic solutions that are both action-based and emotionally healthy for both the provider and the recipient.

Research into the efficacy of the ECMHC model confirms that teachers receiving ECMHC were more sensitive to the needs of the children in their classrooms and have demonstrated improvements in their classroom management skills (Raver et al., 2008). Classroom climates became more positive and teachers reported more confidence in their ability to work with children exhibiting challenging behaviors (Alkon, Ramler, & MacLennan, 2015; Olmos & Grimmer, 2005). Teachers also reported lower levels of job stress after receiving ECMHC services (Green, et al., 2006; Langkamp, 2003; Olmos & Grimmer, 2005).

Mental health consultants can be licensed professionals (counselors, therapists, or social workers) or early childhood and special education professionals with training and experience in the mental health field. The Center on the Social and Emotional Foundations for Early Learning (CSEFEL) has developed a series of resources to help mental health consultants and these resources, plus many others, that promote social and emotional competence in infants and young children, are available free of charge on their website (www.vanderbilt.edu/csefel).

Social emotional learning (SEL)

Teachers of young children are charged with supporting the social and emotional well-being of the children in their care, but what support is available for teachers to examine and enhance their own social and emotional competence? Specific social and emotional learning focused on staff development is increasingly becoming a part of teacher preparation at the college and university level and is proving to be highly effective (Hemmeter, Santos, & Ostrosky, 2008; Schonert-Reichl et al., 2016). According to Jennings and Greenberg (2009), teachers who are socially and emotionally competent are able to work more effectively with challenging students because they have better insight into the emotional responses of students as well as to their own reactions. These teachers experience less stress and less burnout.

What are the characteristics of socially and emotionally competent teachers?

High self-awareness

Teachers with high self-awareness recognize their own emotional patterns and feel confident in understanding of their emotional strengths and weaknesses.

High social awareness

Teacher with high social awareness recognize the impact of their emotional expressions on others and have an understanding of the emotions of others. They understand social and ethical norms and make realistic and meaningful attempts to assume the perspective of others from all walks of life including those of diverse backgrounds and cultures.

Self-management

Teachers who are competent in self-management can effectively regulate their own emotions in a range of situations. They manage stress, control impulses, and can delay gratification.

Relationship skills

Teachers with good relationships skills can establish healthy appropriate relationships with diverse individuals and groups. They are good communicators, active interested listeners, and they can successfully negotiate conflict.

Responsible decision-making

Teachers with this competency make constructive choices by assessing the relevant factors with an understanding of how their decision will affect themselves and others. These teachers take responsibility for their own decisions. (CASEL, 2014; Jennings & Greenberg, 2009).

Much emphasis has been put on student social and emotional development, but in the past, little attention has been placed on the value of a teacher's own social and emotional development. Some of these skills come naturally, while others might require more attention and additional development. When teachers have inadequate social and emotional competencies, they are less able to handle classroom challenges and more likely to experience job-related stress (Jennings and Greenberg, 2009). Intentional training for teachers in social and emotional competence creates healthier classroom climates.

Summary

The effects of early childhood teacher stress are significant, although the sources of teacher stress vary. Direct action, proactive strategies are likely the most effective in addressing stress in the workplace. It is essential for teachers to have opportunities to reflect, communicate, share ideas, and participate in decision-making. They need to be heard and their input thoughtfully considered. This is vital to the mental health of the staff and to school morale. When teachers have a better understanding of themselves and their reactions, they are also better equipped to handle challenging situations more constructively and with less stress. Short-term or palliative stress-relieving techniques have their place, but in the long run, self-reflection, intentional training in social and emotional competence, and professional consultation can yield sustainable effects that will serve teachers in both their professional and personal lives.

Authors' note

We have worked in over 150 childcare centers and preschools and much of what we have written reflects what we see and what we know to be successful. Teachers first need to know that their needs are understood. The recognition that professionals other than themselves realize their challenges is essential as a starting point. When teachers develop better reflective competencies, their perspectives change, and their problem-solving capacities evolve. Opportunities for social support increase as teachers share their insights and personal discoveries. System changes are unwieldy and slow, but ECMHC programs are growing in number as are SEL programs in institutes of higher education.

Teachers, this is your "call to action." Be proactive in raising discussions with directors and opening dialogue for change within your schools and centers. Teacher stress is a school and system problem every bit as much as an individual burden and we are working hard (here in North Carolina) to make system changes for more permanent teacher support.

References

Alkon, A., Ramler, M., & MacLennan, K. (2015). Evaluation of mental health consultation in child care centers. *Early Childhood Education Journal*, 31(2):91–99. doi:10.1023/B:ECEJ.0000005307.00142.3c

Barford, S., & Whelton, W. (2010). Understanding burnout in child and youth care workers. *Child and Youth Care Forum*, 39:271–287. doi:10.1007/s10566–10010–9104–9108

Baumgartner, J., Carson, R., Apavaloaie, L., & Tsouloupas, C. (2009). Uncovering common stressful factors and coping strategies among childcare providers. *Child and Youth Care Forum*, 38(5):239–251. doi:10.1007/s10566–10009–9079–9075

Betoret, F. (2006). Stressors, self-efficacy, coping resources, and burnout among secondary school teachers in Spain. *Educational Psychology*, 26(4):519–539. doi:10.1080/01443410500342492

Berkman, L.F., & Glass, T.A. (2000). Social integration, social networks, social support, and health. In L.F. Berkman & I. Kawachi (Eds.), *Social epidemiology* (pp. 137–173). New York: Oxford University Press.

Biglan, A., Hayes, S., & Pistorello, J. (2008). Acceptance and commitment: Implications for prevention science. *Prevention Science*, 9(3):139–152. doi:10.1007/s11121–11008–0099–0094

Carson, R., Templin, T., & Weiss, H. (2006). Exploring the episodic nature of teachers' emotions and its relationship to teacher burnout. Paper presented at the American Education Research Association Annual Convention, San Francisco, CA.

CASEL (Collaborative for Academic, Social, and Emotional Learning). (2014). *Effective social and emotional learning programs*. pp. 9–14. https://static1.squarespace.com/static/513f79f9e4b05ce7b70e9673/t/526a220de4b00a92c90436ba/1382687245993/2013-casel-guide.pdf

Cohen, E., & Kaufmann, R. (2005). *Early childhood mental health consultation*. Washington, DC: Center for Mental Health Services of the Substance Abuse and Mental Health Services Administration and the Georgetown University Child Development Center.

Dorman, J. (2003). Relationship between school and classroom environment and teacher burnout: ALISREL analysis. *Social Psychology*, 6(2):7–127. doi:10.1023/A:1023296126723

Downer, J., Locasale-Crouch, J., Hamre, B., & Pianta, R. (2009). Teacher characteristics associated with responsiveness and exposure to consultation and on-line professional development resources. *Early Education Development*, 20(3):431–455. doi:10.1080/10409280802688626

Dworkin, A. (2001). Perspectives on teacher burnout and school reform. *International Education Journal*, 2(2):69–78.

Elfer, P., & Dearnley, K. (2007). Nurseries and emotional well-being: Evaluating an emotionally containing model of professional development. *Early Years*, 27(3):267–279. doi:10.1080/09575140701594418

Faulkner, M., Gerstenblatt, P., Lee, A., Vallejo, V., & Travis, D. (2014). Childcare providers: Work stress and personal well-being. *Journal of Early Childhood Research*, 14(3):280–293. doi:10.1177/1476718x14552871

Feldman, P., Cohen, S., Lepore, S., Matthews, K., Kamarchk, T., & Marsland, A. (1999). Negative emotions and acute physiological responses to stress. *Annals of Behavioral Medicine*, 21(3):216–222. doi:10.1007/BF02884836

Gilliam, W. (2008). *Implementing policies to reduce the likelihood of preschool expulsion* (Foundation for Child Development Policy Brief No. 7: Advancing PK-3). New York: Foundation for Child Development.

Gold, E., Herne, D., Hopper, L., Smith, A., & Tansey, G. (2010). Mindfulness-based stress reduction (MBSR) for primary school teachers. *Journal of Child and Family Studies*, 19(2):184–189.

Green, B., Everhart, M., Gordon, L., & Gettman, M. (2006). Characteristics of effective mental health consultation in early childhood settings: Multilevel analysis of a national survey. *Topics in Early Childhood Special Education*, 26:142–152. doi:10.1177/02711214060260030201

Hamre, B., & Pianta, R. (2001). Early teacher-child relationships and the trajectory of children's school outcomes through eighth grade. *Child Development*, 72:625–638. doi:10.1111/1467–8624.00301

Hastings, R., & Bahm, M. (2003). The relationship between student behaviour patterns and teacher burnout. *School Psychology International*, 24:115–127. doi:10.1177/0143034303024001905

Hemmeter, M., Corso, R., & Cheatham, G. (2006). Issues in addressing challenging behaviors in young children: A national survey of early childhood educators. Paper presented at the Conference on Research Innovations in Early Intervention, San Diego, CA.

Hemmeter, M., Santos, R., & Ostrosky, M. (2008). Preparing early childhood educators to address young children's social-emotional development and challenging behaviors: A study of higher education programs in nine states. *Journal of Early Intervention*, 30:321–340. doi:10.1177/1053815108320900

Jennings, P., & Greenberg, M. (2009). The prosocial classroom: Teacher social and emotional competence in relations to student classroom outcome. *Review of Educational Research*, 79(1):491–525. doi:10.3102/0034654308325693

Johnston, K., & Brinamen, C. (2006). *Mental health consultation in child care: Transforming relationships among directors, staff, and families*. Washington, DC: Zero to Three Press.

Kyriacou, D. (2001). Teacher stress: Directions for future research. *Educational Review*, 53 (1):27–35. doi:10.1080/00131910120033628

Langkamp, D. (2003). *Evaluation of the early childhood mental health initiative*. Akron: Ohio Department of Mental Health, Office of Program Evaluation and Research.

McGinty, A., Justice, L., & Rimm-Kaufman, S. (2008). Sense of school community for preschool teachers serving at-risk children. *Early Education and Development*, 19(2):361–384. doi:10.1080/10409280801964036

McGrath, N., & Huntington, A. (2007). The health and wellbeing of adults working in early childhood education. *Australian Journal of Early Childhood*, 32(3):33–38.

Montgomery, C., & Rupp, A. (2005). A meta-analysis for exploring the diverse causes and effects of stress in teachers. *Canadian Journal of Education*, 28(3):458–486. doi:10.2307%2F4126

Moriarty, V., Edmonds, S., Blatchford, P., & Martin, C. (2001). Teaching young children: Perceived satisfaction and stress. *Educational Research*, 43:33–46. doi:10.1080/00131880010021276

Olmos, A., & Grimmer, M. (2005). PEARL: Lessons learned from collaboratively delivering mental health services in early childhood settings. In C. Newman, C. J. Liberton, K. Kutash, & R. M. Friedman (Eds.), *The 17th Annual Research Conference proceedings: A system of care for children's mental health: Expanding the research base* (pp. 247–252). Tampa: University of South Florida, Louis de la Parte Florida Mental Health Institute, Research and Training Center for Children's Mental Health.

Perrier, C.., Boucher, R., Etchegary, H., Sadava, S., & Molnar, D. (2010). The overlapping contributions of attachment orientation and social support in predicting life-event distress. *Canadian Journal of Behavioural Science*, 42(2):71–79. doi:10.1037/a0018337

Pianta, R. (1999). *Enhancing relationships between children and teachers*. Washington, DC: American Psychological Association.

Raver, C.C., Jones, S.M., Li-Grining, C.P., Metzger, M., Smallwood, K., & Sardin, L. (2008). Improving preschool classroom processes: Preliminary findings from a randomized trial implemented in Head Start settings. *Early Childhood Research Quarterly*, 63(3):253–255. doi:10.1016/j.ecresq.2007.09.001

Reffett, A. (2009). *Exploring sources of teacher stress in Head Start*. (Unpublished doctoral dissertation). Wheaton College, Illinois, United States of America. http://search.proquest.com/pqdtft/docview/305135181/abstract/13C73462B353F1E79A/1?accountid=14541

Ruble, L., Usher, E., & McGrew, J. (2011). Preliminary investigation of the sources of self-efficacy among teachers of students with autism. *Focus on Autism and Other Developmental Disabilities*, 26:67–74. doi:10.1177/1088357610397345

Substance Abuse and Mental Health Services Administration, Office of Applied Studies. (2007). *The NSDUH report: Depression among adults employed full-time by occupational category*. Rockville, MD.

Schonert-Reichl, M., Kitil, J., LeRose, M., Sipl, M., Sweiss, L., Zuhra, T., & Sauve, J. (2016). Social & emotional learning and teacher education: What do we know and where do we go from here?www.hopelab.org/wpcontent/uploads/2016/05/SELinTeacher Education_WhitePaperforHopeLab_April152016KSR.pdf

Schwarzer, R., & Hallum, S. (2008). Perceived teacher self-efficacy as a predictor of job stress and burnout: Mediation analyses. *Applied Psychology*, 57(1):152–171. doi:10.1111/j.1464-0597.2008.00359.x

Sorenson, R. (2007). Stress management in education: warning signs and coping mechanisms. *Management in Education*, 21:10–13.

Ware, H., & Kitsantas, A. (2007). Teacher and collective efficacy beliefs as predictors of professional commitment. *The Journal of Educational Research*, 100(5):303–309. doi:10.3200/JOER.100.5.303–310

Whitaker, R., Dearth-Wesley, T., Gooze, R., Becker, B., Gallagher, K., & McEwen, B. (2014). Adverse childhood experience, dispositional mindfulness, and adult health. *Preventative Medicine*, 67:147–153. doi:10.1016/j.ypmed.2014.07.029

Zinsser, K. (2013). *Early childhood directors' impacts on social-emotional teaching and learning* (Doctoral dissertation). George Mason University, Fairfax, VA. Retrieved from http://digilib.gmu.edu/dspace/handle/1920/8234

Zinsser, K., Bailey, C., Curby, T., Denham, S., & Bassett, H. (2013). Exploring the predictable classroom: Preschool teacher stress, emotional supportiveness, and student's social-emotional behavior in private and Head Start classrooms. *NHSA Dialog: The Research-to-Practice Journal for the Early Childhood Field*, 16(2):90–108.

Zinsser, K., & Curby, T. (2014). Understanding preschool teachers' emotional support as a function of center climate. *SAGE Open*, 4(4):1–9. doi:10.1177/2158244014560728

AFTERWORD

Jill Bellinson

And so, we come to the end of our journey into the inner lives of youngsters in the early childhood classroom, using psychodynamic concepts and developmental theories to understand and support early childhood education.

Along the way, we have described play as a vital part of children's development. Play fosters cognitive, emotional, and social development in children while increasing their creativity and expressiveness. Play is the way children express thoughts, practice skills, and work through anxieties. Earliest games of peek-a-boo are used to work out children's fears of being abandoned and their budding knowledge of object constancy. Building with blocks and Legos provide opportunities to test theories of physics and feel the power of destroying one's own (or others) creations. Play in the house area allows children to try on the roles of adults and feel what it's like to be a caregiver, decider, or even punisher. The presence of the other children in the classroom requires children to negotiate their places in the world at large—cooperatively, collaboratively, or conflictually.

When children have experienced trauma, play becomes both more difficult and more important. Children who are chronically stressed never have the freedom to use their imaginations—too much of their energy has to be used in calming themselves and managing the dangers in their world. Their daily struggles and pains leave them caught in reality and blocked from the freedom that imaginative play requires. This makes the small moments of play even more vital for their growth and inner peace, yet harder for them to accomplish.

Play in the early childhood classroom is all this and more, since it is there that children play in interaction with others and as witnessed by caring adults. Those adults are positioned to foster children's emotional development by listening carefully to children's wishes and needs and providing the accepting environment they all need.

This book has tried to explain and develop these ideas.

We have presented the development of play, from youngest babies' peek-a-boo using their own bodies, through toddlers' play with wooden telephones and plastic food, to preschoolers' creation of whole worlds of fantasy. And we have described the ways children gradually include peers in parallel, conflictual, and, eventually, collaborative play. We have discussed play as communication, both with others—so teachers can read what's on children's minds by watching their play—and with themselves—so children can think through confusions and work out challenges by incorporating those into play situations.

We have tried to demonstrate the wide variety of circumstances and modalities of expressive play. Art, music, and cultural narratives all serve to reveal children's experience and help both teachers and children themselves to make sense of them. The interaction of children's cultural background with the cultural norms of the classroom can stifle or inspire children's experience.

Traumatized children—those our hearts go out to most—are often unable to play. They are likely to act out aggressively or refuse adamantly or cling needily, and they frustrate their caretakers. Yet they do play, a little, in the ways they can, and that little play serves the same functions and requires the same response as the play of children with wilder imaginations and more liberty to create.

Most of all, we have talked about the nature of teachers' and caregivers' responses to children's play. We encouraged understanding over controlling, accepting over restricting, sensitivity over indoctrination. We focused on mentalizing—thinking about states of mind—as the way to understand what children are showing us in their play. Children need to be listened to and heard. Early childhood educators spend long hours every day with young children and are uniquely positioned to listen and hear. When children come from calm and happy homes, they easily attach to teachers, express themselves freely, and make good use of teachers for support and aid. Teachers of these children serve as additional parenting figures to add to the support they receive at home. When children come from conflict-laden and traumatizing backgrounds, they bring fears and angers into the classroom and are harder for teachers to reach—but, of course, are the most in need of being reached. Teachers of these children may be the only calm and accepting adult these children know, and teachers' warm demeanor and understanding reception may equip them with the resilience traumatized children need to survive.

In this book, we have tried to provide some thoughtful approaches to children, all children, in hopes that early childhood educators and caregivers can be the lifeline that helps every child thrive and that traumatized children so desperately need. Our psychoanalytic backgrounds lead us to understand that unconscious, unspoken, and familial experience influence behavior and that teachers should be looking for the ways children express these underlying feelings in their observable actions.

We are aware, certainly, of the toll this work can take. We encourage the practice of good self-care for teachers, who need to monitor their own reactions and triggers so they can be at their best for this challenging and vital mission. We describe the way teachers can explore their own motivations for becoming teachers, and how those motivations manifest in the classroom. We recommend that teachers recognize their own states of mind—mentalizing for themselves—so they can monitor their reactions to children's behaviors. We support teachers freeing themselves to play, to create art and music, and to understand their own cultural backgrounds and biases, so they can bring their best selves into the classroom. And, most of all, we understand the need for teachers to provide for their own best care and stress release, for themselves and for each other, because we recognize how challenging and exhausting the work they do can be, and how crucial it is that they do it.

We hope this book proves useful to you, the teachers and caregivers who are so critical to the development of the minds and hearts of our young ones. Our children are our future, and teachers are paramount in helping to form our children.

INDEX

Page numbers in **bold** refer to tables.